Advance Praise for
JUSTICE NEVER RESTS

"Always riveting, sometimes raw, and often relentless, *Justice Never Rests* is an extraordinary achievement that stands alongside F. Lee Bailey's *The Defense Never Rests* and Alan Dershowitz's *The Best Defense* as classic masterworks of real-life courtroom drama. Not only does justice never rest, neither will you until you finish this book."

—*Reader's Digest*

"*Justice Never Rests* is certain to be devoured by law students and legal junkies alike, as well as fans of John Grisham, Scott Turow, and Michael Connelly craving real-life courtroom theatrics. The verdict: An instant classic that's the best work of legal nonfiction in generations and maybe ever."

—*Los Angeles Tribune*

"*Justice Never Rests* sprints out of the gate and never lets up or slows down, informing even as it entertains. A mesmerizing, mind-numbing masterpiece of an evolving criminal mindset that William Kolibash was equal to at every turn. He's Frank Galvin from *The Verdict* without the alcohol problem, Michael Connelly's Mickey Haller without the Lincoln, and Perry Mason without the theme song."

—*San Francisco Post*

JUSTICE NEVER RESTS

A U.S. ATTORNEY'S BATTLE AGAINST MURDERERS, DRUG LORDS, MOB KINGPINS & CULTS

WILLIAM KOLIBASH

with JON LAND and
SHARIANE KOLIBASH TAYLOR

Post Hill
PRESS

A POST HILL PRESS BOOK

Justice Never Rests:
A U.S. Attorney's Battle against Murderers, Drug Lords, Mob Kingpins & Cults

ISBN: 979-8-88845-706-1
ISBN (eBook): 979-8-88845-707-8

Cover design by Cody Corcoran
Cover photo by: Joe Ravi - CC-BY-SA 3.0
Interior design and composition by Greg Johnson, Textbook Perfect

All photographs appearing herein are from the author's personal collections, unless noted otherwide.

This book, as well as any other Post Hill Press publications, may be purchased in bulk quantities at a special discounted rate. Contact orders@posthillpress.com for more information.

All people, locations, events, and situations are portrayed to the best of the author's memory. While all of the events described are true, many names and identifying details have been changed to protect the privacy of the people involved.

Post Hill Press

Post Hill Press
New York • Nashville
posthillpress.com

Published in the United States of America
1 2 3 4 5 6 7 8 9 10

For the staff of the U.S. Attorney's Office
for the Northern District of West Virginia,
and all the law enforcement agents and officers,
who made the content of this book possible.

The only thing necessary for the triumph of evil
is for good men to do nothing.

—EDMUND BURKE

Contents

The official portrait picture of Bill Kolibash that hangs in the U.S. Attorney's Office for the Northern District of West Virginia.

PROLOGUE

Wheeling, West Virginia; January 1991

As soon as I slid the contents from the envelope, I knew it was a bomb. The mail had arrived that morning before my assistant did, so I grabbed the pile off her desk on the way back from a meeting. The thick legal-size envelope rested on the bottom, and I opened it first as the morning sunlight streamed through the windows that overlooked Chapline Street. My second-floor U.S. Attorney's Office for the Northern District of West Virginia was housed in the ornate stone-and-granite Federal Building that still contained a post office on the first floor. This letter bomb had made it to my desk without being inspected, because this was before the era of metal detectors and scanners. The return address was the Ohio County Jail on the other side of town, and it wasn't at all unusual for inmates to file forms in envelopes like this themselves.

Small, jagged pieces of steel spilled out with the yellow legal pad I had eased partway from the envelope. In that moment, I didn't know the only thing saving me from being swallowed by an explosive fireball was that the accelerant, believed to have been lip balm, had failed to trigger the blast. The bomb was designed to detonate when the legal pad was removed from the envelope and the wires of the improvised switch touched. The resulting electrical current was supposed to heat the wire and ignite the detonator, which then would melt the plastic casings of two lighters, free the butane, and ignite it. If it had gone off, the bomb would have produced a thousand-degree fireball up to three feet in diameter. I was forty-seven at the time and came that close to not seeing my next birthday.

The sender was an inmate named Rodney Curtis Hamrick, and my life had been saved by the fact that he was unable to find an accelerant better than lip balm that would have left my wife a widow and my children fatherless. Believe it or not, Hamrick had managed to obtain all the items with which he'd rigged the bomb from the jail commissary that had, fortunately for me, lacked a better accelerant in its inventory. If he had opted for hamburger grease from the cafeteria, I would not be here today.

This wasn't the first time Hamrick had sent bombs and threats through the mail, not even the first time he'd done so from jail or prison. He was in state prison in 1987 when he mailed letters threatening to murder then president Ronald Reagan, was caught in possession of a letter containing a "smoke bomb" addressed to George H. W. Bush, and built five improvised bombs while he was serving time in the Federal Correctional Institution at Petersburg, Virginia. He also threatened to blow up the courthouse in Elkins, West Virginia, a United Airlines flight, and the headquarters of the NAACP in Washington, DC (twice) if he wasn't released. In April 1990, Hamrick mailed a letter to the judge who had sentenced him, William M. Kidd, vowing to kill the judge and his family on behalf of "the Nazi Socialist Republican Party." An avowed white supremacist, Hamrick on another occasion had facilitated an escape by fashioning what looked like a pistol out of duct tape. He successfully fired the improvised gun at a fellow inmate and threatened a guard.

The legal pad had been hollowed out in the center in a six-inch square to allow for the placement of his improvised explosive device. A wire had been connected to the clasp, rigged to release the accelerant as soon as I opened the envelope, triggering the blast that could have been powerful enough to blow my head off.

More shards of what I realized was shrapnel leaked from the envelope as I cautiously laid it down on my desk and backed out of my office. My assistant had just arrived but stopped short of greeting me when she saw the look on my face. I picked up her phone and dialed the number for the offices of the Bureau of Alcohol, Tobacco, and Firearms a block away.

"This is U.S. Attorney Bill Kolibash," I said, after the receptionist's greeting, "calling from my office down the street."

"Good morning, Mr. Kolibash."

"Not really. There's a mail bomb in my office."

"Please stay on the line."

Seconds later, a male voice I recognized came on. "Bill, this is Special Agent Kerse. Is the bomb secured?"

"It's sitting on my desk, Frank. It was delivered from the Ohio County Jail."

"I'm heading your way with a team. Move everyone on the floor as far as possible away from your office."

I'd just finished doing that when the ATF's Frank Kerse, a big, rawboned man who served in the U.S. Army as a military policeman, exited the elevator with his advance team. By the time he completed a visual inspection of the device exactly as I'd left it, another team had arrived with protective sandbags in tow. It took five elevator trips to haul them up to the second floor! The ATF team piled the bags around the desk and secured the office, as if it was something they did every day.

"I've got an army bomb-disposal team on their way from Chambersburg, Pennsylvania," Kerse said, ending a call he'd made on his mobile phone, a rarity back in 1991.

That team, consisting of the bomb-disposal expert and his commanding officer, were flown to Wheeling from Chambersburg. Upon arriving about two hours after the call, the expert ordered the evacuation of the entire wing of the Federal Building in which my offices were housed. I stayed behind and watched him suit up in a full-body Kevlar bomb suit and a Kevlar helmet with an inch-thick Plexiglas shield. ATF agents moved the sandbags aside so he could enter my office, where he used a portable X-ray device to examine the bomb. He clipped the X-ray device back to his belt, covered the bomb with a bomb blanket, and attached a hook-and-line set to the device itself. Then he retreated thirty feet down a flight of stairs and remotely pulled the bomb's components apart. Only then did I breathe easy again.

"Go buy a lottery ticket, Bill," Frank Kerse told me. "Today must be your lucky day."

Hamrick was identified from the commissary log listing the bomb components he'd purchased. He had targeted me because I was slated to prosecute the case against him for making those threats against Judge Kidd. He was arrested inside the Ohio County Jail and transferred to federal custody. Months later, I stared directly into Hamrick's sunken eyes through the whole of my testimony in district court. He stared back at me indignantly. It was chilling. His eyes were vacant, as dark and empty as a shark's, a smirk worn beneath his slicked-back hair. With tattoos adorned up and down his arms and swastikas on the back of both hands, he sat there unapologetic and soulless. He was pure evil and one of the scariest criminals I'd ever encountered, a psychopath without conscience who would never stray from the path that had brought him to where he was that day.

A jury found Hamrick guilty on all counts, and the district court sentenced him to 210 months in prison on the convictions for attempted murder and mailing of that bomb. They tacked on a concurrent 120-month sentence for assault with a deadly or dangerous weapon as well as the unlawful manufacture, transfer, and possession of a destructive device. The court also imposed the mandatory sentence of thirty years imprisonment to run consecutively with Hamrick's other sentences, only this time he would be serving his hitch at the ADX Supermax prison in Florence, Colorado, that's reserved for the nation's most heinous and dangerous criminals, including the Boston Marathon bomber and the infamous Mexican drug lord El Chapo.

While in Supermax, though, Hamrick proclaimed himself a jihadi and was transferred to the Communications Management Unit in Terre Haute, Indiana. The CMU was one of several prisons created by the U.S. Bureau of Prisons in response to 9/11, which generally house terrorists and significantly restrict the communications of inmates. But that didn't stop Hamrick from killing, and nearly beheading, a fellow inmate named Robert David Neal in 2018.

Hamrick wasn't the first criminal to threaten my life during my service as the United States Attorney for the Northern District of West Virginia and he wouldn't be the last. In my twenty years of service, initially as an Assistant U.S. Attorney, I faced all manner of villains from organized crime bosses to corrupt public officials to moonshiners turned marijuana distributors to drug kingpins and even the corrupt swami of the Hare Krishna movement. Many of those I prosecuted were criminal Goliaths who believed themselves to be beyond the law, free to pursue their ill-gotten gains to the detriment of ordinary people like you and me.

Someone had to stand against them. Someone had to be David, even if it meant receiving an envelope with a bomb inside. Because justice never rests, starting with the first case I ever prosecuted in 1973 as an Assistant U.S. Attorney.

AUSA

Bill Kolibash (right) being given an award for his service as an Assistant U.S. Attorney by United States Attorney General Benjamin Civiletti in 1980.

CHAPTER 1

Wheeling, West Virginia, 1973

That case focused on fraud committed by a tax preparer named Tony Lobise, who was falsifying the tax returns of his clients to assure they would get a bigger refund. It was part of the sales pitch that lured customers through his door, kind of like the H&R Block of tax-fraud preparers. Of course, he never told them that his means for getting them more money back from the IRS was illegal.

Initially, I had handled civil matters and appeals of criminal cases to the Fourth Circuit Court of Appeals after taking the position of Assistant United States Attorney (AUSA) for the Northern District of West Virginia. The appeals involved fairly routine violations of the federal criminal statutes, which made me the perfect AUSA to represent the United States since I had served my last year in the military's JAG Corps in the Appellate Government Division.

Although that tax-fraud case was simple and straightforward, it highlighted a pervasive nationwide trend that became a harbinger for some of the biggest and most important cases I tried over the years. According to the 1973 annual report issued by the Commissioner of the Internal Revenue Service, "A total of 4,977 tax returns were prepared for Service employees posing as clients during the 1973 filing period. Of these returns, 1,112 (or 22%) appeared fraudulent. From January 1972 to June 30, 1973, the Intelligence Division filed complaints, arrested or obtained indictments against 420 tax return preparers. So far 209 preparers have been convicted or have pleaded guilty."[1]

Another of my early cases was an attempted bank robbery. The culprits, who had a history of violent crime, were coming into Wheeling from Pittsburgh. Thanks to an informant's tip, we knew the route they were taking and had FBI agents stationed around the bank they intended to target. And when they got near the site, the agents closed in on foot and surrounded their car when it was stopped between other vehicles at a red light.

"Federal agents!" an agent screamed as the Tac Team rushed in with guns brandished. "Show me your hands! Show me your hands!"

The men inside the car obeyed and were arrested without incident. I prosecuted them in the district court in Elkins, West Virginia, before a sequestered jury that didn't have much trouble convicting them on all counts. That was especially meaningful to me, because I hadn't had a lot of luck with the firearms cases I'd brought before the same court. Elkins, West Virginia, was about as redneck country as you can get. When new babies were born, rumor had it that a toy deer rifle was put in the crib instead of a football, basketball, or baby doll. I learned the hard way that it wasn't easy to get a conviction on a firearms case in Elkins because jurors were not exactly the friendliest toward these cases. Fortunately, they felt differently about bank robbers.

* * *

I tried my first major case as an AUSA in 1977. A Charleston, West Virginia–based DEA agent named Randy James noticed from drug-trafficking intelligence reports that the same names he was familiar with while stationed in Chicago had begun to show up in our neck of the woods. He knew the source was a drug network out of Mexico but hadn't latched on to the particulars of the operation yet. This was before the birth of the actual Mexican drug cartels that can be traced back to the 1980s, and the Mexican gang responsible had recently engaged in a violent shoot-out with officers of Mexico's federal police force, so we knew we were up against some pretty bad hombres.

The key witness in the case was a woman named Karen Pappas. Police were summoned to her home by neighbors who had heard shouting and sounds of a struggle. When they arrived, they found marijuana strewn all over the apartment. That gave them probable cause for a search, which included Pappas's car, where they found an additional 165 pounds of marijuana in the trunk.

By then, Pappas had been hospitalized for injuries suffered in an altercation with her then boyfriend Eric Walton. She spoke willingly and without counsel present to Randy James from her hospital bed through a swath of bandages and swelling, her speech garbled at times.

"I just want this to be over," she started.

"That's why I'm here. Tell me about the marijuana police found in the apartment and the trunk of your car."

"It was part of the same shipment."

Randy leaned forward in his chair.

"It comes into New Mexico from Mexico," Pappas continued. "I fly down regularly to make the pickup."

"How regularly?"

"I don't know. Often. A lot."

"How much?"

"This particular shipment was three hundred pounds."

"Did you drive it all the way back to West Virginia yourself?"

"No, we use an older couple who hides the stash in their camper. Nobody ever pulls them over. You know, who stops Grandma and Grandpa?"

"You said 'we,'" Randy noted. "Did this involve Eric Walton, the man you allege beat you up?"

"Allege? Look at my face. And, yes, it involves Walton. He's the boss, the man in these parts when it comes to drugs."

"And you'll testify to that in court?"

"As long as I don't have to go to jail, I'll testify about anything."

It turned out the fight had been spurred by Pappas finding out Walton was seeing another woman. We gave her immunity and moved her into the Witness Protection Program to keep her safe. She was about to expose a massive drug network supplying the Midwest and West Virginia, which meant the danger she faced was very real to the point we even put a guard on her hospital room door.

Randy started connecting all the dots, which led us to realize Walton's weed was being distributed out of Belmont County, Ohio, by way of Chicago and Indianapolis. The Belmont County Sheriff's Office, backed up by the FBI, raided the storehouse and confiscated all the marijuana that had come up from Mexico by way of New Mexico.

Eric Walton was arrested on a ten-count indictment returned November 7, 1977, against him and six other defendants. Our case rested squarely on the shoulders of Karen Pappas, whom we kept shielded even from defense attorneys up until the time she arrived in court. Walton had hired a very prominent local attorney, while several of his codefendants were represented by an out-of-town attorney who arrived wearing a long leather coat, expensive jewelry, and a flashy suit. As soon as the judge emerged from chambers, I saw him snicker at the lawyer's appearance. His message was clear: you don't come to Elkins, West Virginia, to defend a drug dealer dressed like a wiseguy yourself.

I spent hours getting Pappas prepared for that trial. I knew our entire case rested on her shoulders and that defense counsel was going to try and impeach her credibility. Walton's case centered almost entirely on convincing the jury that Karen had set him up in order to seize the drug operation from him. To prove that, they insisted her actions stemmed from a turf war currently underway between the Belmont County, Ohio, part of the organization and the Morgantown, West Virginia, group. The word was Belmont County was making a move to take over Morgantown's operation. In response, to put the message out that Morgantown was not to be messed with, a couple of thugs headed into Ohio and shot the Belmont County drug kingpin in the anus to make their point—supposedly that way of shooting him was meant to stoke fear in potential rivals and send a message to everyone else to steer clear of the Morgantown drug operation. The Belmont County kingpin wasn't supposed to die, but he did, so Walton's defense made use of that internecine conflict to cast aspersions on Karen Pappas's testimony. But she proved unflappable on the stand, great in direct testimony, and held her own in strong fashion during cross-examination.

Following a four-day trial, a jury found Eric Walton guilty on two counts: possession with intent to distribute fifty pounds of marijuana and actual distribution of ten pounds of marijuana. He was fined $15,000 and sentenced to five years imprisonment on each of the two counts on which he was convicted, the sentences to run consecutively.

As for the murder investigation up in Belmont County, Ohio, the alleged shooter turned out to be a Walton enforcer named J. B. Brown. The Belmont County prosecutors handled that case, so my involvement was limited. Prior to the Walton trial, though, we did encounter a problem when we went to pick up the marijuana to use as evidence. A raid conducted by the local sheriff's department had netted thirty-six pounds. But several pounds of that, consisting of a stronger strain called Acapulco Gold, had gone missing at some point between the evidence locker and the crime lab in Columbus, Ohio, where it had been tested.

Back then, Kathy Crumbley was the sheriff up there, a kind of legend for being the first woman ever to be elected county sheriff anywhere in the country. In 1977, the song "The Lady Sheriff of Belmont County," sung by Adolph Anthony, was released as a 45 RPM single by Gold Star Records and included the line, "Where they got a lady sheriff, the only one of her kind."

Indeed, she was. Kathy stood a couple inches over six feet and weighed well over two hundred pounds. She gave no quarter to any man, especially those who served under her, and I think she fancied Randy James quite a bit. If she ever found the guy who stole the marijuana from her evidence locker, standing trial would have been the least of his problems. I once heard that Sheriff Kathy's hairdresser had to stand on a Coca-Cola carton to cut her hair because she was more than a foot shorter. She died in 2011 and will forever be remembered for colorful appearances she made on *The Mike Douglas Show* and *The Tonight Show*.

Meanwhile, I turned my attention as an Assistant U.S. Attorney to a scourge that rivaled drug dealing: public corruption.

CHAPTER 2

Hancock County, West Virginia, 1977

It all started with gambling. There are currently five casinos operating legally across the state of West Virginia. There were far more, though, sixty to seventy years before that operated illegally. The vast bulk of them were located in the panhandle area of West Virginia where the state borders Pennsylvania and Ohio. There was a street up there called the Strip where gambling casinos operated with impunity. By the time I became an AUSA for the Northern District, my predecessors had done such a good job prosecuting them that the casinos were gone, in stark contrast to their peak era in the 1950s and 1960s.

The underworld was committed to changing that. In 1976, a Hancock County resident named Ron Donell, running for sheriff in the county, was approached by a mobster from Steubenville, Ohio, named Silvio "Berdie" Pinciaro. Pinciaro ran gambling in those parts for the Steel City mob out of Pittsburgh under the auspices of Joseph "JoJo" Pecora.

"How do you feel about gambling, Mr. Donell?" Pinciaro asked.

"It's not for me, but I've got no problem with it so long as it's on the up-and-up."

Pinciaro cast Donell a wry grin. "Well, if you get elected and allowed gambling in Hancock County, you'd stand to make a lot of money."

"Last time I checked," Donell told him, "gambling was illegal."

Pinciaro, the textbook definition of a low-level gangster, didn't smile this time. He just winked. "That's why you stand to make a lot of money."

Indeed.

"A hilly section of the 63-mile panhandle that runs between Pennsylvania and Ohio," *Reader's Digest* wrote in an April 1980 article entitled "Sheriff Donell Beats the Racketeers," "Hancock County was ideal for racketeering. Its casinos drew high rollers from Cleveland, Youngstown and Pittsburgh; area steel mills provided many more eager players. Illegal gambling had become a way of life in the county, leading many residents to assume there was corruption. 'Get elected in Hancock County,' Donell had heard, 'and retire rich in four years.'"[1]

But he'd been an Eagle Scout in his teenage years, as well as president of his high school class—a solid citizen, in other words, who came from an equally solid family that had deep roots in the community. Donell reported his encounter with Birdie Pinciaro to the FBI, at which point the Bureau, along with the U.S. Attorney's Office for the Northern District and the West Virginia State Police, started an undercover operation. The FBI special agent in charge of the case was one of the very best I ever worked with, Tom Burgoyne.

Before long, the case blossomed into something significantly bigger than just a gambler from Ohio trying to expand his business into West Virginia. Once Donell was elected in Hancock County, he agreed to pose as a crooked sheriff. With Donell's apparent cooperation, Pinciaro and his boys moved in and approached a whole bunch of local bars on the pretext of putting pinball and cigarette machines in their establishments.

"And while we're at it," they'd tell the owner, "we can put in gambling machines, even loan you the money you need to create space for them."

So this was never about bringing full-fledged casinos back to Hancock County; it was, instead, about packing the back rooms and basements of bars with video gambling machines and setting up bookmaking operations. This was a working-class area where the bulk of residents worked in steel mills or the retail stores supporting the families that called the area home. Men would get out of work on Fridays, cash their paychecks, and head to their favorite watering holes. Except if Birdie Pinciaro had his way, they'd have something else to spend their money on in those establishments besides alcohol.

Of course, Pinciaro knew plenty of these mom-and-pop establishments wouldn't be able to pay the loans they'd taken to build their gambling rooms, so the mob guys would come in and take over. There were kickbacks paid to Donell in his guise as a corrupt sheriff to protect the operations and keep any competitors out of the gambling business. In turn, Donell passed that money up the food chain to the prosecuting attorney of Hancock County, Robert Altomare, thereby implicating the highest local official responsible for dispensing justice in the sting. Pinciaro and his associates must have figured they were covered from on high with both the sheriff and head prosecutor on the take. The kickbacks Donell received and distributed, accordingly, became one of the most vital elements in making our case against Altomare since the evidence was pretty much indisputable.

Here, for example, is an excerpt from a conversation between Sheriff Donell and county prosecutor Altomare, recorded on December 19, 1978, that became one of the primary pieces of evidence used to prove our case at trial:

> DONELL: Come in, hi, Bob.
>
> ALTOMARE: Just take a couple minutes of your time to talk about a couple things with you.... Now, here is—no one knows anything about this but you, Dingbat and me—what I think I've put together real clean, for a thousand dollars a month each. I mean clean. Ron, we could go into a takeover of slot machines [with] Dingbat, and listen to how we're gonna do this. Beautiful, Ron, it's beautiful. I mean I love this.
>
> DONELL: Okay.
>
> ALTOMARE: Let me start at the beginning. These machines are owned by the clubs, under a service contract.
>
> DONELL: Twenty-five percent. [Benny] Phillips.
>
> ATORMARE: Okay, that means, according to Dingbat [Delong], about four grand a month to Phillips. I'm talking a *month*.
>
> DONELL: Just one club.
>
> ALTOMARE: Total—Newell Legion, Chester Legion, Lawrenceville Legion, Chester Vets.
>
> DONELL: Un-huh.
>
> ALTOMARE: Dinger's telling the guy [who cleans out the machines], Harry, or whoever Harry is, "Don't come back. After today I'm servicing my own machines." In other words, Dinger's not paying Benny 25% anymore, okay, and Dinger owns the machines. Can't be a problem because Benny can't go to the State Police, can't go to you, and it's not a federal violation so what are they going to do [to] Dinger?

DONELL: Uh-huh.

ALTOMARE: Benny's out. The problem comes in when we try to go to Sam Graham at the Chester Vets and whoever else is at the Lawrenceville Legion or Chester Legion. I just can't send you in there and say, "Quit dealing with Phillips and start dealing with Dingbat, okay?"

DONELL: Uh-huh.

ALTOMARE: No way you can do that, which means there was to be a way to get around that. Here's what we do.... Dinger throws them out of the Newell Legion today.

DONELL: Okay.

ALTOMARE: And Dinger's not saying a word to anybody else, yet.

DONELL: Okay.

ALTOMARE: I want you to get the deputy or deputies, out of uniform between now and Monday, to go into those three places and play the slots, okay, and I think that can be done. If you need [ID] cards, Dinger has cards, give me a call. Now you have your boys make the buys, they know what to do.

DONELL: Right.

ALTOMARE: Okay, right, now we will prepare search and seizure warrants based on that, but I don't want a big explosion in the newspaper about your picking up slot machines. It doesn't look good, Ron.

DONELL: Right.

ALTOMARE: I tell Dinger, "Dinger, Ron has search warrants and he's going in Wednesday night." Now Dinger goes to these three places: "The prosecutor and sheriff are pissed off at Benny. I already threw Benny out of my place. I don't want any trouble. There are warrants for these slot machines." You make the raid at 10 o'clock that night—the slots are gone. No publicity, nothing, return the warrants, no property found, we don't call the press, nothing, okay?

DONELL: Okay.

ALTOMARE: Next morning, Dinger goes in: "See what I'm telling ya, these guys are putting Benny out of business. Now if you guys will come over to me, let me handle the service contract, I think I can talk to Ron and Bob. I'm not promising but I know this—if you continue to deal with Benny, you're finished, 'cause they'll come back." If they don't buy that, then we'll do the same thing one more time.

DONELL: Sounds good.

ALTOMARE: Dinger takes those four places over, okay, and we starting getting a piece a month.

DONELL: Yeah, that sounds better.

ALTOMARE: That's a lot better.[2]

So we had Altomare on tape not only admitting his participation in the crime and making himself a party to it but actually ordering Sheriff Ron Donell to *commit* a crime. But the tapes would be useless if we didn't have the physical evidence to back them up in court. To obtain that physical evidence, our team planned a sweeping raid on all the local gambling establishments on January 26, 1979. Nearly a hundred federal agents and West Virginia state policemen entered those establishments within minutes of each other and seized the machines. That was a Friday night. On Monday morning, I began presenting evidence to a federal grand jury to gain the indictments we sought.

This was Pinciaro's operation, but it had been blessed by the Steel City mob out of Pittsburgh in the person of JoJo Pecora, who'd been heavily involved in casino operations along the infamous Strip back in the '50s and '60s. He basically controlled all gambling in the panhandle area and saw an opening to do so again throughout Hancock County. While Altomare was the primary target of the U.S. Attorney's Office, the FBI prioritized Pecora along with numerous other mob types who were seeping into the area.

All that was standing in the way of Pinciaro's, and Pecora's, attempted move into Hancock County in the late 1970s was the federal investigation we'd opened, thanks to Ron Donell coming to us about the corruption. And we had an innovative, then little-known tool at our disposal…

RICO.

According to the Department of Justice, the Racketeer Influenced and Corrupt Organizations Act, which had passed in 1970, was meant "to strengthen the legal tools of evidence gathering by establishing new penal prohibitions and providing enhanced sanctions and new remedies for dealing with the unlawful activities of those engaged in organized crime." The power of RICO lay in its conspiracy provision, based on an enterprise rationale, that allows tying together apparently unrelated crimes with a common objective into a prosecutable pattern of racketeering. In addition, RICO provided for severer penalties and permitted a defendant to be convicted and separately punished for both the underlying crimes that constitute the pattern of racketeering activity as well as for a substantive violation of RICO.

In RICO, "enterprise" is defined as "any individual, partnership, corporation, association, or other legal entity, or any union or group of individuals associated in fact although not a legal entity." The terms of the RICO law enabled prosecutors like me to tie numerous crimes together into one case, even if they had covered an extensive period of time. By combining individual crimes into a broader context, law enforcement was able to pursue those in charge of an organization rather than just those who reported to them and were not the ones ordering that the crimes be committed.

RICO, for instance, allowed for the pursuit of a mob boss who ordered underlings to commit crimes in furtherance of the organization but who hasn't personally pulled the trigger, set a fire, or committed a burglary. But we discovered there was one problem with the law as we began a RICO investigation into public corruption in Hancock County: it had never been successfully utilized on a case of this complexity and magnitude in the nine years since its passage. In fact, the highest profile case to rely on RICO up until that point had failed to produce a conviction against the Hells Angels motorcycle gang despite attaining sixty-four indictments.

"The trial proceeded tensely," CAFE reported in November 2021. "194 witnesses presented harrowing stories of the Angel's violence and misdeeds. Many Angels, known for their brutality toward those who testified against them, sat in the courtroom in the San Francisco Federal Building, where 8-foot high Plexiglass walls were installed around the bench. The sprawling portrait of the Angels' misdeeds, however, did not convince the jury that there was a centralized meth distribution scheme, the charge on which the indictments depended."[3]

The failure of those prosecutors to win a conviction against the Hells Angels meant we were attempting to become the first investigative body to ever successfully prosecute a RICO case of this magnitude. Good thing that the intelligence and evidence Donell provided checked every single box we needed to accomplish that.

Living a double life, meanwhile, couldn't have been easy for Ron. Plenty of the people who'd voted for him had no problem with illegal gambling taking place in the back rooms of bars; it was ingrained in the Hancock County culture and the residue left by the heyday of those casinos along the Strip that had never totally gone away. This was the epitome of a working-class area where men would yank down the handles of those poker machines with hands no amount of soap could clean and the hard hat they'd worn all day resting on the other side of the table. The steel mills were running three shifts back then.

Many of the bars were located right next to those mills and never closed, which meant they could be as busy at 7:00 a.m. as 7:00 p.m. The same held true for the gambling rooms. If someone wanted to spend a few hours feeding poker machines with nickels, dimes, or quarters or place a bet with a bookie who made a table in the bar his office, that was their decision. One of those bookies, Emilio "Hambone" Julian, had a son who played running back for the University of Pittsburgh. One game, the kid was running down the field for a touchdown when Hambone jumped up in the stands yelling, "Tackle him! Tackle him!" It turned out he had a bet on the other team.

The evidence we accumulated against all the defendants was really strong because we had some of them on tape owning up to what they did, like a local bar owner named Constantine Karas admitting to bribing local police officers. We had the cash seized from the establishments in which the gambling was taking place. And we also had guys who worked under the kingpins testifying against them to save their own butts, a common feature in all mob trials and RICO cases.

Ron Donell's testimony linked everything together. He essentially played the role of a confidential human source for us while he was serving as sheriff of Hancock County. It could have gotten him killed, but that didn't faze Donell because he saw it as his duty, part of his job as a law enforcement officer. Had he not reported being approached by Birdie Pinciaro to the FBI, there might well have never been a case at all. Ultimately, Donell received $100,000 in bribes to buy his acquiescence in a plot he had actually exposed.

"Under cover," the *Pittsburgh Press* reported in February 1979, "Donell accepted cash payments from alleged co-conspirators and turned payments over to Robert Altomare."[4] Altomare had presented a novel defense, if nothing else. Vociferously maintaining his innocence, he claimed that he was the one conducting an investigation into *Ron Donell* toward launching a state prosecution, without any police or law enforcement involvement or corroboration in the form of investigative files, reports, memoranda, or any record whatsoever of all the money that was exchanged. But we had 150 tape recordings Donell had made that proved otherwise. Those tapes outlined the various illegal ventures that Altomare as prosecuting attorney had concocted, involving bribery and illegal gambling activities in Hancock County.

Ron Donell spent the two months between the arrests and subsequent trials in a motel room to prep for his testimony and for his safety. The block of rooms was rented under false names and the federal agents protecting him were paid personally so as not to leave any trail back to Washington, or the U.S. Attorney's Office for the Northern District, for that matter. Even Altomare was in the dark about Donell's true whereabouts, believing sheriff's business was taking him regularly to Martinsburg. He didn't realize the truth until Donell walked into court to testify.

In addition to Altomare, the grand jury indictments named twenty-four defendants. Multiple trials were held in the Northern District of West Virginia from April 12, 1979, through July 24, 1979, resulting in nineteen convictions. Our trial team consisted of myself, United States Attorney Steve Jory, and Bill Wilmoth, who would succeed me as United States Attorney during the Clinton administration.

The attorneys on the defense side made for a who's who list of criminal defense counsel from Charleston, Wheeling, and Pittsburgh. Robert Altomare was represented at trial by Rudy DiTrapano, one of the two best criminal attorneys in Charleston, West Virginia, at the time. One of his codefendants in that particular trial before a visiting judge named Franklin Taylor Dupree Jr. from North Carolina was represented by Stanley Preiser, the second of the best criminal lawyers out of Charleston. Preiser and DiTrapano despised each other so much that whenever Preiser left the courtroom during a break, he instructed his associate Fred Fahrenz to stay at the table so Rudy wouldn't pilfer any of the strategy notes from his legal pad. We'd have a bench conference in front of Judge Dupree and Preiser would always pronounce RICO properly, whereas DiTrapano made it a habit to say "ry-ko" instead. And when they got to arguing about a legal issue, the judge would say, "Gentlemen, there's another section of the United States Code called I-95. It goes to Richmond, and if you have an issue with any of my rulings, you want to look at I-95." Richmond was where the Fourth Circuit Court of Appeals was located.

Speaking of which, when it came time to appeal, it was Stanley Preiser who represented Robert Altomare. Preiser would go on to appear in court in twenty-five different states and is generally considered to be one of the finest defense lawyers of his time, hardly ever losing a case. But he lost this appeal.

That proved to be small consolation to Sheriff Ron Donell, who became a pariah in the community and ended up with West Virginia state policemen as permanent house guests to protect his family. The blinds were drawn in his house pretty much all the time, and he lost his bid for reelection strictly because he had done his job and refused to look the other way. In response, those who believed gambling was a victimless crime regarded him differently. They weren't thinking about the bar owners who forfeited their establishments when they couldn't pay the loans the mob had made to them, or where the money that had paid off the corrupted officials like Altomare had come from, any more than where the profits made off those back rooms ended up. Drugs maybe, or money laundering and, maybe, loan-sharking. There's no such thing as a victimless crime.

Some of the biggest tests we faced were challenges to how we prosecuted the cases under the RICO statute. After all, there wasn't a lot of successful precedent to rely on; basically, none. During the trial, for example, Judge Franklin Taylor Dupree had ruled that certain evidence alleging Pecora's involvement with slot machines was inadmissible. In his closing argument, defense counsel reminded the jury that the government had promised, in its opening statement, to prove that Pecora had slot machines, then stressed that no such evidence had been put before the jury regarding this allegation. In rebuttal, I stated that the trial court had prevented the government from presenting any evidence of the slot machines but that in any event such evidence was not needed for a conviction because other testimony established three acts of bribery by Pecora, which was more than enough to win a conviction under RICO.

To a large degree, those nineteen convictions we scored in court were thanks to the vital role the West Virginia State Police (WVSP) played in our operation when it came to surveillance, wiretaps, and all the arrests. One of the lead troopers on the case, Ron Shiflett, was nicknamed Shifty, and he had a minor stuttering problem. On the day of his testimony, though, he appeared extremely nervous and could barely get a word out. Ron had always been a good witness, and I wondered what had caused his nervousness. I'd later learn that his wife had come to court to watch him testify.

Speaking of the WVSP, the superintendent of the state police back then, Harley Mooney, was a retired U.S. Army general and took no guff from anyone. It was right around this time that, for some reason, the Carter administration's Justice Department became very circumspect about arresting white-collar criminals. When we told General Mooney about the new Justice Department policy, he said, "Well, that policy does not apply to the West Virginia State Police. Damn, I'm gonna go up there and arrest these guys, put them in handcuffs, and have a tank roll down Main Street with them trailing behind it."

JoJo Pecora, in his appeal, threw all kinds of mud at the wall in the hope that something would stick. He stated, for instance, that "the RICO statute is not applicable to the allegedly illegal activities because there was no 'enterprise or impact on interstate commerce regarding the bribery and misuse of the offices of the county law enforcement officials.'" His attorneys also claimed that "the evidence failed to show that he engaged in a pattern of racketeering activity; i.e., commission of at least two of the acts outlined in § 1961(5)." His contention here was that he had committed only one act of bribery, because the other bribes had been provided by underlings who were, of course, beholden to him. He and just about all the defendants challenged the admission of the taped conversations because those recordings meant we had them dead to rights discussing everything with their coconspirators.

There were approximately 150 transcripts that I had placed in a binder separated by inserts with different colored tabs. Stanley Preiser thought that the tabs meant we had some color code since we knew the contents of the tapes almost verbatim. Stanley told Fred Fahrenz they needed to find out what our code, which really never existed, was.

All of these appeal efforts failed, affirming not only the convictions we'd obtained but also the RICO statute in general. Our public corruption case became a model of how to prosecute a RICO case, and many such investigations began to follow our lead immediately. Sometimes history makes you and sometimes you make history, but this was truly a team effort that established the precedent for how I would try some of the biggest cases I handled when I moved up to U.S. Attorney.

All of which goes back to my years in the JAG Corps. I cut my teeth there in military courtrooms, where lives literally hung in the balance.

The JAG Corps

Bill Kolibash kissing his daughter Shariane, one of this book's coauthors, in 1972 while stationed in Fort Hood in Texas as a member of the JAG Corps.

CHAPTER 3

Benwood, West Virginia, 1966

I wasn't born to be a lawyer. In fact, becoming one wasn't even on my radar through high school and my first two years or so in college.

I came to Brown University as a member of the Class of 1966, intending to concentrate in mathematics and physics. That is, until my second semester when my learning curve started to straighten out. The textbooks would fill a backpack on their own, and for physics there were weekly four- or five-hour labs on top of the regular class load. One day I was walking back into the fraternity house where I lived, lugging those textbooks, when I ran into a fraternity brother carrying all of one paperback.

"What's that?" I asked him.

"My history textbook."

I nearly dropped the big books I was carrying. That was all I needed to hear. I changed my major to history. My course load, as well as my book load, lightened considerably.

I was slated to graduate from Brown just as the draft lottery for the Vietnam War was really ramping up. At the time, the two best ways to be granted a deferral were either to become a teacher working in select underprivileged areas or enroll in law school. One of my advisors was a professor named Jim Barnhill, who was in the process of establishing what would become the school's Department of Theater Arts and Performance Studies.

"What are your plans after graduation?" Professor Barnhill asked me during my senior year.

"I'm thinking about law school," I told him, even though nothing in my background and coursework suggested I'd be a good fit, and I don't think I'd ever even met a lawyer in my entire life to that point.

Professor Barnhill shook his head, scowling. "Stop. Forget about it. You can't talk. You've got a West Virginia accent, coupled with a New England brogue [which I had acquired in my four years in Providence], and your diction is horrible. You'll never make it as a public speaker, let alone manage the trials and tribulations of a courtroom."

I didn't listen to him, fortunately. And years later, when I came back to Brown for my twenty-fifth reunion, I ran into Professor Barnhill on campus.

"Professor, remember me, the guy who couldn't talk clearly? Turns out, I did make it as a lawyer, and I think I'm doing pretty well—as a U.S. Attorney!"

He did indeed remember me and offered his hearty congratulations. It had been nothing personal for either of us. And the truth was Barnhill had taken an interest in me, as he did all his students, staying in touch with many of them long after they graduated Brown.

Senior year, I didn't score very well on my LSATs, the test required for entry into law school, and I only had a C+ average. Brown was in the midst of transitioning to what was then called the "New Curriculum," the brainchild of a visionary education expert named Ira Magaziner. The New Curriculum did away with core requirements and allowed students to take the same classes with only a Pass/Fail grade. Had I come to the school a few years later, I guess I would have left with a P average instead.

My early education was at a small Catholic grade school. My eighth-grade class consisted of myself and three other students. Although the school was very small, it had an excellent basketball program, and several of its graduates attended Linsly Military Institute, the premier college preparatory school in the Ohio Valley at that time that provided athletic scholarships. I was one of the better eighth-grade basketball players in the Catholic parochial league, and Linsly had expressed an interest in me attending the school. By the time late July rolled around, though, I had yet to hear back from anyone associated with the school.

So I prepared to attend the local high school where my brother was a senior and began to train informally with the football team. A great season was in the offing, since the team was led by a star player who later received a scholarship at Ohio State and played four years for Woody Hayes.

As I was hanging out with some of my friends over the summer, a Linsly alumnus who knew me was riding by in his vehicle and pulled over.

"You ever hear back from anyone at Linsly?" he asked me out the window.

"No, sir. I'm going to the local high school."

"Why don't you hold off on that decision. Let me see if I can have someone from Linsly contact you."

A few days later, Linsly football coach Etz Rine contacted me, and we arranged a meeting with him at my house with my parents in attendance. Coach Rine asked me what my plans were, and I told him I was going to attend the local high school.

Sitting at the kitchen table in our three-room house, Coach Rine, in his typical no-nonsense tone, said, "Son, if you want to go to college, the best opportunity for you would be to attend Linsly."

He told me I would receive a full scholarship and that there might be some other funds available for uniforms, books, and the like. I looked at my parents, both of whom had grown up with limited education opportunities, and they nodded, indicating their approval of Coach Rine's offer.

At the time, Linsly was accessible primarily to the prominent families in town since the tuition and related costs were substantial. Linsly also doubled as a boarding school for out-of-state kids of doctors, lawyers, and executives—clearly not my demographic, making this a great opportunity.

Although I was an A student, I knew there would be an adjustment to my new scholastic environment, attending a school of such high academic standards after being part of an eighth-grade graduating class of four. Of course, you wouldn't know who was who, or which was which, because we all dressed in the same military uniform, unless you looked at the cars in the parking lot. I knew I was going to have to work hard, because many of my classmates had been at Linsly the previous four years as well, or came from bigger junior high schools that boasted more resources. That fueled the underdog mentality that saw me graduate as the salutatorian of my class and serve as captain for both the football and basketball teams in my senior year. I started on the football team as a sophomore playing defensive end.

Before my first game against a team from New Martinsville, West Virginia, my uncle Mickey pulled me aside.

"I'll give you five bucks for every fumble you recover."

I went on to recover a fumble in that game and ended up five dollars richer. I moved to the offensive line for the rest of the year and played there and linebacker the following years, calling all the defensive signals. We were a good team that won our share of games. But as a small school that played a tough schedule against AAA high school teams with far more students than we had, we took our lumps from time to time before winning the city championship my senior year.

For some Linsly Military Institute cadets, the next natural step was West Point or the Naval Academy at Annapolis. But I wasn't a candidate for either because I had really bad vision, and the military academies didn't allow corrective lenses at the time. So I applied for an ROTC scholarship to attend college, but my poor vision also precluded me from that too.

One of my history teachers at Linsly, Mr. Mead, was a Brown University graduate. His father was also a prominent lawyer and politician in the area. When seniors started weighing their options for college, Mr. Mead told me, "You would be a perfect fit for Brown."

I agreed and submitted my application. I had several other football and basketball scholarships from colleges in Ohio and Pennsylvania as a backup, so I had nothing to lose by shooting for the Ivy League. And then, lo and behold, my academic record and my talents on the football field helped secure me a spot at Brown, where I was eligible for enough financial aid to make up for the lack of scholarships in the Ivy League.

I knew Brown would be challenging but was confident I could be successful because of my academic and athletic success at Linsly. I enjoyed my four years there, which prepared me for all future challenges that followed. In addition to receiving an excellent education, I made lifelong friends, many of whom I remain in contact with to this date. I remember my band, Little Otto (my nickname) and the Pixies, playing during parties in our fraternity house. Over Thanksgiving and Christmas, I didn't have the money for a bus or train ticket, much less a plane, so I'd always hitchhike home, and the adventures I had on the road would fill another book.

Good things, though, do come to an end, which for me was June 1966 when I graduated to face a slew of new challenges. The Vietnam War was raging, the draft had been reinstated, and no one's future was secure. I ended up applying to West Virginia University College of Law. Being a West Virginia resident and a Brown graduate, I figured that school gave me my best chance of admission, but I fell short. I got the rejection letter in the mail and read it a bunch of times, as if it might change the outcome.

When it didn't, I figured the West Virginia University College of Law must have made a mistake. I couldn't get anyone on the phone to plead my case to, so I just drove the two-hour distance from my house to the school's Colson Hall, which had been home to the law school since 1923, to see the man in charge of the school, Dean Paul Selby.

"May I help you?" his secretary asked me.

"Thank you, yes. I'm here to see Dean Selby."

She looked miffed. "Do you have an appointment?"

"No. But I want to talk to him about this," I said, producing the now well-worn rejection letter.

She didn't have to view the letter long to know what it was. I could tell she was ready to tell me to write a letter myself or something, but I wasn't going anywhere until I got to see the dean.

"Let me see if he has a few minutes," she said, having gotten that sense.

Paul Selby had been dean of the West Virginia University College of Law for only two years at that point, but he'd go on to do great things for the school that included shepherding the construction of a new venue on campus that became known as Law School Hill, which opened in 1974, two years after he departed the school. On the day of my visit, he did something great for me as well.

"Dean Selby, look, I know I'm not the greatest student," I said of my 2.5 grade point average at Brown, "and that my LSAT scores weren't the greatest either. But you've got to consider the competition. You're accepting people from colleges that I don't think have the academic standard that Brown has. If I'd gone to one of them, I would've been starting here in the fall and wouldn't have needed to come to see you."

"I'll tell you what," Dean Selby offered, more impressed than taken back by my show of bravado, "take the LSATs again, and if you improve your score, we'll reconsider our decision."

I took the LSATs a second time on the day President Lyndon Johnson's daughter Luci got married. I improved my score a little, and it proved enough. I got my acceptance letter from Dean Selby personally on the very same day another envelope came for me in the mail. It didn't contain a mail bomb, but easing the single page from inside was a still bit mind-blowing…

My draft notice.

CHAPTER 4

Charlottesville, Virginia, June 1969

Since I was accepted into law school, I was eligible for a three-year deferment, which I decided to take advantage of. I was a lot more successful academically in law school than at Brown and was a member of the *West Virginia Law Review*. While I was in law school, I married my wife, Rita, prior to my final year. Upon graduation from law school and admittance into the West Virginia State Bar in June1969, I was offered a commission as a captain in the United States Army, which I accepted.

I became a member of the Judge Advocate General Corps, serving a four-year stretch. My daughter, Shariane, was born three days after I became a JAG officer. On the day she was born, I was at Fort Lee, Virginia, undergoing basic training but was allowed several days' leave to come home and see her. We watched Neil Armstrong walk on the moon the following month from Charlottesville. My son Bill was born while I was based at Fort Hood in Texas, assigned to the Second Armored Division. When I was at Fort Lee, we did some cursory weapons training, but since I was going to spend my military career in a courtroom, there wasn't a lot of need to master the M14 rifle or drive any tanks.

"Excuse me, Captain," the range instructor asked after inspecting a target I'd missed with every shot, "but can you see?"

"No," I told him, "not really."

Needless to say, my marksmanship left a lot to be desired. Good thing I was bound for a courtroom and not Vietnam.

I gained great legal experience in the JAG Corps, the kind of training junior associates seldom get with big, prestigious law firms. Mostly those young men and women do little more than carry a partner or senior associate's briefcase into court or lug boxes full of evidentiary material from one room to another. By contrast, here I was in my midtwenties trying cases before a military court in Fort Hood that went all the way to capital murder.

Among the most positive experiences I took from the JAG Corps was the opportunity to serve as both defense and prosecuting counsel at different times according to a rotation. There were occasions where I tried a case from the defense table in the morning and then prosecuted another case in the afternoon. This was the early 1970s, and we still had tens of thousands of troops fighting in Vietnam. Thanks to so many soldiers stationed at Fort Hood who'd tried drugs over there, especially marijuana, a lot of the cases I handled on both sides of the room involved search-and-seizure arguments. In the morning, I'd be filing a brief and offering arguments as to why the evidence in question should be excluded. In the afternoon on a different case, I'd file a brief and offer arguments as to why comparable evidence should be allowed.

I had felt from the beginning that my future was as a prosecutor. But the time I spent serving as defense counsel made for invaluable experience because it helped spotlight the limitations that role brought with it. Understanding your opponent's weaknesses can be a priceless commodity, as is understanding a defense attorney's psyche. As my career progressed, it was always a lot easier for me to get inside the heads of defense counsels, because I was well practiced with the mindset.

In those days, taking a single puff of marijuana could result in a twenty-year sentence in Texas, so these were serious cases. Once, to make a point, the case investigator actually lit up a joint in the courtroom to illustrate that he could indeed identify the smell, supplying the probable cause to arrest the defendant. Even if the accused wasn't sentenced to years in the stockade, he could be court-martialed and given a bad conduct discharge from the army. Try getting a job with that on your record.

Because of their nature, many of these cases had multiple defendants, and I couldn't represent them all due to conflicts of interest. Once, we had this JAG officer who'd come back into the service as a retread, and he took on a client I wasn't allowed to represent. He had a problem with alcohol and spent the bulk of his time in the Officers' Club, while I was preparing my client's defense. Then his client ended up getting acquitted, while mine was convicted.

The capital murder case I tried as prosecutor involved a noncommissioned officer who had too much to drink one night at the NCO Club. A bouncer threw him out. The NCO returned to the club, pulled his gun, and shot the bouncer, killing him. A panel of officers and NCOs determined that the alcohol eliminated the intent to kill and found him guilty of second-degree murder. He'd still be going away for twenty-five years or so, but he didn't face a death sentence, which first-degree murder carried in the military at that time.

Another interesting case I tried involved a defendant from Fort Sam Houston in San Antonio, Texas, where conscientious objectors who'd ultimately joined the military were trained as medics, nurses, or physical therapists so they wouldn't have to man a combat position in Vietnam. A few of these young men had some disciplinary problems, mostly disobeying orders and that kind of thing. Because they were going to be court-martialed and Fort Sam Houston didn't have a military stockade, their trials were held at Fort Hood. I was assigned to represent one of the conscientious objectors as military defense counsel.

Since the trial was scheduled during the holiday season, I had to stay behind while Rita and six-month-old Shari flew from Killeen to Dallas to catch anther plane to return home to West Virginia. Well, the plane encountered a serious mechanical problem, and Rita told me they had to assume the crash position upon landing. To this day, she's still mad at me for not being on board that plane with her.

One of my fellow JAG officers, Oliver Barber, was a very effective prosecutor. Unfortunately for Ollie, he had a thick mustache that our commanding staff judge advocate told him to shave off. When Ollie refused to comply, our judge advocate repeated his order a while later and added a caveat:

"Shave off your mustache, or I'll send you to Vietnam."

Ollie held his ground, kept the mustache, and was sent to Vietnam.

Years later, when I was working in the U.S. Attorney's Office, we had a prisoner case out of Kentucky. I called to get some additional information and learned the defense attorney was none other than Ollie. I reached out to him and he provided the information that I had requested on this particular case, in which his client would be serving as a potential witness. We didn't talk about Vietnam at all, but at least he made it home safe and alive.

After I finished three years in the JAG Corps, I had the opportunity to accompany my commanding officer to his new post in Hawaii, but I respectfully declined because the reassignment would have required me to re-up for another three years. I was eager to put all this courtroom experience I'd gained into action, given that I'd had no previous experience of any kind with litigation. The West Virginia University College of Law lacked a trial advocacy class; that meant, once you got into court after graduation, it was sink or swim. Thanks to the experience I had gained in the JAG Corps I was swimming in the deep end, but I still had another year as a JAG before that came to pass.

I had assumed the position of Chief of Military Justice at Fort Hood, which meant that I reviewed all the court-martial proceedings and prepared reports for the commanding general. This provided great experience for reviewing and drafting legal arguments for appeals. After those three years at Fort Hood, an opening came up in the Appellate Government Division, which was located in Falls Church, Virginia, and I applied. My current position made me a solid fit, and I welcomed the opportunity to move back east and be that much closer to home.

One of the first cases I handled on appeal in my new position as an appellate government lawyer was a case very much like the infamous My Lai massacre case in which Lieutenant William Calley was found guilty of personally murdering twenty-two Vietnamese civilians and sentenced to life in prison. The case I handled was on a much smaller level than that, but the guilty party was appealing his conviction nonetheless. On appeal, I employed the same arguments that resulted in Lieutenant Calley's conviction being upheld, and this conviction was affirmed as well. Precedent, I learned, is a prime component of trials in all courtrooms.

Other cases I dealt with often involved the practice of "fragging," described by journalist Eugene Linden as "a macabre ritual of Vietnam in which American enlisted men attempt to murder their superiors. The word comes from the nickname for hand grenades, a weapon popular with enlisted men because the evidence is destroyed with the consummation of the crime."[1] Most of these incidents occurred because of the alleged incompetence of senior NCOs who did not enjoy the faith or respect of their men and were seen as more dangerous to their survival than the Viet Cong. The cases I handled mostly involved a subtler method of fragging where the grenades were rigged to explode, which provided at least the possibility that the blast had been triggered accidentally. Most of the appeals challenged the veracity of the evidence, and not a single one was reversed on my watch.

I also argued cases before the United States in the U.S. Court of Appeals for the Armed Forces, which is the highest military tribunal and presided over by civilian judges. The decisions made by the judges on the Military Court of Appeals create precedent for all military court proceedings, similar to U.S. Supreme Court decisions, only on military matters. So needless to say, this was not just a great honor, it also provided incredible experience.

One of the cases I argued was if a canine alerting military police officers to an item in a vehicle provided probable cause for a search of that vehicle for drugs, and the Military Court of Appeals ruled that it was. Although this was a military case argued before a military tribunal, the ruling was one of the first by any court of appeals setting the precedent that a drug dog alert could, in fact, establish probable cause for search of a vehicle and other types of containers.

As my four-year army commitment drew closer to an end in 1972, I entertained the notion of becoming a military judge, due to the obvious need. But all of us JAGs back then were stuck in the rank of captain, since there was very little movement on the promotion list, and you needed to be a major or higher to be considered for a position on the bench. Meanwhile, the Department of Justice at the time was looking for lawyers to be part of an Organized Crime Drug Enforcement Task Force. That would have been a viable option for me, if it hadn't meant relocating to Detroit.

Fortunately, an opening had come up in the U.S. Attorney's Office for the Northern District of West Virginia, and the U.S. Attorney there, Jim Companion, an appointee of President Richard Nixon, hired me as an Assistant U.S. Attorney to fill the slot. I was twenty-nine and happy to be able to settle close to home with my wife and two young children.

Jim stepped down in 1976 and was replaced by my friend and fellow AUSA at the time Steve Jory. Steve had been a classmate of mine at West Virginia University College of Law. We were both AUSAs under Jim

Companion, me at the Wheeling office while Steve worked out of Elkins County. When he took over as the U.S. Attorney for the Northern District, we kept our offices the same. Steve served his entire tenure under the "court-appointed" label, since no one President Jimmy Carter put forth was ever approved. That gave him great freedom to operate apolitically and run the office as he chose, which afforded me a great deal of independence to pursue the cases I wanted to. Steve was very deferential to my thinking, which was how we started to get into some of those major criminal investigations, like the Eric Walton and Hancock County public corruption cases, in my tenure as AUSA.

Steve similarly stepped down in October 1981 after Ronald Reagan was elected president. Someone had to be appointed in the interim, a responsibility that fell on a presiding federal judge named Robert Maxwell, who chose me to be the court-appointed U.S. Attorney. I assumed that Judge Maxwell anticipated that my appointment would last only until the Reagan administration's presidentially approved United States Attorney took over the reins. After all, there were several lawyers in the Northern District of West Virginia who expressed an interest in the position who had the support of some of the state's leading Republican politicians. However, for various reasons, none of these candidates were able to meet the criteria set forth by the Reagan administration for becoming a U.S. Attorney, whereas I clearly did.

At that time, Bill Tyson was the director of the Executive Office for United States Attorneys and was familiar with the background and successes our office had been having in prosecuting those major cases when I was an AUSA. In fact, on May 11, 1980, I was presented with a special commendation award by Attorney General Benjamin Civiletti for my outstanding service. Bill indicated that the Department of Justice was committed to seeking a presidentially appointed U.S. Attorney for the Northern District of West Virginia, since Steve Jory was never presidentially appointed and had never been confirmed by the Senate.

Being in the army for four years and an Assistant U.S. Attorney for seven years, I was never politically active and, in fact, was prohibited from engaging in any type of political activity during those time periods. Growing up in West Virginia, which was heavily Democratic at the time, I registered as a Democrat when I became eligible to vote, consistent with the political atmosphere locally and statewide. I subsequently changed my political registration to Republican when I was offered the position of Assistant United States Attorney, since that appointment would be coming during a Republican administration.

Since there was no statewide Republican representation in Congress, the Department of Justice decided I met the criteria set by the Reagan administration and that they would send my name to the White House. The prime West Virginia Republican politician in those days was former governor Arch Moore. I met with Governor Moore, at which point he raised the issue that I at one time had been a Democrat. He candidly expressed that created some issues for him and indicated he probably would not support me. The best I could reasonably hope for was that Moore would, at the very least, not oppose my appointment.

As I said, I had developed a strong personal and professional relationship with the defense lawyer Stanley Preiser, who had successfully represented former governor Moore in a previous criminal prosecution. Stanley was very supportive of my candidacy for the United States Attorney, and when I told him of my discussions with Moore, he said that he would take care of it. I later found out that Stanley convinced Governor Moore not to oppose my candidacy for the position of United States Attorney at a golf outing in Florida. Once that matter was resolved, the appointment process moved smoothly. I was interviewed by Rudy Giuliani, who at that time was the associate attorney general. Our interview consisted mostly of discussing Yankee baseball. One of Rudy's most prized possessions was an actual bleacher seat he'd obtained during the renovation of Yankee Stadium. He kept it prominently displayed in his office.

Ultimately, I was formally nominated by President Reagan and confirmed by the United States Senate on May 13, 1982. My friend Stanley Preiser had come through in a big way, and we went on to enjoy several other interesting dealings both on a professional and social basis. After assuming the position of U.S. Attorney, I had a meeting in southern Florida, where Stanley had a home. Although I wasn't much of a golfer, Stanley invited me to play with him at the Doral Country Club. I ended up getting lost trying to find the club and was late for the tee time. When I finally arrived, there was a line of golfers waiting to tee off because

Stanley had held them all up until I got there so we wouldn't lose our place on the course. He had the golf cart set up with the club pro's clubs and an appropriate pair of golf shoes for me. At some point, Stanley said he lost the scorecard, maybe because I was winning. As we approached the eighteenth hole, he said, "I think we're tied, Bill," even though I was probably ahead. "Means this hole is for all the marbles. Watch how you hit your tee shot, because there's water to the right."

So I clubbed my tee shot to the left, where it promptly landed in a pond.

"Did I say right?" said Stanley. "I meant to say left."

That was Stanley. He loved to win and hated to lose just as much in court. He was in the same conversation as F. Lee Bailey as the best criminal attorney of that time. Bailey was a brilliant showman, but Stanley was a much better lawyer in my opinion.

Up until my formal appointment in May 1982, I wasn't able to bring on additional administrative and attorney resources, and that allowed Judge Robert Maxwell, who had opposed my nomination, to do his best to run herd over me just as he had done through Steve Jory's entire tenure since Steve was neither presidentially appointed nor Senate confirmed. Maxwell had signed off on my interim appointment only because he never expected it to become formal.

It was the worst mistake he ever made.

Judge Robert Maxwell: Justice Not Served

Bill Kolibash being sworn in as U.S. Attorney for the Northern District of West Virginia in March of 1981 as his family looks on. (Reprinted with permission of the Wheeling Newspapers.)

CHAPTER 5

Wheeling, West Virginia, 1982

Judge Maxwell didn't like me, and his comments and rulings reflected that. Take the Sammy Iaquinta case, for example. Iaquinta was a career criminal who was arrested on a federal narcotics charge in December 1980. Subsequent to that, he was also arrested on a firearms charge. In district court before Judge Maxwell, Iaquinta's counsel argued in convoluted fashion that his arrest by local authorities triggered a violation of the federal Speedy Trial Act of 1974, which, of course, it didn't. Not even close. But that didn't stop Maxwell from ignoring my counterargument and ruling in Iaquinta's favor, dismissing the charges. We appealed the decision to the Fourth Circuit Court of Appeals, which reinstated the indictments and, ultimately, Iaquinta was convicted before another judge.

Numerous rulings issued by Maxwell were overruled by the Fourth Circuit because they were low on merit and high on vindictiveness. Maxwell only liked prosecutors and investigations he could control, which meant he must have hated me and didn't even bother disguising that fact. To that point, he'd selected my immediate predecessor, Steve Jory, but never allowed him to be presidentially appointed, so Steve would remain beholden to Maxwell or risk being replaced. There was another judge named Glen Williams, who liked to come to West Virginia because his son practiced law in Clarksburg. I was told whenever Judge Williams came to Elkins, Maxwell would bad-mouth me and my office to him.

Maxwell had grown up in Elkins, among a group of wealthy, entitled elites. Staying close to home, he served as prosecuting attorney for Elkins County from 1953 to 1961, after which he served as U.S. Attorney for the Northern District from 1961 until 1964, when he left office involuntarily at the request of Attorney General Robert Kennedy. However, he later rode his Elkins elite status, and his friendship with Senator Jennings Randolph, to power. It was Senator Randolph who pushed his appointment to the federal bench with President Lyndon Johnson. And I was told Johnson acceded because he needed Randolph's support to assure the passage of the landmark Civil Rights Act of 1964.

When I first started as an AUSA, Maxwell was the only full-time federal judge in the Northern District, which meant almost all cases brought were heard by him. There was no getting around it. The Marion County Bar Association opposed his appointment, and out of spite, he made sure the judicial council shut down the federal courthouse in Fairmont instead of the courthouse in Clarksburg. Members of the bar would have to travel all the way to Elkins to litigate their cases. Winter weather in Elkins and the surrounding areas could get pretty extreme; it was prone to getting a lot of snow, which proved great for the Canaan Valley and Snowshoe Mountain ski resorts but not so much for lawyers forced to negotiate miles of icy roads. Maxwell, meanwhile, used his power to get a new courthouse built in Elkins in November 1983 so he wouldn't have to commute to the other district courthouses located in Wheeling, Martinsburg, and Clarksburg. It was all about making things more convenient for him. That's the kind of sway he held, and as a result, he was used to having everyone, especially the U.S. Attorney's Office, kowtow to him.

"For years attorneys who have come before Federal District Court Judge Robert Maxwell have been struck by the domination he has over all that occurs in his Elkins, West Virginia courthouse," the *Washington Post* wrote in November 1980. "As chief judge of the state's Northern District, he has been able to tailor the way he administers judicial duties to fit his own needs and whims. From the hiring of the U.S. attorney to the makeup of the docket sheet, the 56-year-old judge is in command."[1]

Maxwell was also chairman of the judicial budget committee, which meant anything the other federal judges wanted to requisition had to be approved by him. He got away with it because he had Senator Randolph backing him.

"Normally," that same *Washington Post* article continues, "the president selects the U.S. attorney, acting on the advice of a senator. But that's not the way it works in Maxwell's district. In 1976, with the U.S. attorney's position in the Northern District vacant and before President

Carter had been sworn into office, Maxwell used his statutory power to name Stephen Jory U.S. attorney for the district. Usually such an appointment lasts until the senator recommends a U.S. attorney. But Carter never received any name from Senator Randolph; four years later, Jory remains a court-appointed U.S. attorney arguing before a judge who can replace him at any time."[2]

Maxwell made no secret that he didn't like gun cases, student loan collection cases, or car cases where dealers rolled back odometers put before him. And he made it plain that if we did bring those cases, we'd probably lose. No other full-time judge had been appointed to serve the Northern District since 1938, in spite of the fact that our caseload had more than tripled, which was just the way Maxwell wanted it. Allegedly, he even turned down an appointment to the Fourth Circuit Court of Appeals on several occasions because he wouldn't be able to run roughshod over cases the way he did in the Northern District.

"What that really means," one plaintiff's lawyer told James Cramer of the *American Lawyer*, "is delay, delay, and more delay."[3]

That included a case against Weirton Steel Company that was filed on behalf of ninety-four women in 1971. Brought before his court, Judge Maxwell slow-walked the case for seven years by taking months to issue rulings on one defense motion after another. The plaintiffs finally succeeded in getting the case moved to a different court, where they prevailed in a settlement in 1979.[4]

Of the ninety-five federal court districts in the United States, Maxwell's ranked ninetieth in its disposition of civil cases and seventy-fourth when it came to criminal cases. I tussled with him regularly for years. I believed he had the *Exponent* newspaper behind him, because it was owned by some of his connections in Clarksburg. I, meanwhile, had a good relationship with the media, including the TV stations and newspapers in Charleston, Wheeling, Clarksburg, and Martinsburg, to name a few. When our office received favorable media coverage, an editorial praising Maxwell would inevitably appear, usually in the Clarksburg paper.

Maxwell tried to get rid of me, even after I was officially appointed by President Reagan. Sam Roberts, a doctor and member of the Elkins elite, was under investigation by our office for illegal drug activity. Dr. Roberts's wife was a lawyer and one of Judge Maxwell's law clerks. Roberts was contacted by a customer of his who was about to be arrested by the West Virginia State Police for buying drugs from the doctor, among his many clients who purchased cocaine. According to this individual's testimony, "Sam told me to relax and be cool, not to sign any plea agreement with the government. Sam told me to stall for time, that something was coming down with Bill Kolibash. Sam said that the person who might be indicted would be Bill Kolibash. Sam told me that Bill Kolibash was being investigated for wrongdoings involving some drug case that he had worked on. Sam Roberts told me that Bill Kolibash was the problem and if we could get rid of him, we'd have a chance. Sam said that if there was another U.S. Attorney appointed, he would be easier to deal with. Sam told me that he would never tell on me, and he hoped that I would never tell anything on him. He told me not to admit to anything other than recreational use involving him. Sometime later after I talked to Sam, I called his wife [Maxwell's clerk] to attempt to confirm what Sam had told me about Kolibash being in trouble and to see if there was anything she could add to what Sam told me about stalling for time and about Kolibash being in trouble. She said that she had heard what Sam had told me or she had heard some talk to that effect."

What Sam Roberts's wife was referring to was an ethics investigation against me and one of my Assistant U.S. Attorneys that Maxwell obviously had knowledge of and would have certainly encouraged. The charges were based on the fact that prior to becoming an AUSA, the lawyer involved briefly represented three defendants in an investigation when they were issued a subpoena to appear before the federal grand jury. Upon joining the office, this AUSA tangentially participated in the investigation of persons who were later indicted in the case as codefendants with his former clients.

The initial complaint, in which I was not named, by one of the defendants against the AUSA in question was rejected by the state bar association. The criminal case proceeded to trial, and the individuals involved were convicted. On appeal to the Fourth Circuit, the same defendant raised the issue of conflict involving the Assistant U.S. Attorney. Although the Fourth Circuit found that there had been no misconduct, the court did find that there was an appearance of impropriety and reversed the convictions of the defendant who had contacted the same Assistant U.S. Attorney when he was in private practice.

Following the reversal, the West Virginia State Bar reopened the inquiry and eventually filed charges against the AUSA and me. The AUSA was charged with wrongfully accepting employment with the United States Attorney's Office and with misrepresenting evidence to the district court. I was charged with failing to adequately supervise the AUSA and also with failing to fully inform the district court of particular facts at a subsequent hearing. The bar concluded that the conduct did not constitute a violation of the West Virginia Code of Professional Responsibility, and the charges against the AUSA were dismissed, except for a simple admonishment to avoid any appearance of a conflict of interest in the future.

Despite that finding, the state bar continued to pursue these allegations against me. In an order entered on March 30, 1984, even U.S. District Judge Maxwell ruled that "no impropriety existed on the part of the Assistant United States Attorney or the United States Attorney's Office for the Northern District of West Virginia." Similarly, United States District Judge William M. Kidd also entered an order on August 3, 1984, finding that "the Office of the United States Attorney did not conduct its affairs in an improper and illegal manner, but to the contrary, and at all times has been fair and dedicated in the undertaking."

On October 25, 1984, Judge Maxwell and Judge Kidd entered a joint order adopting the findings and conclusions contained in their original orders. In two opinions issued by the Fourth Circuit, including the case in which the complaining defendant's conviction was reversed, the court applied a *pro se* rule with no suggestion that neither the AUSA under fire nor anyone else had violated any ethical duties. In a second opinion in a related case, the court found "on the records in this case there was a basis for the conclusion that there was no prosecutorial wrongdoing, and not even an appearance of impropriety."

There is a provision in the United States Code that if a federal official is charged with misconduct that involved the performance of his federal duties in a local jurisdiction, the case can be removed to federal court to avoid any unfair prejudice from the local venue. This certainly appeared to be the case here, so we filed a motion to remove the case to federal court. That request case was denied by a district judge in the Southern District of West Virginia who was assigned the case because two judges in the Northern District had been disqualified. We appealed the case to the Fourth Circuit, arguing that the federal officer removal statute permits the state charge to be adjudicated on the merits in federal court. The Fourth Circuit agreed and reversed the district court's decision, allowing the case to indeed be tried in federal court. This decision was landmark, even groundbreaking, since in previous cases, jurisdiction over bar complaints remained under local jurisdiction. The state bar, having lost their home-court advantage, eventually capitulated and dismissed the charges. Even though justice had been done, I continued to ruminate on what had motivated the bar to pursue charges against me in the first place despite overwhelming evidence to the contrary. Sometimes you never learn who your enemies really are or their motivations.

Meanwhile, Judge Maxwell was informed of the allegations against Dr. Roberts early on and that the investigation was continuing. At various times, Judge Maxwell required the U.S. Attorney's Office to update him on the status of the investigation, and at several of the hearings, he also included counsel who was representing Dr. Roberts. During grand jury sessions, Judge Maxwell's clerk was present in the hallway where witnesses were waiting and therefore would know who was testifying on the Roberts investigation. On several occasions, the clerk of the district court would be seen on the third floor, where the U.S. Attorney's Office was located, using a vending machine even though the same type of vending machine was also located on the second floor, where the district court clerk's office was located. It was obvious that Judge Maxwell and his staff were keeping a close watch on me and my investigation into the allegations against Dr. Roberts.

Eventually our office was recused from any further investigation, and the case was assigned to a Special Assistant United States Attorney from the Southern District. When this attorney, who was one of the more experienced attorneys in the Southern District of West Virginia, first appeared before Judge Maxwell, he questioned her certification to appear as the Northern District, even though this was a routine procedure used in numerous cases throughout the U.S. Attorney offices across the country. Maxwell also continually delayed ruling on motions she filed. Eventually,

Maxwell transferred the case to Judge Knapp in the Southern District, and Roberts pled guilty to five misdemeanor drug counts.

Further evidence of Maxwell's hostility toward me personally, my assistant in the U.S. Attorney's Office, and the law enforcement agents who worked with the U.S. Attorney's Office was demonstrated by his effort to basically shut down investigations by refusing to impanel an investigative grand jury. The Civil Rights Division of the Department of Justice, for example, had been conducting a criminal civil rights investigation of allegations against the U.S. Marshals Service in the Northern District of West Virginia. Judge Maxwell had convened a grand jury solely dedicated to that investigation and prevented my office from using that same grand jury for any of our investigations. At the same time, Judge Maxwell inexplicably refused numerous requests by my office to convene a grand jury so we could investigate several major criminal organizations in the Northern District.

Maxwell's pattern of conduct interfering with grand juries didn't stop there. During the morning of the first day of one grand jury that had been convened, the court informed me that we may have "done something wrong" and that to prevent any problems his court reporter would record the grand jury. Maxwell stated that the chairman of the Judicial Conference had indicated to him that only court reporters employed through the judiciary may now record grand jury proceedings. I responded to him by bringing certain procedures of the Department of Justice to his attention, particularly the attorney general's requirement that grand jury court reporters receive a security clearance by the Department of Justice, which his court reporter had not received. That didn't sway Maxwell in the least, and his court reporter remained in place.

"Are you ordering me to disobey the Department of Justice order, Your Honor?" I asked him.

"As I would review the options you have, I would leave this entirely up to you. You can proceed with the official court reporter who is available or you can decide not to take any testimony."

I contacted the Department of Justice, who proceeded to call the court's administrative office. Apparently, after being told by the Administrative Office of the U.S. Courts that I was correct, Maxwell told me that we could go ahead and use the court reporter retained by the Justice

Department, adding a stipulation that this was a fact that could be brought up at a later time in the form of an objection to the validity of the grand jury proceedings. He also required the grand jury to meet in the courtroom each morning and at the end of each session, despite objections from the foreman of the grand jury that these meetings were a waste of time. On numerous occasions, Maxwell would tell the grand jury it was time to adjourn, even though the grand jurors were in the middle of hearing testimony from a witness and wanted to stay on.

Maxwell also required all grand jury witnesses to report to the clerk's office and remain in the witness room until they were signed out to appear before the grand jury. Such an egregious procedure prevented agents from interviewing cooperating witnesses before their appearance at the grand jury, a normal procedure we were no longer able to follow. On one occasion, Judge Maxwell even entered the grand jury room while a grand jury was in session, a clear violation of secrecy rules.

When I reported his unprofessional and nonsensical actions, Maxwell retaliated by filing allegations of misconduct against me and other prosecutors within my office, claiming no "ill will" was involved and going on to tell the *Charleston Gazette* newspaper, "I don't know that we have had any differences of opinion. These matters will be determined on issues of law."[5]

Which they were.

"Having found no misconduct," the Justice Department's Office of Professional Responsibility concluded after investigating, "we consider the matter closed."

Judge Maxwell, of course, didn't, and our conflict continued unabated. "Time after time," the *Charleston Gazette* wrote in October 1988, "the Fourth Circuit Court of Appeals in Richmond has reversed Maxwell and ruled that the prosecutors were in the right.... The battle between Maxwell and the prosecutors is bewildering. It is complicated by the fact that the U.S. attorneys obtained a cocaine conviction against a doctor who is the husband of Maxwell's law clerk."[6]

Maxwell's lack of jurisprudence, along with his penchant for slow-walking civil cases especially, were on display so often over the years that it began to attract welcome attraction from the likes of James

Cramer writing for the *American Lawyer* in an article called "Maxwell's Silver Hammer:"

"Federal district judge Robert Maxwell is at it again. Last November *The American Lawyer* reported that the chief judge of the Northern District of West Virginia had ruled in favor of a natural gas company, even though that company held leases for gas drilling on some of Maxwell's property. Now the judge has once again ruled in favor of a business associate—except that this time the issue is coal, the stakes are much higher, and the plaintiffs in the case say they may ask for a new trial on the basis of Maxwell's conflict."[7]

In an internal report prepared by our office, we concluded Judge Maxwell's incessant interference was aimed at undermining our cases. "His conduct," the report stated in the summary, "has worked to undermine the effective administration in the district. He has spared no opportunity to publicly condemn the U.S. Attorney's Office, particularly U.S. Attorney William Kolibash, and to provide forums for others to do the same. Kolibash and his staff have been faced with interference and obstruction of virtually all their investigative efforts and the Judge has used his position to try and learn the details of ongoing criminal investigations."

Maxwell tried to reduce the effective administration of justice in the Northern District, particularly in central West Virginia, but the successful prosecutions described in this book and the numerous putdowns by the Office of Professional Responsibility in the Justice Department and the Fourth Circuit indicated that he failed miserably. In fact, our office successfully obtained guilty pleas and convictions in over 90 percent of our prosecutions. Regardless of his motives, Maxwell's actions were beyond unprecedented for a federal judge.

And the same can be said for Maxwell's behavior. Rules, decorum, and protocol only mattered to this judge for how they might serve him. This wasn't about corruption as much as ego and power. I sought to go around Maxwell at every juncture I could. If I wasn't going to let myself, my staff, and law enforcement agents be intimidated by the killers and criminals we were pursuing, we certainly weren't going to be intimidated by a judge. And his egomaniacal approach to the bench only strengthened our resolve to run the U.S. Attorney's Office for the Northern District with the kind of meticulous attention that could pass any scrutiny.

No high-ranking politician had my back, so I had to have my own.

Marijuana Moonshiners

Bill Kolibash pictured in a courtroom drawing next to a pile of marijuana, created for and gifted to him by the courtroom artist.

CHAPTER 6

Wheeling, West Virginia, 1980

Understanding how a klatch of longtime North Carolina moonshiners morphed into a major marijuana distribution ring in central West Virginia requires some historical context.

"Moonshine holds a particular and somewhat conflicting place in the American mythos," the *Bitter Southerner* reported in June 2020. "An illegally-produced spirit borne to the Appalachian frontier from Scots-Irish immigrants who wanted some good drink and didn't see any reason the government should interfere with things they made on their own land, its name has come to embody both the cheeky pioneer spirit of American rebellion, and no-good, rotten-scoundrel, tax-evading drunks. The reality is somewhere in the middle."[1]

"The image of a moonshiner in the Blue Ridge Mountains," adds Virginia.org., "tends to bring to mind an impoverished backwoods farmer, but in reality, some moonshiners would turn an incredible profit, especially during Prohibition."[2]

The moonshine underworld continued to flourish after Prohibition was repealed as well. "In the decade of 1954 to 1964," according to the website Moonshiner28, "more than 72,000 stills were destroyed by federal agents in North Carolina, South Carolina, Georgia, Tennessee, Alabama and Mississippi."[3]

"Moonshining, once the province of hillbillies operating small stills in the secluded backwoods of the South, is taking on some of the trappings of big business," the *New York Times* picks up in a June 3, 1973, article. "The stills are getting bigger, and the illegal distilling of liquor appears to be handled increasingly by well-organized, well-heeled entrepreneurs."[4]

There was another issue the *Times* makes no mention of that I learned early in my career as an AUSA. In the military courts, there were no grand juries. Instead, there are what's called Article 32 investigations. So my first experience with grand juries came when Jim Companion had me present a moonshine case. Because the defendant had already agreed to plead guilty, all we needed to do was get a formal indictment so the judge could sign off on the deal. But then the grand jury returned a no true bill, meaning they refused to return an indictment even though the subject had agreed to plead guilty. I had to go back in and present the case from scratch instead of just asking the grand jury to produce the indictment I needed. In the mind of those jurors, moonshining was a part of West Virginia history and culture. So they produced a no true bill because they didn't accept a guilty plea for something they didn't consider to be a crime.

Maybe so. But something else was happening too. Starting in 1971 and continuing through the entire decade, prices of crops like grain, wheat, barley, and corn—the primary ingredients of moonshine—rose considerably, reaching record highs in 1974. Sugar, another primary ingredient, also peaked.

"The untaxed whisky market seemed to dry up at around the same time the illegal drug trade picked up," according to an article in the *Richmond Times-Dispatch*.[5]

Which brings us to the case of the Marijuana Moonshiners. The primary allure of moonshine was that it could be made, and thus sold, cheaply. Take away those components and moonshiners found themselves in direct competition with traditional liquor stores because the price gap had closed considerably. That dealt a major setback to operations, which now had incentive to turn their criminal pursuits in another direction.

As the *Washington Post* reported on August 8, 1977, "Hard-pressed by revenooers, high sugar prices and a changing Southern culture, Appalachian moonshiners are turning from marketing mash to marijuana. Federal Treasury agents, who in the past year have smashed the smallest number of stills since the repeal of Prohibition in 1933, report they are finding more and more marijuana patches as they crawl through the hills and gullies where they used to find the high-octane product that contented an older generation. Like local and state officials, John Westra, special agent in charge of ATF's North Carolina bureau, said he is finding a 'tremendous interest increase' in evidence that 'our liquor-law violators are pursuing careers in marijuana.' In the past year, Westra's agents have found only 90 stills—down from 1,200 annually 15 years ago, he says. However, the veteran still-chasers have found at least 20 patches of marijuana this year, some of it planted inconspicuously in the rows of corn that used to end up being hauled from the ridgetops in liquid form."[6]

There was a North Carolina element to the Marijuana Moonshiners case I prosecuted because that's where the drugs coming into West Virginia were grown by a coconspirator of the man at the top of this particular food chain, Robert Foster. Foster was raised in the best traditions of West Virginia moonshining, and his family might well have qualified as our state's version of the Bondurant brothers or the Stanley family, who both infamously operated in the Franklin County area of Virginia.

"The Stanleys are the most prominent family in the county's most notorious business—making moonshine whiskey," the *Washington Post* wrote in August 1998. "Known for drinking and brawling, they amply fulfill the stereotype of backwoods bootleggers, but they're part of a proud tradition here. As long as there's been an America, there's been a market for cheap, untaxed hooch. Franklin County, a beautiful stretch of rolling hills in the Blue Ridge south of Roanoke, likes to be known as the Moonshine Capital of the World."[7]

Robert Foster, by comparison, sought to make West Virginia at least a hub of marijuana distribution. Already gone were the days when moonshiners moved their products in the trunks of cars with NASCAR drivers behind the wheel. In the first decade or so of NASCAR racing, the transportation of illegal liquor in the south was huge business, and a lot of the sport's early stars were responsible for getting it from the stills to the people. That would have been the 1950s, and it was sometime in the 1970s that Foster's grandfather killed his father with a shotgun for allegedly cheating him out of his share of the profits. Foster had sided with his grandfather in the dispute and ended up learning the moonshine business at his side.

He learned it well enough to know that by the mid-1970s, there wasn't enough profit to be had any longer for someone as ambitious and business-minded as he was. He had never gone to college, had barely graduated from high school, but maintained a savant-like sense of balance sheets and profit margins that would make any Harvard Business School graduate proud. Not only did Foster reckon that the move from moonshining to marijuana was mandated, he also ultimately realized that the best his growers could manage was an inferior strain of weed that paled in comparison with the product coming up through Mexico.

By then, moonshine distribution had become far more sophisticated and business-oriented. A few of the drivers he employed either had direct experience with transporting marijuana for the cartels or were connected to the shipping networks that trafficked in that product. It was through them that Foster struck a deal with drug syndicates from Mexico and Colombia to provide seedlings for their best product to mix with his far lesser-grade marijuana to create hybrid strains that rivaled the best on the black market.

Pretty much everyone knows that, in the end, the infamous gangster Al Capone was nailed by income tax violations he'd committed. In the case of Robert Foster and his marijuana moonshining operation, it was the fact that all the arrangements were made over telephone lines we had obtained warrants to listen in on, thanks to intelligence provided by underlings we turned to our side as we climbed the food chain closer and closer to Foster himself. None of this would have been possible, though, if not for another factor that also made this case stand out...

The Internal Revenue Service.

Up until that point, no investigative body, neither federal nor local, liked working with the IRS, so they avoided the agency at all costs because of bureaucratic red tape and the anticipated slog before anything really got done. But we had a couple of IRS supervisors in the region, Jimmy Connell and Bill Clevenger, who were determined to change that by streamlining the process. Jimmy had helped the feds make some cases out in San Francisco and felt he could do the same for us, a perfect scenario given the experience we'd gained in working across multiple jurisdictions in the Hancock County case detailed earlier.

But the man who really helped us make the Foster case was Larry Mincks, a special agent with the IRS's criminal division who was also a former Ohio state trooper. By the end of 1985, Mincks's dogged work following the money had led to the indictment of nearly three hundred suspects, narcotics seizures of over $6.7 million, and forfeiture of almost $3 million in assets before forfeiture laws had fully taken hold. But the Marijuana Moonshiners case was the one that got the ball rolling.

"It has to be a joint effort of the agencies involved," Larry told the *Exponent Telegram* around that same time, in his typically humble fashion. "There is no way that any one individual or one agency could have accomplished these goals."[8]

In that sense, the Marijuana Moonshiners case became potentially the first-ever federal prosecution to utilize a multijurisdictional task force cooperative approach, combining the efforts of the IRS, West Virginia State Police, FBI, and U.S. Attorney's Office, in addition to law enforcement in local municipalities. I'll bet Larry liked to put puzzles together when he was a kid, because that's the way he attacked our investigations, putting the cases together one piece at a time. And the Marijuana Moonshiners case became a template nationwide for assembling task forces that could achieve together what the component agencies would likely never have been able to on their own.

"The Northern District of West Virginia," the *Exponent Telegram* reported in that same 1985 article, "was the first area in the nation to utilize the concept which President Reagan ordered nationwide in 1983."[9]

The case also debuted the concept of an investigative grand jury, through which we were able to take more and more blocks out of the Foster organization pyramid. Once we identified who the bad guys were, we'd pick someone identified as a weak spot—maybe a girlfriend, wife, or participant who was disgruntled. We'd haul that person in front of the investigative grand jury and start gathering information.

The IRS was vital in that sense because they loved paper. Their specialty was documents, something other agencies were less prone to and effective at. And those documents became crucial to us making our case to the investigative grand jury so we could issue subpoenas and warrants for those wiretaps that proved so vital. Assembling the information that Larry Mincks was able to gather in this case gave us a very clear picture of criminal activity, the financial aspect of which became a dead giveaway. If a guy is living in a half-million-dollar home with no visible source of income, for example, you can bet he is up to no good. And the Marijuana

Moonshiners was basically a document-dominated case, as many of the biggest are. Follow the money and the trail will always lead to where you need to be.

"Foster had those five or six people driving for him in Lincoln Continentals with four hundred pounds of dope in the trunk," Larry recalls. "His growers would call Foster and tell him the dope was ready to be picked up in North Carolina, where all his fields were located, and his drivers would go out and get it. There were no cell phones back then, but there were toll records of every call made out of the local area. So once we knew who Foster's drivers were, we'd get their toll records and program every call they made into a computer, dump them all together. That allowed us to collect who had called what number and how often, so we knew exactly who in Foster's organization was calling who. That told us who was picking up the dope and who was going to be on the receiving end. Foster's toll records were what gave up much of his organization, and once we had those guys dead to rights, we worked our way up the pyramid all the way to the peak. Because the frequency of those calls and when they were placed also gave us a clear idea of who the players were and where they ranked in Foster's organization."

Thanks to Larry, we figured out exactly how Foster was moving his drugs through a pretty ingenious process in which a courier would load up his car with his family and their suitcases, like they were going on vacation. They'd check into a motel in North Carolina and leave the keys in the car. Then, while they were asleep in their rooms, another driver would show up and load up to four hundred pounds of marijuana in the trunk, usually a late-model luxury car. The next morning the "vacationing" family would then drive the car to Foster's house or another prearranged location in Morgantown, deliver the drugs, and then go about their business.

We locked onto that pattern, thanks to those telephone toll records Larry Mincks was so adept at analyzing, particularly calls placed from the motels where the couriers stayed. When we arrested them, we'd flash the motel receipts and registration records before them and ask what were they doing there on that date. Their mouths would usually drop at that point, because they knew we had them.

And those couriers, Larry notes, were transporting more than just marijuana.

"They would deliver the marijuana to Foster and then cash back to the sources stuffed in Kroger grocery bags with real groceries on top. These bags would be laid out right in the back seat all the way to North Wilkesboro, or somewhere else in North Carolina, where the marijuana was coming from. Again, thanks to those telephone toll records, we were able to figure out who was talking to who and when. That gave up their pattern, and that was another way we built our case."

Using computer analysis from records obtained by an investigative grand jury, we were able to identify who the major players were and what exactly the organization was doing. All telephone and motel records were inputted into a computer to establish patterns and identify the participants at all levels. We then issued a slew of subpoenas that resulted in lower-level guys testifying against their superiors before the investigative grand jury. And the Marijuana Moonshiners is generally cited as the first case to mark the successful use of telephone records analysis.

Some of Foster's marijuana also came from supplies smuggled into North Carolina aboard oceangoing freighters, but it all made its way back to Foster's hub in Morgantown. And Foster allegedly used the trucks belonging to a major chicken products manufacturer to ship his product throughout the region stretching to the Ohio Valley and beyond. His moonshining family's history of violence more than prepared him for the often cutthroat (literally) world of drug dealing, particularly when dealing with the kind of drug kingpins who would later build the cartels responsible for Mexico's blood-soaked streets.

Our investigation also turned up something that would become a harbinger for the future in the form of evidence suggesting Foster wasn't the only one who'd brought Mexican elements into his organization. As the *Washington Post* reported, "In Tennessee, senior state narcotics officer Taylor Bettis believes there is a mountain moonshiner–Mexican marijuana connection. 'One of our people who began in moonshining 45 years ago got a Mexican connection and was flying in two tons a month,' Bettis said citing other evidence that the 'white whiskey business' is intertwined with the green weed. 'Growing is a trend on the green weed. Growing is a trend on the way up,' he added. Bettis believes the Mexican connection is necessary to mix the better Latin product with the poorer quality mountain-grown marijuana. Sheriff Anderson says the Wilkes County, N.C., variety is mixed with those from Columbia and Missouri to bring it up to snuff."[10]

In May 1982, another federal grand jury indicted twenty-eight individuals with sixty-four violations in connection with our eighteen-month investigation of a drug ring that spanned six states. The kingpin, though, was West Virginia's own Robert Foster, and he eventually pled guilty to federal drug violations as well as, of course, income tax violations. His chief lieutenant, Marvin Leifried, was convicted too, notable because it marked the first time a defendant had ever been convicted of violating the Continuing Criminal Enterprise (CCE) and Drug Kingpin statutes in the Northern District of West Virginia.

The Marijuana Moonshiners case proved to be as successful as it was groundbreaking. But the final act, and trial, was still to come thanks to my old friend Stanley Preiser. Stanley called and told me that the daughter of a fugitive who'd slipped from our grasp had contacted him and said her father wanted to turn himself in and plead guilty in Anderson, South Carolina. His name was Dob Pyle, and he was the ringleader in North Carolina, responsible for supplying Robert Foster with the bulk of his marijuana. I wondered why Stanley wanted to have his client plead guilty in Anderson, South Carolina, since there was no connection with the case. Well, I found out that the federal judge in Anderson was Ross Anderson, who, prior to taking the bench, was a very successful plaintiff's attorney whom Stanley knew from their membership in the American Trial Lawyers Association. Stanley may have thought he had a little advantage, but he really didn't since Judge Anderson knew Stanley's tactics well.

When Stanley called me, he asked, "You're not recording this, right? You're not going to charge me with obstructing justice or harboring a fugitive, are you?"

"No, Stanley, we can work out a plea agreement."

"Well, my client wants to plead guilty, and he wants to do it in Anderson, South Carolina."

"Okay," I said, "we've done that before. It's fine. I don't have a problem with that."

"And my client is an older guy. He has physical problems that need to be considered."

"That's fine, too."

"He's very sick."

"The Bureau of Prisons has some fine facilities where he can be treated."

So we set up a meeting down in Anderson. I got in the night before to go over everything with Stanley's client Dob Pyle and get the plea agreement worked out ahead of our court appearance the next day. We went to his very sick client's hotel room, and the client had this much younger blonde woman with him who definitely wasn't his nurse.

We got everything worked out and reconvened in court the next day before Federal District Judge Ross Anderson.

"So we have a plea agreement," Judge Anderson said in chambers.

"We do, Your Honor."

Anderson, an affable, friendly guy who didn't like surprises or conflict in his courtroom, nodded. Stanley was quiet through it all, but his reputation preceded him into the courtroom.

"I'm waiting for your acquiescence, Mr. Preiser."

"Yes, Your Honor."

"We're going to go into the courtroom to hold a hearing and not argue the case."

"Yes, Your Honor," Stanley repeated.

Stanley and I walked into the courtroom together and sat at our opposite tables. Judge Anderson followed us.

"I understand a resolution has been reached in the matter before this court," he opened.

I rose. "It has, Your Honor."

Then Stanley rose. "If I may, Your Honor."

I could see Judge Anderson's expression change. "Proceed, Mr. Preiser."

And with that Stanley started to argue a case he had promised not to argue.

"Your Honor, my client Mr. Pyle has severe health problems that must be taken into account when—"

I didn't have to object on the grounds of the young blonde woman being in the hotel room of Stanley's client the night before, because the judge cut him off right there.

"Do we have a plea agreement, Mr. Preiser?"

"We do, Your Honor," Stanley said, softer.

"Then please sit down."

Stanley retook his chair, flashing me a look that said, *Hey, I had to try...*

Judge Anderson accepted the plea agreement and later sentenced Dob Pyle in accordance with its terms. Case closed.

Meanwhile, I continued trying to break the back of organized crime in West Virginia, which had reached a level not seen since the days of a legendary gangster named Big Bill Lias and the original Wheeling mob.

Cocaine Cowboys

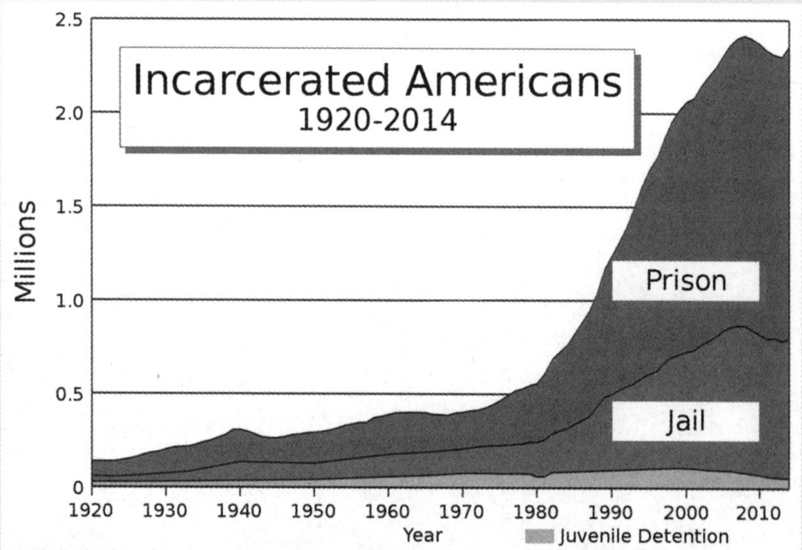

U.S. Bureau of Justice Statistics via Wikipedia, Public Domain, https://commons.wikimedia.org/wiki/File:US_incarceration_timeline-clean.svg

A graph showing a spiked rise in the number of Americans incarcerated that coincides with the explosion of drug dealing and related crime circa 1980.

CHAPTER 7

Morgantown, West Virginia, 1981

In July 1981, *Time* magazine ran a cover story entitled "High on Cocaine" with cover art of an elegant martini glass filled with white powder. The article reported that cocaine's use was spreading quickly into America's middle class as "the drug of choice for perhaps millions of solid, conventional and often upwardly mobile citizens."[1]

"When cocaine came to town it was so ridiculously profitable," Roben Farzad, author of *Hotel Scarface: Where Cocaine Cowboys Partied and Plotted to Control Miami*, told PBS News Hour correspondent Jeffrey Brown in 2017. "It was so seductive, it made people do such crazy things in the name of money and power and blood lust that you had something approximating a failed state by 1981 in Miami."[2]

I mention Miami because that's where the cocaine that reached West Virginia mostly came from. And it was right about that time that the first major cocaine case I ever prosecuted came across my desk in the person of West Virginia state trooper Thom Kirk, who at the time was working undercover. At the center of the investigation was a young man named John Pankulics, only twenty-seven years old when we began our investigation. He was distributing the cocaine not only in West Virginia but also across the border in Pennsylvania according to Thom, who was working with state authorities there. That's when another key member of our task force, IRS agent Jeff Sandy, began an investigation into him.

Jeff uncovered the fact that Pankulics had no real source of income but lived in a million-dollar-plus home on the outskirts of Morgantown on Cheat Lake, a 1,730-acre man-made reservoir located in the northern part of Monongalia County, about ten miles east of downtown Morgantown and West Virginia University's main campus. Back in those days, the bucolic area was still a well-kept secret beyond West Virginia. Locals gravitated to a section known as the Backwaters, where there were quiet spots for swimming, canoeing, kayaking, and fishing. The more commercial areas of the lake, favored by those like Pankulics, were rife with powerboats dragging inner tubes and water skiers. Jet Skis were becoming increasingly popular back then, and you could hear them coming a mile away. Nobody was better at ferreting out targets whose assets didn't at all match up with their apparent resources than Jeff Sandy.

"The cocaine Pankulics was moving tested as ninety-eight percent pure, which made it the purest cocaine that our labs had ever tested," Jeff recalls today. "It was also the purest cocaine that was being brought into the United States at the time, which was more than enough motivation for us to take this guy down. I worked seven days a week for ninety days until we submitted what's called a net worth method of proof. And I documented every single thing that John Pankulics had bought, like that beautiful home overlooking Cheat Lake where very distinguished, reputable people live. He drove a Mercedes. He owned boats, antique cars, and would buy cases of Dom Pérignon. He'd throw these lavish parties where people would ask him, 'My God, where did all this money come from?' And Pankulics would tell them, 'Well, my parents are very influential and rich.' That was just the front. His parents lived in New Jersey and didn't fit that profile at all. The net worth statement I put together on Pankulics revealed the guy had never worked a day in his life. So his reported income was zilch, which meant everything that he bought must have come from unreported income from the sale of cocaine. All we had to do was prove it."

Jeff documented every single thing Pankulics had purchased as far back as he possibly could. These days, that may not sound challenging given the electronic trail that follows us everywhere. Back then, though, Jeff had only a hard paper trail to follow and that's what he did, tracking down receipts, bills of sale, registration records, tax bills—pretty much anything that had John Pankulics's name associated with it.

"That," Jeff says, "is how you make a drug case."

And that's where Thom Kirk, the West Virginia State Police, the DEA, and my office came in. The investigation was centered in the Northern District and revealed several major players in Pankulics's operation.

Among them were Louis Colasanti and Jo Anne Rind, who conducted their business as a partnership during the period of the conspiracy case we would ultimately make. They had developed an entire network of drug dealers to move Pankulics's product throughout their territory, which included West Virginia University and its thousands of students who went there.

"I got a call from Thom Kirk, who I'd never met at the time," Jeff Sandy reminded me recently. "He said my supervisor Larry Mincks had told him to call me."

"'I want to meet you tonight at eleven p.m. at the West Virginia University basketball arena.'

"'Okay, I'll be there,' I said. 'How will I know you?'

"'Don't worry about that,' Thom told me, 'I'll know you.'

"So I'm walking through the parking lot, waiting for him to come up to me, when I hear, 'Hey, Sandy, get in.' I turn around and there's this guy sitting in a beat-up Chrysler Cordoba. I mean, it looked ready for the junkyard. But I climbed in the passenger seat and ended up sitting on the car's headliner, which had peeled off the underside of the roof and dropped to the fabric. So we start driving around Morgantown and the whole time I'm holding up the headliner, while Tom explained that an informant had come in to the West Virginia State Police and told them he owed John Pankulics thirty thousand dollars for a kilo of cocaine he brought from him. The guy was scared because the state police told him that Pankulics had ties to organized crime in New Jersey, which was a lie."

"'Can you get Pankulics on the phone?' Thom asked him.

"'Not unless I've got the thirty thousand I owe him.'

"Tom looked at him and said, 'What if I can get the money for you?'"

Larry and Thom arranged to get the $30,000 the informant needed to pay off his debt, at which point they'd have Pankulics dead to rights. Pankulics told the informant to bring the money to his house on Cheat Lake, unaware the guy was wearing a wire with Thom and Larry parked just down the road. Because the informant had paid his debt, Pankulics fronted him another kilo, over two pounds, of coke, which the informant tossed through the passenger-side window and hit Larry right in the head.

"We went back to the hotel room and started working on an affidavit for a search warrant," Larry says, picking up the story from there. "And then we headed to West Virginia University School of Law, because there was a professor up there who was a part-time United States magistrate, and he was the one who signed off on the search warrant. And I believe it was December 6 of 1982 when we executed the warrant on Pankulics's house on Cheat Lake. He was incredibly cool about it, like it was business as usual, and our guys were well into their search when I said to him, 'Listen, we don't want to tear up your house. Just tell us where the cocaine is.' He looked at Thom and me right in the eye and said, 'There's no cocaine in this house. That's the truth.'

"Just then the head of the assault team comes into the room decked out in full camo gear with his face blacked out and says, 'He's telling the truth. We've searched everywhere. There's no cocaine in this house.' So Pankulics looked at us and said, 'I told you I was telling the truth. There's no cocaine in this house because it's in a brush pile out in the back.' And, sure enough, we found sixteen million dollars' worth of pure cocaine in stainless steel containers hidden exactly where Pankulics told us they were."

In retrospect, Pankulics knew he was looking at life in prison, so by cooperating he was able to get his sentence reduced to thirty years, which meant, under the then current sentencing guidelines, he could get out in half that time. This case was a sad one in the sense that it involved professors and students from West Virginia University. And it ended up stretching all the way to Wheeling, where the arrests made were all from the well-to-do set, upper-class white people on top of those WVU professors and students.

That was the biggest difference between a case like this and the drug cases I'd prosecuted up until that time, like the Marijuana Moonshiners. The culture was changing. Drugs were going mainstream, reaching upper-middle-class suburbia. Using cocaine was not just socially acceptable, sometimes it was socially expected. People would pass it out like shots in a bar. Users had been fed images of the rich and glamorous snorting it. Studio 54 had closed back in 1980, but trendy establishments like that fed into the mythology of coke too. It just took a little bit longer to get to West Virginia.

The exhaustive study Jeff Sandy performed on Pankulics's financial records, meanwhile, yielded a detailed inventory of large transfers of money, in keeping with the scope of Pankulics's operation. Colasanti and Rind, for example, turned over around $300,000 to him from 1978 through 1982, pocketing a like sum for themselves. Others in Pankulics's chain of dealers paid him back as much as $440,000, meaning their profits from selling not only powder but also rock cocaine were off the charts.

One of those dealers pled guilty in exchange for a deal that put us on to Pankulics's source for the coke in Florida, a man named Robert Monty. Monty was worth enough to live on the posh Jupiter Island, a barrier island that's part of Florida's Treasure Coast, named for a Spanish treasure fleet that was lost in a 1715 hurricane. One of his neighbors was none other than Vice President George Bush, who'd been tasked by President Reagan to oversee an effort to win the war on drugs at long last. Until that time, the only infraction on Monty's record was a disturbing the peace complaint filed against him for cutting his grass too early in the morning, which roiled his Jupiter Island neighbors.

This turned out to be a pretty big case, with somewhere around fifty defendants either pleading out, going to jail, or both. That's a lot of dealers, and drugs, taken off the streets. One of those to enter into a plea agreement was John Pankulics's brother Tom, a conduit who, it turned out, was the one who dealt directly with Robert Monty in Florida. Our investigation revealed that Monty was supplying Pankulics, through his brother, with a large portion of the drugs he was moving, including the cocaine that tested 98 percent pure. Tom Pankulics made several trips south, delivering cash sometimes approaching $100,000 to turn over to Monty in exchange for drugs.

It turned out Robert Monty's legitimate business was running concessions for major events, which had the added advantage of providing a vehicle for laundering cash through. And we learned he was headed to New Orleans with the intention of bribing then Louisiana governor Edwin Edwards, long considered the heir to the traditions espoused by Huey "the Kingfish" Long. Monty wanted the concession for the 1984 World's Fair, which was being held in New Orleans, and was willing to pay big for it.

I flew down to New Orleans and learned from the locals that Monty had rented a yacht to entertain the powers that be, inviting the governor and the various other politicians he needed to cajole into giving him the

World's Fair concession. I wanted to put someone, an informant or confidential human source, on that yacht, thinking of the treasure trove of intelligence he or she might be able to come back to shore with. But the FBI nixed the idea because they thought it was too dangerous. Which, I guess, it was.

We garnered enough evidence against Monty to coax him into becoming a cooperating witness. He saw distributing cocaine as a victimless crime, not unlike the corruption and bribery that were business as usual for him. Cooperating with us allowed him to keep his home on Jupiter Island we would have seized otherwise, in addition to keeping him out of jail. All the same, I would have loved to have gotten someone on that yacht, even though by that time Monty had already served up Pankulics to us on a silver platter.

We pinned a Continuing Criminal Enterprise label on Pankulics's operation under Title 21, because it had forfeiture provisions. In spite of his directing the West Virginia State Police strike team to where they could find his stash of cocaine, that was enough to make John Pankulics change his plea to innocent. As ringleader, though, he was facing life in prison, so he ultimately ended up cooperating to preserve a measure of his future. If memory serves me correctly, Rind, Colasanti, and John's brother Thomas ended up pleading guilty too, since we had all of them dead to rights.

That might have been my first major case involving cocaine, but it was far from my last. Prosecuting drug cases marked the formation of our multijurisdictional task force that included the aforementioned pair of IRS agents who were among the best investigators I ever worked with.

The Task Force: The IRS—Larry Mincks & Jeff Sandy

IRS super agents, and task force members, Larry Mincks (left) and Jeff Sandy.

CHAPTER 8

Washington County, Ohio

Larry Mincks can tell you exactly why he decided to go into law enforcement while still in elementary school.

After his military service ended, Larry's father came home and joined the Ohio State Highway Patrol, but as a reserve officer. In that capacity, he wasn't allowed to carry a gun but still rode with the troopers who did. Oftentimes, he'd bring them back home to eat after their shift was over, usually in the predawn hours, and his wife would get up to serve them breakfast around an often-crowded table where the evening's exploits became fodder for discussion. Larry would listen for the sound of his dad's car pulling into the driveway and voices entering the house and then scramble to get downstairs.

"What'd you do tonight?" he'd asked the officers as they ate. "Who'd you arrest? How many bad guys?"

The officers inevitably indulged the young boy's questions. Call it a kitchen full of heroes, and eventually, Larry's childhood obsession birthed a career as soon as he returned from an overseas military deployment himself. Law enforcement had seeped into his blood, and there was no getting it out.

Things, though, didn't go exactly as Larry Mincks expected, in large part because of a new phrase he learned in his one semester at Ohio University.

"That phrase," he recalls, "was 'academic probation.'"

Growing up poor on a small farm in Washington County, Ohio, left Larry with no choice but to work on the family farm, as well as take a second job at a gas station. As a result, there was no time to become an exemplary honor roll–type student, though his ambition was still to go to college. Attending Ohio University made for his first big adventure in the world, with more people living in his dorm than in the town where he'd grown up. Being placed on academic probation, though, left him to follow the same path his father had by joining the military.

"I was born in 1942 and was four hours old when my father left for Hawaii in the wake of the bombing of Pearl Harbor," Larry shares. "It was really tough to make ends meet in those three and a half years my father was away, and I never saw that as the road for me. When I found myself with no choice, I took the military-placement testing and scored high enough in the intelligence category to join the air force, where I was assigned to air force intelligence."

Larry went through boot camp at Goodfellow Air Force Base in San Angelo, Texas, and then spent a year training in such areas as cryptanalysis and code breaking, among various other topics covered in a U.S. Air Force intelligence officer's arsenal. He spent most of his time situated near the Black Sea where the then Soviet Union was developing its missile program. It fell to Larry's unit to keep close tabs on the Russians over the two years he served overseas and then two and a half more serving stateside, where his responsibilities included occasionally reporting directly to the National Security Agency.

Upon leaving the air force, he took advantage of the GI Bill to return to college at Ohio's Marietta College, earning his degree over a nine-year period. It took that long because Larry also served as a trooper with the Ohio State Highway Patrol through the same period, working the very same county where he had grown up and where his father had served as a reserve officer.

"I ended up working with some of those troopers who ate breakfast in our house back when I was a kid, and they never let me forget all those questions I'd always ask them."

One of these, a mentor of sorts, was Charlie MacLeish.

"He was a big guy, big enough for people to be scared of, but he wasn't all brawn; he also had brains, and he could talk his way in and out of any situation. One of the things Charlie told me was to always treat people with respect and dignity no matter how big a dirtbag they were. He used to say they all had mothers and were human beings regardless of what they'd done and deserved to be treated as such. Charlie went to church every Sunday, even if he'd been out working the night before and had to sit in the pew in his uniform. Years later, when I ran for sheriff, he was my campaign manager. Charlie's pushing ninety now, and we play in the same poker game the second Thursday of every month. Our wives rotate making the desserts."

Of course, attending college while working full-time as a trooper presented its own set of challenges for Larry.

"Back then," he recalls, "the night shift started about three or four o'clock in the afternoon and wasn't over until eight o'clock the next morning. It was mostly us young guys on that shift, which suited me just fine because I could attend classes during the day. As much as possible, I'd schedule them in the morning; that way, I could get home by noon so I could get some sleep before I went on duty."

At heart, though, Larry was a numbers guy.

"I majored in accounting at Marietta," he recalls. "But the problem was the state patrol didn't have an opening for somebody in accounting. I started looking around and took the exam to get into the Treasury. At the time the Treasury Department had an intelligence division that was looking for both accountants and lawyers, just like the FBI was. So I applied to both, and the Treasury people came back first. I guess I could have pursued a career in the private sector, but that wasn't what I wanted. I couldn't give up law enforcement."

Larry spent six months in the Treasury Department training program, mastering the intricacies of tax law and criminal investigative techniques. He graduated from the Federal Law Enforcement Training Centers (FLETC) in Glynco, Georgia, taking a position in the intelligence division of the Treasury Department for two and a half years before it was swallowed up by the Criminal Investigation Division of the IRS. That's where he ended up spending the rest of his career, starting as a certified fraud examiner at the IRS offices in Parkersburg, West Virginia, a stone's throw away from his native Ohio to the west. He also claimed the title of forensic accountant, since that was the label applied to his particular area of expertise whenever he was testifying in court.

"My job was to follow the money wherever it went," he recalls today.

And there was plenty of it to follow when drugs came to dominate the scene in West Virginia in the late 1970s and early 1980s. A whole new breed of criminal required a whole new methodology of investigative work, which was pioneered by the task force I formed with Larry as one of the centerpieces.

Back then, bottom-up investigations in which lower-echelon criminals, once arrested, gave up higher-echelon ones was nothing new. Drug cases, though, allowed Larry to take it to a whole new level, thanks to how many potential targets actually handled the drugs before they reached the street.

"If we arrested a guy with an ounce of coke on him, we'd debrief him thoroughly and, sooner or later, he'd say something like, 'You know I bought that ounce from this person.' So the strategy was to round up as many low-level dealers as we could and get them to roll on who their suppliers were. And from there we just kept scaling the pyramid all the way to the top to make our case."

The investigative grand juries came in especially handy in that regard, because they enabled us to provide immunity to dealers as a route to get to the kingpins we really wanted. Those grand juries also allowed us to secure indictments and make plea deals with the lesser figures to keep them out of jail if they cooperated.

"Maybe we'd charge them with misdemeanor possession instead of wholesale distribution," Larry explains. "A difference between serving no time in jail versus five years or more. And, of course, the way we made our cases ironclad was through tax evasion prosecutions."

It was Larry who got the call from Florida when Peewee Tenant, a pilot from Fairmont, West Virginia, crashed on his way back from picking up a hefty shipment of drugs in Lima, Peru. Among the recovered belongings was a contacts book filled with names and addresses. There was also a book that listed an assortment of deals that had been made, how much of the cocaine had been provided to this person or that, and how much they owed in return.

"None of these people, of course, were reporting the money they made on their taxes," Larry says. "So we were able to make strong tax evasion cases against them to spur them to cooperate with us and give up dealers like Robert Foster."

Larry was exceedingly patient in making those cases, as comfortable nestled in the office as he was in the field, and helped the task force make great use of both the RICO and CCE statutes. In fact, I'd go so far to say that the great success we encountered in prosecuting cases under both or either of those was due to the task force concept in general and the participation of the IRS in particular, thanks to dogged agents like Larry and his team. Sure, he carried a gun, but paper proved to be his greatest weapon against criminals.

"Computers were just coming into use back then," Larry recalls. "I had filing cabinets, but there was so much paper I had a lot of it stored in boxes and boxes full of reports and financial records on anyone we were investigating or had investigated. I'd inventory those records and highlight all the names and what box or drawer they could be found in. And then we put all that information into the computer, so when you entered the name of your target, you'd know where all the records and reports we had on him could be located. So if you were getting ready to interview somebody, everything you possibly needed to know about them could be found by reading all the documents we'd already accumulated."

Larry retired from the IRS in 1999 and went to work as a financial detective for the Washington County Sheriff's Office. Then, five years later, he was elected sheriff, an office he still holds to this day, going on twenty years now.

"I've got sixty-one thousand people in my county. I'm responsible for a one-hundred-and-twenty-four-bed jail and maintain a seven-million-dollar budget as Washington County sheriff. It takes a lot of accounting to stretch the money as far as I can, so I've never really let go of numbers. And I think the thing about accounting is that it teaches you to be very tenacious. Leave no stone unturned and no question unanswered. If you don't do all those things, you'll end up missing something. When you're working a case, anything that comes up, you've got to follow through on it. The young deputies I preach that to remind me of when I was doing patrols at night and going to college in the morning."

Larry treats his young deputies like his own kids. He and his wife had three boys of their own. Their oldest, Larry Jr., graduated from the University of Cincinnati with a degree in aerospace engineering and had followed his father's path into the U.S. Air Force when tragedy struck. In 2000, he was attending the wedding of a fellow young air force officer when Larry, Jr. excitedly dove into the hotel pool. He struck the bottom and his neck broke on contact, paralyzing him from the neck down. Larry and his wife spent close to five months at Ohio University Hospital while their oldest was in the intensive care unit.

Thanks to therapy, Larry Jr. was able to operate a wheelchair, and Larry retrofitted their home as much as possible to accommodate his needs before they brought him home. Larry, Jr. still had all his mental faculties, so Larry got him a job in the sheriff's department working directly for him.

"Larry Jr. had a machine that took voice dictation so he could work on a computer, and it made him feel like a contributing member of the community. During my campaign runs, he'd even write a lot of my speeches for me."

Larry Jr. lived for fifteen years after the accident, ultimately succumbing in 2015. Meanwhile, Larry's middle son has staked out a career with Amgen Pharmaceuticals, while his youngest followed in his wake into the Criminal Investigation Division of the IRS. As for Larry...

"I'm eighty-one and still at it, still serving as sheriff. This is what I like to do. It's in my blood. It's what gives me satisfaction. We even have this cadet program to give high school seniors the ability to experience what it's like to work in law enforcement. I feel good about that, but I'm really concerned about the amount of drugs coming into the county. So much of it is laced with fentanyl that we've had more than our share of overdoses, which goes for the whole state of Ohio. Well, I have a sixteen-year-old grandson and a fifteen-year-old granddaughter, and every time I take a parent to identify their child in the morgue, all I can think of is them. We've got to get these drugs off the street, whatever it takes."

Spoken like a true lawman.

CHAPTER 9

Dallison, West Virginia

Jeff Sandy grew up in Dallison, West Virginia, a town that boasted a population of all of sixty people. Growing up in a small town, though, did nothing to stymie Jeff's big ambitions. Early on, he dreamed of becoming a big-league ballplayer.

"My father was a car salesman and my mother was a stay-at-home mom. We weren't poor, but money wasn't exactly flowing in."

Indeed, Jeff recalls using dental floss to re-stitch the laces on the baseballs he was prone to wearing out. As a boy, he might have known his father best as a car salesman, but that changed later in life.

"My dad served in General Patton's Third Army. His unit liberated the airborne troops who were under siege in the Belgian town of Bastogne. That would become known in the history books as the Battle of the Bulge. His unit started out with around one hundred and ninety-three troops, but only twenty-seven of those were alive when World War II ended."

One of the accomplishments Jeff is most proud of is that he and all four of his sisters graduated from college, an amazing feat for a family from an impoverished Appalachian town. Another thing he's proud of just as much was painstakingly re-creating his dad's entire journey through his service in the war.

"I was able to reconstruct it because about ten years ago, the U.S. Army's daily logs for World War II were declassified. So I was ultimately able to trace my father's path starting in Normandy Beach, all the way through France, Belgium, Luxembourg, Germany, and Austria over two hundred and seventy-seven days of combat."

Being one of the twenty-seven survivors of his unit allowed Jeff's father to watch his kids grow up and attend college. Even though he never had that experience himself, he was always partial to nearby West Virginia University, where two of Jeff's older sisters went. But Jeff's future lay along a different path.

"We were watching our old black-and-white TV one day when the announcement of the plane crash that killed all of the Marshall University football team came on. And I told my dad that I was going to go to Marshall instead."

But there was another reason why Jeff thought Marshall, which was located in West Virginia as well, proved to be the perfect school for him.

"We were a really poor family that struggled to make ends meet. I didn't even know if I was going to have to put college on hold to get a job. One day I got a call from a close friend who suggested that I go down to the unemployment office because they had a program designed to keep kids like me in school by helping them find part-time after-school jobs."

It turned out that the U.S. Treasury Bureau of the Public Debt was hiring high school kids for six dollars an hour, so Jeff decided to apply.

"'Hey,' I said to this woman behind the counter at the local unemployment office, 'I'm going to be a high school senior next year, and I hear you have jobs at the Bureau of the Public Debt.'

"She looked at me and said, 'Oh, I'm sorry, sir, but those jobs are all taken. But how would you like to work for the IRS for two dollars an hour?'

"And I said, 'Sure!'"

Jeff went to work for the audit division, turning enough heads to make his supervisor reluctant to let him go after he graduated from high school.

"'Are you going to college?' she asked me.

"And I said, 'Yeah, I'm going to Marshall University.' She told me to give her a few minutes and then called me back into her office and asked me, 'How would you like to work two days a week in Huntington, West Virginia, for the audit division down there?'"

Again, Jeff made quite the impression to the point that, not long into his part-time tenure, a man he'd never met before stopped by his desk.

"'Are you the new guy?' he wondered.

"'Well, yeah, I guess so.'

"'I want to talk to you about a career with the IRS in the Intelligence Division.'

"'What would I be doing, sir?'

"'You'd be an investigator, like a detective.'

"'I didn't know the IRS had detectives.'

"'We think you'd make a great one.'

"'Police detectives carry guns.'

"'So do IRS investigators, son.'"

Jeff went on to work part-time for the IRS through all four years of college. After college he attended the Federal Law Enforcement Training Centers, where he got into great shape and learned how to shoot. Upon graduation, he moved to Cleveland, Ohio, to take a job as a special agent with the IRS's Intelligence Division there. Then, a few years later, he transferred to an office close to home back in West Virginia, where his supervisor was none other than Larry Mincks.

"No one wanted to work estate cases," Jeff recalls. "But that's where I ended up, and I worked estate cases where people were defrauding the IRS on their estate taxes. Back in those days, the Treasury Department was also in charge of the Secret Service, and Ohio had become a very important state in presidential elections, so in 1980 I found myself working protective details for both Ronald Reagan and Jimmy Carter. Hey, Ronald Reagan and his wife, Nancy, even called me by my first name."

It was the investigative work, though, that Jeff had the most zest for. Further breaking the established paradigm for IRS agents better known for wearing pocket protectors than packing pistols, one of those cases Jeff was assigned to by Larry involved the mayor and police chief of the town of Osage, West Virginia. Once Jeff made the case, the plan was for Larry to arrest the mayor while Thom Kirk simultaneously arrested the chief of police. It turned out that the mayor owned and operated a bar where he would be taken into custody. Interestingly enough, the mayor could do more than talk the talk; he was a true tough guy who had boxed at the Golden Glove level and was known for starting more bar fights than he broke up.

"We're going through the front door," Jeff recalls, "and Larry Mincks says to me, 'You make the arrest. I'll be backup.' So I figure he doesn't want to get his ass kicked and that I'm gonna get mine kicked instead. In we go and I move straight to the mayor and yell out, 'Federal agents! Up against the wall!' And, much to my surprise, he obliges and presses himself against the wall, lets me take his right hand and then his left into position to slap the handcuffs on. And I imagine the bar patrons watching the scene, thinking that Jeff Sandy is a real badass.

"After I got the mayor to the West Virginia State Police barracks, he looks at me and says, 'Oh my God, who was that guy behind you?'"

"'That was my boss,' I tell him, 'Larry Mincks. Why?'

"'Because he was waving his gun around like crazy. I thought he was gonna kill both of us.'"

Jeff remained a vital part of the task force all the way up to my departure from the U.S. Attorney's Office in 1993. That coincided with him being promoted to a supervisory special agent for the IRS Criminal Investigation Division. It was in that role he was dispatched to Iraq in 2003, not long after the war's outbreak. His mission was twofold: find the location of the weapons of mass destruction that everyone was looking for, and trace the money Iraq had squirreled away across the globe to fund the purchase and manufacture of those weapons. To that end, a meeting was arranged for Jeff with Saddam Hussein's imprisoned right-hand man and number two ranking official in the Iraqi government, Tariq Aziz, the country's deputy prime minister, whose association with the dictator went all the way back to the 1950s.

"They were taking sniper fire at the airport," Jeff recalls, "and the C-130 that brought me in didn't want to linger any longer than it absolutely had to. So upon landing the rear cargo door lowered into a ramp, and I was told to take off out of the plane running as fast as I could as soon as the plane touched down. That didn't go too well for me. I ended up taking a tumble and then stumbled on as best I could."

At that point, the white-haired, sedate-looking Aziz was easily the highest-ranking government official in United States custody, but he had thus far refused to speak to any of the interrogators who took their shot with him. Jeff had been warned to expect the same, along with something else: a peculiar and revolting trait Aziz had come to practice to demonstrate that he still held the upper hand in his own mind.

"And sure enough when he was escorted into the interrogation room at Abu Ghraib prison, he walked to a corner of the room, pulled down his pants, and took a crap right there. Then he wiped his butt with his hand and extended it toward me to shake before he took a seat at the table. He did that with all other interviewers who'd attempted to coax information out of him. I don't know about the other guys, but I told him I wasn't about to shake his hand."

"'Who are you?' Aziz asked from across the table.

"'Let's get off on the right foot. I'm the one asking the questions here, so why don't you tell me who you are?'

"'I'm Tariq Aziz, deputy prime minister of Iraq.'

"He put his hand out to shake mine again. 'I'm not going to shake your hand,' I told him again. He looked at me smugly and said, 'How many languages do you speak?'

"'Again, sir,' I said, 'I'm here to ask the questions. So how many languages do you speak?'

"'I speak seven,' Aziz told me.

"'In that case, I can tell you I speak two: English and Appalachian-eese.'

"'There's no such language as Appalachian-eese.'

"'That's because you've never been to West Virginia, sir.'"

Jeff didn't get anywhere the first two days. On the third day, he changed things up by bringing Aziz grapes and Cuban cigars.

"How'd you like to get out of prison for the day, Mr. Aziz?" Jeff asked him, while Iraq's deputy prime minister gobbled up the grapes between puffs of a cigar.

Jeff had arranged to take Aziz to one of Saddam Hussein's palaces. Upon entering and being led to a room where the interview was to take place, they passed a conference room where a college football game happened to be on television: powerful Kansas State against Jeff's beloved Marshall University. Marshall was winning, and if they held on, it would mark the first time the school had ever beaten a top-ten ranked program.

"Mr. Aziz," he said, "would you mind sitting with me in there to watch the game for a few minutes?"

"Where else do I have to go, except back to jail?"

They watched the end of the game and, sure enough, Marshall upset Kansas State, and Jeff circled the room giving high fives to everyone there... except Aziz, who still hadn't washed his hands after defecating in the corner earlier that morning.

"Why do you get so excited over a simple game?" Aziz asked Jeff, once they were ushered into their interview room.

Jeff explained how Marshall's football program had risen from the ashes after that plane crash and that he was a proud alum.

"I understand now," Aziz said, wiping a tear from his eye. "What do you want to know?"

Jeff repeated what he'd said on the first day. "I want to know about the weapons of mass destruction, and I want to know where all the money went."

"You were too early for the weapons. We were just getting ready to start the program when you declared war on us. As for the money, I will help you all you want. What would you like to know?"

Aziz's other interrogators had been hard-core military, CIA, or some combination of both. On the other hand, Aziz loosened up considerably once he learned Jeff was neither of those things and worked for the Internal Revenue Service instead. The Iraqi regime, he explained, had hidden billions of dollars in individual bank accounts scattered across the world, either in the names of fictitious people or real people who had no idea their names were being used. They spent days and days together, during which Aziz explained to Jeff everything about the process, along with how and where the accounts could be found, explaining, according to *Counter Terrorist* magazine in the summer of 2016, "how Iraq circumvented United Nations sanctions and moved money in and out of Iraq. How oil was sold in violation of United Nations sanctions. How front companies were used to conceal and disguise the movement of money."[1]

The whole time, Aziz sounded like he was boasting, as if trying to impress a fellow financial professional, and Jeff left Iraq having accomplished what no one else had been able to manage.

That trend continued, even after he retired from the IRS in 2005.

"A very good friend of mine in Baltimore called me and said, 'Hey, I heard you were retiring. How would you like to work on terrorism projects for a company based in Washington?'"

Upon hearing that the pay was $120 per hour, Jeff jumped on board and went to work for the company, specializing in uncovering how terrorists moved their money around and where they tended to park it. After that stint was over, he became sheriff of Wood County, West Virginia, which neighbored Washington County in Ohio where Larry Mincks was serving in the same role.

"I had this informant back from when I was an IRS agent who called to tell me that a woman approached him about having her husband murdered for the insurance money. So I called the West Virginia State Police and we set her up with an undercover trooper masquerading as a hit man. We ended up with video and audio recordings—the works, basically everything we needed to make the arrest. After she was in jail, I went to her husband's place of business to talk to him."

"'Sir,' I said. 'Your wife has been arrested for placing a contract to have you murdered.' He looked at me—I'll never forget the look on his face, almost like he was about to start crying—and he said, 'Where can I go to bail her out of jail? I love her.' Can you imagine that?"

What Jeff is most proud of these days, though, came a bit later when he had the honor of serving on Governor Jim Justice's cabinet as West Virginia's homeland security secretary. One day, he was sitting in his office with Thom Kirk, his deputy secretary, and Jack Luikart, who was a retired Putnam County sheriff's deputy.

"You know," he said to them, "for years we've been putting people in jail on drug offenses. What if we changed things up? What if while they're incarcerated we put them in a drug rehabilitation program to get over their addiction lifestyles so they won't use again when they get out?"

Candidates deemed right for the six- to nine-month program were selected by a combination of defense attorneys, prosecutors, and judges. Jeff himself went to the Western Regional Jail to address the prisoners who'd been chosen to partake in the pilot program.

"How many people in here know someone who's died from a fentanyl overdose?" He'd start those meetings with that question, and inevitably, every single person in the room would raise their hands. Then he'd tell them, "I'm coming back here in sixty days to have a pizza party for everyone who sticks with the program."

And sixty days later, Jeff recounts, the men and women who'd looked like zombies two months before, to put it mildly, looked like normal human beings. The next time he returned was graduation day, during which a young woman from the very first group to go through the program came up to him.

"I wanted you to know that you and the governor saved my life," she said, "and I wanted to thank you for that."

"Would you stay in touch with me if I give you my business card?" Jeff asked her.

"I'd love to."

For the next four years, she called and told him she was still clean and sober, along with something else.

"Mr. Sandy, I want you to know I'm helping women in Huntington, West Virginia, get off drugs."

The following year, Jeff met her in person on the campus of his beloved Marshall University for an altogether different reason.

"'How would you like to become an employee of the state of West Virginia?' I asked her," he recalls. "And today she's still counseling prison inmates to prepare them for when they get out of jail."

Big Bill Lias & the Friendly City

The legendary Wheeling, West Virginia crime boss William "Big Bill" Lias pictured in his heyday. Reprinted with permission of the Wheeling Newspapers.

CHAPTER 10

Wheeling, West Virginia

Nobody seems to know how Wheeling earned the nickname "the Friendly City." While not disputing the basic tenets behind that, such a moniker belies a historical truth about a city the author George T. Sidiropolis writes "would become nationally recognized as a bread basket of crime and political corruption" in *Murder Never Dies: Crime and Corruption in the Friendly City*.[1]

"At the turn of the twentieth century," Sidiropolis continues, "the United States was producing thirty percent of the world's goods. Wheeling was cited as one of 832 trading centers in the United States and a city that would be involved in one-half of the nation's business. It had one thousand nine-hundred and ninety-two wholesale and retail establishments within its borders and was recognized as the first wholesale distribution point west of the Allegheny Mountains. The city of Wheeling was a target of opportunity. Within this distinguished metropolis, a wanton sub-culture would soon emerge from beneath the veneer of its Victorian respectability."[2]

To understand when and how that happened, we need to go all the way back to 1914, when a fourteen-year-old boy named Basil Kokoliades sold bottles of his uncle's moonshine whiskey out of the back of a bread wagon. He'd been indoctrinated into the business by his father, who would take the boy with him on moonshine runs, even before he started selling it himself out of the back of that bread wagon in his early teens. It was an early and inauspicious start to an underworld career that made the boy who would grow up to be William George "Big Bill" Lias, the father, or grandfather, of crime in the Friendly City.

Big Bill turned twenty the same year Prohibition became the law of the land, and he took advantage of it by quitting his family's grocery business to sell alcohol to all comers, eventually building a criminal network that kept the city of Wheeling drinking. He maintained a fleet of cars and trucks with the floorboards jerry-rigged to allow for secret compartments to hide the liquor and even retrofitted a fuel tanker to haul Canadian whisky all the way to Wheeling.[3] When Prohibition was repealed, Big Bill turned to numbers running after that and then, in 1939, launched a string of casinos across the county.

He was also, not surprisingly, no stranger to violence. In 1937, Big Bill's cousin turned rival Mike Russell was gunned down in front of the Lias family home on 15th Street in East Wheeling, shot once in the head and three times in the chest. He had been operating a gambling club in Bridgeport, Ohio, and trying to muscle in on the numbers game in Steubenville that Big Bill controlled. Three years earlier, Russell's wife had shot and killed Big Bill's first wife, Gladys, during an argument, which makes you wonder how Russell had managed to last that long.

Big Bill rose not only in stature and power but also in size, topping out at 350 pounds by the time he became the godfather of Wheeling crime, as wide, it was said, as he was tall. Since Italians were not part of the picture, the term "Mafia" was never employed. It was simply the Wheeling mob, founded and built into a criminal juggernaut by Big Bill.

"Before the end of his life, he would become a multi-state real estate magnate, the owner of one of the most modern and extravagant racetracks in the country and amass millions from his bootlegging, lottery numbers, horse bookmaking, casino, slot machine and vending operations. During his meteoric rise to power, this 350-pound anomaly's appetite was accommodated by federal judges, governors, congressmen, a United States senator and the President of the United States."[4]

Big Bill ran his operation out of his sprawling half-mile racetrack, Wheeling Downs, which he had purchased in 1945 for $250,000 at a bankruptcy auction. He ended up investing twice that to turn the track into what became known as "Little Churchill Downs." He'd emerge from the racetrack with a stack of two-dollar bills in his hand, culled from the two-dollar bets placed that day, and pass them out to the hefty group of kids that were inevitably waiting for him on weekends. Plenty of Wheeling residents were struggling in the 1950s, so every Christmas he'd bring in truckloads of groceries to pass out, along with just as many truckloads of toys for kids whose families were down on their luck.

Big Bill drove a big Cadillac with a front seat equipped with a swivel so he could twist it all the way to the left and set his feet down on the pavement. That's how he conducted a lot of his business. Instead of getting out of the car, he'd just sit there and talk to whoever was alongside the Caddy. And when he was finished he'd lock the front seat back into place and drive off.

The city of Wheeling in general, especially South Wheeling, looked at Big Bill Lias as one of those thugs with a heart of gold, a kind of folk hero known for leaving piles of coal in city neighborhoods during the depth of winter for residents who couldn't afford to heat their homes. There were tales about him paying for funerals and weddings for the families of the men who worked for him. And there were stories about him confiscating the paychecks of workers from the steel mills and coal mines and rationing out their gambling money to make sure there'd be enough left over to put food on the table for their families.

But the locals who idolized him didn't talk much about what happened when one of those workers got in hock with Big Bill and fell behind in their debts. Those who revered him had to look past the fact that he was a violent career kingpin. He ran a criminal enterprise that included bookmaking, prostitution, loan-sharking, gambling, and alcohol. If you owned a bar in Wheeling, you got your alcohol, your vending machines, your pool tables, and your one-armed slot machines from Big Bill's Wheeling mob. Those old-school machines could also be found in all the social clubs operated by the Eagles, Elks, and others.

The word was Big Bill enjoyed an understanding with the local prosecutor Theodore "Tad" O'Halloran, who served in office through the bulk of Big Bill's heyday. So long as Bill kept his activities within acceptable boundaries and below the general demarcation point of Wheeling Creek, didn't practice violence against locals, and kept undesirable elements out of the city, O'Halloran would leave him alone. Cops who attempted to enforce the law on their own would find themselves walking a beat in the depth of winter. Occasionally, the state police would raid one of these establishments, but it was mostly for show and the business would be open again the next day. Back then, cops being on the take of gangsters like Big Bill was considered business as usual in Wheeling. They were paid to look the other way, and that's pretty much what they did, including away from the twenty-four houses of prostitution in the center of Wheeling that all fell under the auspices of Big Bill Lias in what became known as Cat House Row.

The federal authorities were far more scrupulous with their efforts, but even so, protocol dictated that they inform locals of their intentions. And whenever those intentions included a raid on any of Big Bill's gambling establishments, word of the crackdown would be passed to owners of the targeted sites. Big Bill maintained a fleet of moving trucks manned by workers capable of emptying out all the machines inside a bar or social club in under an hour. Almost invariably, the establishments were up and running again the following day.

Tad O'Halloran and law enforcement in general looked the other way because Big Bill's racetrack and other establishments brought business into Wheeling. Along with the availability of alcohol, that drew tons of folks to the city, which was good for all business. Those who patronized his gambling halls and scored a successful day at the track would spend their money at local bars, restaurants, and shops. And, all told, he probably employed as many of the locals as any of the big mills or mines. Big Bill might not have been Robin Hood, but he was in close proximity to that for the locals, who appreciated the fact that the streets on which his places sat were the safest in the city because he kept them that way. Even after getting liquored up, men knew better than to cause trouble outside the bars and halls or try cheating at the table games inside them. The punishment he dispensed for either was plenty worse than what the local authorities could dispense.

Big Bill's bulbous figure only added to his larger-than-life stature that stemmed from running the Wheeling mob for upward of three decades. This was a time when the FBI under J. Edgar Hoover hadn't been able to pierce its inner workings since in those days nobody ever talked. The Department of Justice did get him on tax evasion charges in the late 1940s, and Attorney General Bobby Kennedy actually deported Big Bill since he'd allegedly been born in Greece and had never gained U.S. citizenship. Upon reentering the country, Lias was arrested again, but in court the government couldn't prove the status of his birth. Big Bill ended up with a sentence that was little more than a slap on the wrist and emerged from prison after only a few months to again take the reins of his criminal empire.

"The shit got real when the feds came into town, but they weren't really able to get on the inside until they were here for a bunch of years," a former bookie told Steve Novotney for his nine-part series on the Wheeling mob for his website Weelunk.com. "The first group of guys the feds arrested just took it. They went to trial or pleaded out for the best sentence possible, and they went to prison and didn't sell anyone out. When those guys got out, they came back and went back to work. But while the guys were in prison, their wives were visited each week and given cash. They called it unemployment back then."[5]

Big Bill was an old-school gangster with close associations to a crime organization called the Purple Gang of Detroit. He smoked cigars in Chicago with none other than Al Capone and boasted that Capone enjoyed the stogies Big Bill brought up from Wheeling more than the Cuban cigars the head of the infamous Outfit had smuggled in. But he ran his numbers business via New York, which communicated the winning numbers through a Lias associate who, it turned out, was gaming the system by "playing" the winning number before it was transmitted over the wire to Big Bill's headquarters in Wheeling. He was essentially skimming from Big Bill's operation.

"When the enraged Lias discovered the identity of the local conspirator involved in the scheme to steal from his numbers operation, he allegedly summoned the Goldberg brothers, two of his most proficient enforcers, and traveled to Fairmont, West Virginia. There they found their subject, 'Devil' Colantino, operating a tailor shop. The victim's bullet-riddled body was discovered the following day hanging from the clothing conveyor."[6]

Another version of the story adds that the previous day's winning numbers were found written on his forehead.

Big Bill was literally and figuratively larger than life, a paradox of a man who was beloved by the community that cared little or nothing about the ruthlessness he displayed in his illicit business dealings. He helped fashion a culture that persisted into my years not only as the U.S.

Attorney for the Northern District but also coach of my son's eighth-grade basketball team with a man named Earl, who was the brother of a close friend of mine.

There was a pay phone located in the entry hall of the gym where we practiced.

"Hey, Bill," Earl said one day, "can you take over practice? I gotta make a few phone calls."

"Sure, Earl," I said to him, "no problem."

I later found out from Earl's brother that he had calls to make because he was a bookie doing business out of a gym while coaching basketball with a U.S. Attorney. Earl would later receive a visit from FBI agent Tom Burgoyne and a government expense-paid trip to Elkins, West Virginia, where the federal grand jury was meeting.

Stories like that represent the lighter side of criminal activity in Wheeling. But there was also a darker side to the city's criminal culture we owe to the likes of Big Bill Lias. Though he ruled the Wheeling mob with an iron fist until 1970, he did so from the confines of his home on 15th Street in East Wheeling. Around 1965, Big Bill suffered a botched glaucoma operation that forced him to don Coke bottle–thick glasses just to see but did nothing for his depth perception. Stairs had already become a challenge for a man of his girth, and after the operation he could barely get down them. In his sixties now, Big Bill couldn't bear the people of Wheeling—those who revered him as well as his enemies and rivals—seeing him so weak and ineffectual. He became a recluse to the point that many believed he'd moved back to his purported homeland of Greece.

I never prosecuted Big Bill Lias, never even met him. By the time of his death in 1970, he had been pretty much forgotten until a car bombing in the mid-1960s ushered in a new era of crime to West Virginia. There was no shortage of criminals ready to take up the mantle of kingpin in his place. Men who lacked his crass nobility and sense of community spirit, dispensing violence indiscriminately instead of two-dollar bills, coal, toys, and turkeys.

One of them was Carl Lee Gallo, who was the target of my next investigation.

Carl Lee Gallo

Bill Kolibash and daughter Shariane pictured with then vice president George H. W. Bush while Bush was visiting West Virginia University in 1987. The vice president's office had taken an interest a few years earlier in the Gallo case, thanks to Bill's employment of a multijurisdictional task force to wage the war on drugs.

CHAPTER 11

Clarksburg, West Virginia, 1982

In the early 1900s, a significant wave of Italian immigrants arrived in West Virginia, seeking refuge from the sulfur mining industry. Many of these immigrants, predominantly originating from Italy's southern region, settled in Clarksburg, initially finding work in the thriving coal industry. A unique culinary tradition emerged as Italian coal miners brought pepperoni and bread into the mines, eventually leading to the invention of the famous pepperoni rolls, which are now recognized as the official state food of West Virginia.

Talk to any West Virginian, and they'll refer to Clarksburg as a city, even though the population today barely touches sixteen thousand. The population was almost twenty-three thousand in 1982, back when all the coal mines and steel mills were still open and thriving.

Aside from pepperoni rolls, its rich Italian heritage, and being the county seat for Harrison County, the town, or city, is probably best known as the birthplace of General Thomas J. Stonewall Jackson, although it also remains known for the Mountaineer Militia. Seven members of this militant antigovernment group fully intended to blow up the FBI's Criminal Justice Information Services headquarters based in Clarksburg in October 1996. They had obtained blueprints of the FBI facility from a shady local firefighter. Plastic explosives and blasting caps were confiscated by law enforcement officials at five locations in West Virginia, Pennsylvania, and Ohio. Other than that, locals praise the town for its lavish green beauty and easy lifestyle. In short, a great place to live and raise a family.

But that wasn't the case on a spring night in 1982.

* * *

On that night—morning actually at 2:00 a.m.—a wild shoot-out took place in the downtown district. Men with machine guns rode down the streets in separate cars firing rounds at each other. One of those cars had come all the way from Florida, the men inside coming to collect a debt. The other car was filled with soldiers of a local gangster named Carl Lee Gallo, who was running a drug operation with product he purchased, in part, from a crime syndicate in Florida that had sent their gunmen to collect money they believed Gallo owed them. Gallo begged to differ. When the gunmen showed up, his men were ready, and those gunmen left town in a bullet-riddled car with only the money in their pockets. Gallo had made his point, and they never came back.

Gallo had grown up on the streets with other thugs and represented a new wave of criminal element shepherded in by drug crime. With a slight frame, neatly coiffed thick hair, and standing barely five feet nine inches in height, he hardly looked the part. He'd also never been arrested for anything, much less indicted or convicted. He even fought a speeding ticket in court once and got off scot-free. That said, his looks and clean record belied a committed criminal comfortable in the newly violent world of criminal activity fueled by the explosion of cocaine across the country.

Rackets like gambling, prostitution, and numbers running under Big Bill Lias were entirely different from the criminal dealings of Carl Lee Gallo. Big Bill and other crime bosses like him genuinely cared about their community and its people. For men like Gallo, people were no more than cannon fodder to make a profit off of. One time, he told a guy he'd known all his life, but who had rung up a serious marker, to meet him at a hotel in Morgantown that served as one of Gallo's bases of operations. The man got there with an explanation but when he opened his mouth, Gallo stuck a revolver inside and cocked it.

"You better pay up," he threatened.

We've all seen this scene a hundred times in movies, and the guy always yanks the gun out, his point made. Not Gallo. He pulled the trigger and shot the guy through the cheek. The bullet ended up lodged in a wall.

"Next time, it's your face."

The guy paid up the next day. This was atypical behavior for Gallo, who preferred to keep a low profile. He had four or five bodyguards around him, led by Frank Nicholas and David Lee Stout, pretty much all the time. Gallo could call on either of them, or any number of thugs in his employ, to handle the violent aspects of his work, and that violence almost invariably involved guns.

The night of the shoot-out with the contract killers out of Florida led the West Virginia State Police to launch an all-out effort to bring down Carl Lee Gallo and his considerable network once and for all. As trooper Thom Kirk later explained to me, cocaine made up the bulk of Gallo's business, but he also owned a string of coal mines he operated with stolen equipment to make them profitable when no one else could back in those days. With a raised brow and clenched teeth, Thom spoke under his breath, "Rumor has it that there are a whole lot of bodies hidden down in the depths of one or more of those coal mines."

The Gallo case was a defining moment in Thom's career. Recognizing his unwavering dedication and sharp instincts, the legendary state trooper and then WVSP captain Joe Trupo put Thom in charge of the operation.

Joe was a refrigerator-size man, built like an NFL lineman, in both bulk and strength. He commanded respect with his mere presence and was known for settling miners' strikes all on his own. He'd walk into a simmering, taut situation between mine owners and miners and wouldn't walk out until he had a deal. I guess both sides were scared of what Joe might do to them if they didn't settle.

Another time, one of Gallo's thugs accosted a young state trooper during a traffic stop and stole his gun. That was the ultimate ignominy for a cop, especially a raw one. Profoundly embarrassed, the young trooper told Joe the story, but Joe told him not to worry. He got a solid description of the young punk who'd taken the gun and went to the bar where Gallo's gang hung out. He stepped through that door in full uniform like Wyatt Earp without Doc Holliday watching his back and instantly spotted the man sitting smugly on a barstool. Without missing a beat, Joe threw the guy off the stool. The thug, now sprawled out on the floor, glared up at him. Everyone else in the gang's hangout watched with a mixture of fear and apprehension, exchanging glances that asked, *What should we do?* The answer turned out to be nothing. None of them intervened. The thug retook his seat and Joe threw him off the barstool again, only this time he grabbed him by the shirt and jerked him upright like he was a rag doll in hands that were more like slabs of meat.

"You're gonna keep falling off this stool here, son," he told the thug calmly, "until you return that gun."

Joe left the bar with the young trooper's pistol. The message was clear: Joe was a force of nature not to be taken lightly, along with the whole of the West Virginia State Police.

Years later, Captain Joe Trupo sent Thom Kirk to my office in the Northern District to tell me the WVSP wanted to open a full-scale investigation into Gallo's operation. This would have been a great RICO case, but the FBI wasn't doing drug cases at the time, and the DEA didn't have much of a presence in West Virginia. So my first thought was to prosecute the case under the Continuing Criminal Enterprise Act, which was the next best thing. If we did our job, we'd be able to bring the Bureau in to bump the charges up to federal. When we started, though, it was just my office, the West Virginia State Police, and Larry Mincks of the Internal Revenue Service.

We'd already opened an investigation into Gallo with Larry and the IRS, so it seemed prudent to join forces. At that point, Thom had never worked with the IRS, so he headed down to Charleston, where the Southern District office was located, to meet Larry.

"I understand from Bill Kolibash that you're working on the Gallo case," Larry said to him.

"Right, and Bill told me you've got some information I think we could use."

"So Mincks takes me into this back room in the U.S. Attorney's Office," Tom told the *Game of Crimes* podcast just a few years back. "And he's got these boxes stacked all over the place and escorts me straight to an impressive mountain of paperwork. 'Here's my case,' Mincks said proudly, as if unveiling a hidden treasure trove. 'I've got tax forms. I've got surveillance. I've got everything you could think of. Check out anything you want and make all the notes you want. You're not supposed to take any paper out of here, but if you find evidence to help make your case, take it.'"[1]

It turned out Larry had gotten that report of a small plane crashing in Florida, and the pilot, Peewee Tenant, who was killed was a known associate of Rudy Zaccagnini, a midlevel drug dealer from the Fairmont area we had our eyes on too. Larry went down to Florida and met with the customs agents supervising the case, since the plane had come in from the Bahamas. They showed Larry that suitcase containing two kilos of cocaine and that notebook referenced earlier with the names and addresses of all the dealers the shipment would have supplied. Larry brought the notebook back, and we used it as the basis to call witnesses before a grand jury in an investigation we had opened that was now running in tandem with the one the West Virginia State Police wanted to open into Gallo.

Thom couldn't believe it. Intrigued and slightly overwhelmed, he dug in. Like most everyone else, he didn't think of the IRS as anything more than a tax collector. He may have heard how my office had begun making regular use of Larry and his people on task forces, but seeing it up close and personal confronted him with how we'd started to make our cases for the first time. Thom was no stranger to working undercover, and what a guy like Larry Mincks could uncover from afar made for the perfect complement to what Thom could get from in close.

* * *

On July 26, 1982, Judge Charles H. Haden II impaneled a grand jury in Parkersburg to serve as the investigative catalyst that could issue subpoenas for both documents and witnesses. The grand jury went from meeting just one or two days a week to three, four, or even five for the eighteen-month duration of the investigation, allowing us to bring evidence and information before them. If that investigation proved successful, we would go to a separate grand jury to secure the indictments. These investigative federal grand juries became powerful tools to fight crime, and pioneering their use remains one of the proudest achievements of my career.

The grand jury impaneled by Judge Haden included an individual named Robert Neal Raines. Judge Haden instructed the grand jurors, including Raines, on their service and obligation under Rule 6 of the Federal Rules of Criminal Procedure to maintain the secrecy of the grand jury proceedings.

On the day following the impaneling of the grand jury, Special Agent Douglas Miser of the IRS Criminal Investigation Division appeared before the grand jury and provided an overview of the major investigations with which they would be concerned. This included a discussion of the "Gallo organization" as a cocaine distribution network centered in Clarksburg, West Virginia.

Raines later went to Clarksburg and left his business card at one of Carl Lee Gallo's places of business, United Taxi, and indicated that he was in a position to assist Gallo. The card and message were delivered to Gallo at his nearby residence by his bodyguard Frank Nicholas. In the wake of that, Gallo dispatched his other top bodyguard, David Lee Stout, to make contact with Raines. Stout did as he was directed and met with Raines, posing as Gallo. At the first meeting between Stout and Raines, Raines made a statement indicating his vindictive attitude toward the government.

Subsequent to the initial contact, Stout (still posing as Gallo) made numerous contacts with Raines both over the phone and in person. During these contacts, Raines told Stout what was occurring before the grand jury. Raines also delivered microcassette tape recordings of the testimony of various witnesses who had appeared. Gallo and several of his other associates, including Samuel Iaquinta and his girlfriend Valerie Shine, listened to the tapes at Gallo's home, giving them a bird's-eye view of the evidence we were accumulating.

Following one of the grand jury sessions, the court reporter, Frances Warner, came to me and said she had observed strange behavior on behalf of Raines that made her suspicious he was recording the grand jury testimony. Following up on Ms. Warner's information, agents conducted a search of persons outside the grand jury room. During that interval, Raines went into a restroom and threw the tape recorder away. Upon his request, Raines was dismissed from further service as a grand juror on November 18, 1982. He was subsequently convicted of contempt for leaking the grand jury information and also for perjury he committed when he was called to testify before a second grand jury concerning the leaks and denied any knowledge of leaking confidential information.

The more we dug into the labyrinthine underworld of Carl Lee Gallo's crime organization, the more we realized the chilling nature of the men we were dealing with. These weren't two-bit criminals—they were battle-hardened thugs whose very existence thrived on violence and danger.

Gallo, for example, expanded his network to include methamphetamine coming out of Philadelphia. Those drugs were pushed through West Virginia at the time by the Pagans motorcycle gang out of Ohio under the leadership of a criminal lifer named Robert Fitz. The Pagans were not quite as big but just as ruthless and deadly as the Hells Angels. They were the dominant gang for the mid-Atlantic region stretching all the way to Ohio and reportedly had five thousand active members at the time Gallo went into business with them. Gallo outsourced not just the methamphetamine end of his business to the gang but also a measure of the enforcement duties.

We caught a break, though, when Fitz was arrested by FBI agents in Virginia on a case linked to ours. When he testified for us, initially before the grand jury, we made a deal with him that we wouldn't return him to Virginia but instead let him serve his time closer to home in Ohio. Fitz talked and gave up Gallo's people as the ones who'd made a deal with the Pagans on the methamphetamine distribution.

Gallo's drug network was massive, but he didn't realize we also had one of his top dealers, Rudy Zaccagnini, dead to rights thanks to the notebook Larry Mincks had recovered in Florida. Zaccagnini didn't want to go to jail for thirty years, and he had even more reason to want Gallo brought down. Zaccagnini's drug organization was centered in Fairmont, West Virginia. He obtained some of his drugs from Gallo and eventually found himself in debt, so Gallo seized his territory to pay off what was owed to him. He kept Zaccagnini on board as a key cog in his cocaine distribution business, but Zaccagnini always harbored a grudge for having his own turf taken out from under him. When we nabbed Zaccagnini on a drug charge, instead of facing twenty-five to life, he turned cooperating witness in return for a lesser sentence. He knew Gallo's network inside and out, and on top of that, he kept more detailed *written* records of everything, which he turned over to us once he agreed to cooperate.

"Anything else you boys want, just let me know."

I told him I would and then trained my sights on putting Carl Lee Gallo away once and for all.

CHAPTER 12

Clarksburg, West Virginia

Taking Carl Lee Gallo and his organization down was a massive undertaking that required putting a meticulous synchronized operation into motion. West Virginia state troopers, IRS agents, and FBI agents would stage the raids simultaneously. This bust was so big that Vice President George Bush's office flew down in a helicopter to lend the authority and support of his station.

So many people needed to be arrested in so many places, in Ohio and Pennsylvania in addition to West Virginia, that we were afraid the takedowns were going to get bloody. These were criminals, from Gallo on down, who made their living with violence and bloodshed. Just because we never did find any bodies down in those coal mines Gallo owned doesn't mean there weren't any. Word was these were the kind of people who weren't going to go quietly, and things could go to guns in a hurry. Our goal was to minimize the collateral damage that lay in the wake of the pursuit.

We got most of the takedown team together in Jackson's Mill, West Virginia, hundreds and hundreds of law enforcement officers. The feds brought in agents out of Philadelphia, Richmond, and Washington, DC, and we had over a hundred West Virginia state troopers there. This was right before all the indictments, numbering close to a hundred, were unsealed, at which point the cat would be out of the bag. We thought we had every base covered.

Then, the night before the raids were set to go off, we got word from the surveillance team watching Gallo that he was on the move, headed south down Route 79. The surveillance team called Thom Kirk on their bag phone to let them know Gallo might be in the wind, likely headed for Florida, where we knew he had property. But Gallo had one of those original Motorola bag phones, too, which made it possible for someone to tip him off if we didn't move in fast enough. Given his penchant for violence, we needed to avoid a shoot-out on the highway. The stakes had never been higher.

Our first thought was that he'd somehow caught wind of what was going down, in which case we had no idea how bad things might get. But we knew we could no longer wait until the next day to nab Gallo; we had to do it that night, while he was still on the move and before he had the opportunity to warn too many of his guys what was coming.

The next update to Thom Kirk from the follow team was that Gallo was still on 79, approaching exit 57, which led to Route 119 south.

"That's the fastest way to Florida," Thom informed them. "So if he takes that exit, we need to move in."

Thom warned the surveillance team and the other troopers who were already moving in that Gallo was known to travel with two or three guys in a car three or so behind his. Thom happened to have a couple of state trooper friends who flew a chopper for the State of West Virginia Aviation Division, and he called them to see if they could lend a hand.

"We're carrying a couple of politicians up north for a press conference," the trooper in the pilot's seat said. "Just tell me how we can help."

In that moment, Thom got a call from the team on Gallo's trail. He listened to their report and then got back on with the chopper pilot.

"He took exit 57. That means he's headed to Florida, and we need to take him down now."

"In that case, Thom, I guess these politicians we're carrying will have to wait."

Then he got back on the line with his follow team.

"We're a quarter mile back and holding," they told him.

"What's the next town?"

"Summersville."

"Okay. Stand by."

Thom's next call was to the Summersville Police Department. He couldn't tell them a lot but did the best he could.

"Look, we've got a target on 119. We can't let him get past us. We need your help."

Around thirty minutes later, Gallo's car and the surveillance team crested over a ridge, beyond which was a long, straight stretch that was rare in West Virginia. Maybe two miles ahead, two tractor trailers were blocking the highway in what looked like the aftermath of an accident but in reality the local cops had staged. And between the roadblock they'd set up and Gallo was all this traffic that had backed up along the three-lane freeway.

Gallo got closer and closer to that backup, about to get snared among the cars, when he tried to go around it. It was February, and his Cadillac was slipping and sliding in the snow. At that point, the troopers on scene with the locals were ordered to move in. Gallo was still trying to make his way around the traffic jam when this monster of a trooper named Big Bob Cunningham—appeared before him with a twelve-gauge shotgun and pumped two shells into the Cadillac's engine, blowing a hole in its radiator.

The state police chopper had just arrived, saw the shots, and thought a gunfight was going on. So the pilot, Thom Kirk's friend, dropped in real low and spotted a guy wearing a great big cowboy hat getting out of a car a couple lengths behind Gallo's. The pilot thought he was an innocent bystander walking straight into a gunfight, so he dropped in and let the angle of the rotor wash push the guy back inside his car. Then the pilot actually got the door closed and kept it closed by pushing one of the chopper's skids against the frame, pinning the guy inside.

Meanwhile, the troopers and a DEA agent named Lowell Maxey rushed Gallo's car and dragged him out so Lowell could slap the handcuffs on him. At that time, thanks to the staged accident, there were all these people stuck in traffic with nothing else to do but get out of their cars and watch the whole bust go down. It turned out Gallo had no idea what was going on; he hadn't been tipped off after all. He was just headed to South Carolina to pick up some stolen mining equipment to take back to one of the coal mines he owned.

"So why'd you try to go around the roadblock?" Big Bob Cunningham, who'd shot up the car engine, wondered.

"I thought it was just a truck accident," the handcuffed Gallo told him. "I tried to get around it because I was running late, when you stepped out from out of nowhere and blew up my car."

The guy in the cowboy hat that the chopper pilot had pinned inside his car finally emerged, after witnessing all the commotion up close and personal. He approached Big Bob and saw the Cadillac gushing steam and smoke from the radiator, along with the car's driver standing by the side of the road in handcuffs.

"Man, what did that guy do?" the man asked.

Big Bob looked at him and spit a huge wad of tobacco juice from the clump in his cheek to the ground. "Speeding." Then, after a pause, "We take speeding real serious in these parts."

It turned out the guy was a paramedic who'd tried to get out of his car initially to help out in what looked like a serious truck accident.

* * *

Thom Kirk, who had arrived on the scene in a van, called Captain Joe Trupo to tell him they had Gallo and that he and Lowell Maxey would be transporting him to the federal courthouse in Clarksburg.

"That's great," Joe said. "I can't tell you guys how happy this makes me. Let me ask you, is there any way I can pick him up? There's camera crews all over the courthouse here, and I know you guys don't want to be on television, being undercovers and all."[1]

Thom agreed and met Joe out on Route 50, where Gallo was transferred from the van he and Maxey were riding in to the back seat of Joe's cruiser. Joe drove him the rest of the way to the courthouse all by himself, walked Gallo in handcuffs up the steps through all the assembled media, and turned him over to the U.S. marshals who would take things from there. Then Joe, standing right in front of the courthouse, turned back to the cameras and put his hands up.

"I've got two things to tell you folks," he said, according to Tom Kirk's podcast interview. "One is that we just had the successful arrest of Carl Lee Gallo. And the second is that I'm running for sheriff of Harrison County."[2]

That was how Joe kicked off his campaign. And not only did he win, he ended up serving two terms after retiring from the WVSP, remaining in office for eight years.

Meanwhile, we secured a hundred-count indictment on more than fifty members of Gallo's organization, including Gallo himself on charges that included racketeering, tax evasion, and drug dealing. The indictment was the size of a phone book, almost five hundred pages laid out in explicit detail thanks to our investigative grand jury. Meanwhile, Gallo had been arrested so late at night that word didn't spread through his network prior to the raids scheduled for early the following morning. They went off without a single shot being fired.

* * *

Another especially interesting fact about the Gallo case is that it marked the first time we aggressively utilized existing forfeiture laws under the Continuing Criminal Enterprise statute. RICO really wasn't designed for drug cases so much as organized crime, because drug organizations focused on only one thing instead of a myriad of illegal activity. So we stood to do much better prosecuting the case as a CCE. We seized, among other things, the ninety-two-acre coal mine where Gallo allegedly stashed bodies, but we never found any evidence of that and ended up shutting the mine down.

Just after the indictments came down and we made all the arrests, my office got word that members of Gallo's organization who'd escaped indictment were working to liquidate the assets we intended to seize. We had only hours to act before we would potentially lose them for good. We needed a judge to approve an injunction to prevent the sales, but it was Saturday morning and the courthouse was closed. We managed to reach U.S. District Judge William Kidd in Braxton County, who happened to be in his office. He said to come right down and meet him at his house. The problem was it was a four-hour drive, and I didn't think we had four hours before Gallo's associates acted. I met Dave Jividen, a prosecutor who oversaw the activities of the task force, in my office and we drafted the paperwork.

"How the hell else are we gonna get there?" Dave asked me.

"Well," I said, "let's rent an airplane."

He looked at me in disbelief. "So you're going to call the Justice Department to get approval?"

"No, we're not going to do that. We've got an emergency here."

I called up a pilot I knew who owned his own plane.

"Sure, I'll take you," he said. "Do you know where you're going?"

"Braxton County."

We rushed to the airport and boarded the plane.

"How close can you get us to this address?" I said, handing the pilot a slip of paper with Judge Kidd's home address.

"I don't know."

"You don't know?"

"I need to find an airstrip in the vicinity."

So up we went into the air with absolutely no idea where we were going to land. Fortunately, the pilot found an airstrip across from Braxton Academy. I told him to bill the Justice Department and, to this day, have no idea what it cost, but it was an awful lot less than all we eventually reaped in forfeitures.

We also seized Gallo's United Taxi cab company, where his sister worked as a dispatcher and served as a source of methamphetamine for other dealers. We were able to prove that she distributed the substance herself and stored large quantities of cocaine for her brother at her home. There were plenty of stories that Gallo used those cabs routinely to move drugs, but we could never prove that, and we already had more than we needed to nail him.

Meanwhile, the U.S. Attorney's Office found itself operating United Taxi to keep the company running and its drivers employed. Things went bad almost from the start. The company's chief mechanic ended up in jail on alcohol-related charges, and no one in our office really knew a thing about running a cab company. I was standing on the courthouse steps one day next to this young, seemingly sweet lady, who noticed a United Taxi cab cruising by.

"That damn cab company is the worst-run operation in the city," she said to me.

"Ma'am," I told her, "that's *my* cab company."

She must have been right, because after nine months United Taxi filed for bankruptcy. As Clarksburg's *Exponent Telegram* newspaper reported, "U.S. Attorney William Kolibash blamed debts run up by the previous owner for driving United Taxi Service of Clarksburg into bankruptcy."

But a man who was blocked from establishing a competing cab company says the government simply botched it. "People don't want to ride in their cabs because they have dirty cabs," said Tom Surock, a service station owner, validating the sweet young lady's grievances. Interestingly, Surock's efforts to set up the competing service were fought by the feds.[3]

I guess the U.S. Attorney's Office wasn't very good at operating a cab company. And it was the last time our office ever tried to run a business we acquired via forfeiture.

As for Carl Lee Gallo, he got sentenced to thirty years in federal prison but, under the Bureau of Prisons guidelines at the time, served only twelve. He was released on parole in 1996 and was returned to prison on a parole violation for speeding and driving without a license in March 2006. Then, while back behind bars, he was indicted in January 2007 for medical insurance fraud he'd committed from June 2001 through November 2006. Together with the sixteen years he had left on his original sentence, the ten years or so he'd be serving on the insurance-fraud crime should have assured he'd spend the rest of his life in prison.

Recently, though, I was told a Carl Lee Gallo, age eighty-three, was living in Reynoldsville, a town in Harrison County where Joe Trupo had served those eight years as sheriff. Maybe I'll give him a call, just to check in.

In my mind, he still owes the state of West Virginia for that cab company we put into bankruptcy.

The Task Force: The West Virginia State Police—Thom Kirk

The legendary West Virginia state policeman Thom Kirk pictured today.

CHAPTER 13

Wheeling, West Virginia

Thom Kirk had flown as part of a crew on a P-3 Orion sub hunter for the U.S. Navy and then drove a concrete truck while he was waiting for a spot to open with the West Virginia State Police.

His first case on the job was a triple murder. The house where it happened was located right next to a high school, so by the time he got there more than a hundred people had gathered in the parking lot to see what all the fuss was about. Thom worked the southern part of the state, where local law enforcement was responsible for patrolling huge swaths of area and were ill-equipped to conduct a major investigation; in fact, in a lot of those areas the state police served as the only law enforcement. So the troopers of the West Virginia State Police, big and brawny to a man, were very much revered and welcomed when they showed up. I'd say all those spectators would have given Thom a standing ovation when he pulled up in his cruiser, had they not been standing already.

He started working undercover for the state police after only two years as a trooper. At that time in West Virginia, driver's license tests were conducted by troopers. And Thom told me once that several times he'd be working undercover and somebody would come up to him out of the blue and say, "Thank you for giving me my driver's test." I never asked him if that ever blew his cover.

In another of his biggest cases, Thom spent a stretch undercover riding with an outlaw biker gang. He'd go on a "run" with them sometimes for days at a time with little or no opportunity to maintain personal hygiene, even to just take a shower. He'd come home after two weeks or so on the road and either wash his clothes separately or just burn them. He was under strict orders from his wife to take a shower before he so much as touched anything in the house. One time, he had showered, dressed in fresh clothes, and sat down with his wife to watch some television.

"Your beard," she said suddenly, crinkling her nose.

Thom scratched at the scraggly, untamed mess he needed to blend in with the bikers. "What about it?"

"It's moving. I think something's crawling in it."

Just then, Thom heard some buzzing and plucked several nasty bugs from the wild growth.

"The dead ones are easy to get out," he once told me. "The live ones give you a fight."

Thom actually went to law school while he was still in the midst of his career undercover. Because he was working sixty to seventy hours a week, sometimes his wife went to his classes to take notes and record the sessions so he could listen to them later. When he was out on surveillance and couldn't make class, he'd call his wife, who was living in Fairmont at the time. She'd scramble to find a babysitter, grab a tape recorder, and head to the law school. Afterward, they'd meet somewhere like a rest stop or parking lot so she could give Thom the tape, which he'd listen to while on surveillance.

He told me that in one of the classes, a professor, exasperated over not getting the answer to a question, asked Thom's wife specifically for it, and the answer she gave was right! He called her "Mrs. Kirk," so he knew exactly what was going on. When Thom graduated, more people at the ceremony knew his wife than knew him and kept coming up to congratulate her for completing law school.

Thom came from humble beginnings that turned tragic when he was all of seven years old. His father, Robert Lee Kirk, was a highly respected patrol officer who was as tough as they came when he needed to be. One night, he was coming off his shift when he received a radio call that there'd been a car accident. Being the closest unit in the area, Robert and his partner radioed back that they were en route.

Upon reaching the scene, Robert saw that the car had smashed through a guard rail and continued on down a hill toward a natural gas relay plant that was surrounded by a chain-link fence. The damaged car never got that far but did plow over some aboveground pipes and ended up lodged atop them. The resulting damage sent floods of natural gas spewing upward through the vehicle's carcass. Robert and his partner could smell the distinct scent in the air as they clambered down the embankment and heard the gas gushing up from the ground the closer they drew to the scene. Robert pictured the car catching fire and setting all that gas aflame. He also spotted two figures slumped inside the vehicle, unconscious.

"Get back up the hill," he said to his partner, "and call for an ambulance. Then call the gas company and tell them they need to get the gas shut off in these parts before we have a genuine disaster on our hands."

As his partner scrambled back up the hill, Robert shimmied the rest of the way down and edged up to the car, pinching his nose against the stench of gas, and managed to pry the door open. The pair of adults slumped in the front seat were both good-sized. He extracted the driver from the wreck first, eased him over his shoulder, and somehow made it back up that steep hill lugging his weight.

After laying the man down for his partner to tend to, Robert headed back down and repeated the process with a woman in the passenger seat, who was even heftier than the driver. By the time he got the second victim to safety, he couldn't catch his breath and ended up sitting on the side of the road to settle himself down. It turned out that Robert had endured a bout with rheumatic fever when he was about his son Thom's age, and it had weakened his heart to the point where carrying the two victims up that steep hill had led to him suffering a heart attack. In the hospital, though, they wrongly diagnosed his symptoms as being the result of inhaling so much natural gas.

Relieved, another patrolman offered to drive him back to his car at the station, but Robert was feeling better and it was a beautiful day, so he told the officer he'd walk the short distance himself. In the midst of that walk, he suffered what turned out to be a second heart attack and was taken to a larger hospital nearby. Again, he thought he was feeling better and decided to walk down the hill to a bus stop in Fairmont so he could take the next bus back to the station to pick up his car, then suffered a third heart attack on the way that turned out to be fatal.

Years later, Thom's son Kris went to Washington, DC, to attend the unveiling of the name of a fellow Kentucky state trooper who'd been killed in a car accident on a memorial wall dedicated to police who had perished in the line of duty. While there, the young man called his dad.

"How come Grandpa's name isn't on that wall?" he wondered, after being unable to find it anywhere.

"Good question," Thom said to him.

When Thom gets something fixed in his mind, it sticks with him until it gets done, and sure enough, in May 2008, father and son traveled back to Washington for the unveiling of Robert Kirk's name on that memorial wall.

"Although it took nearly a half century, Robert Lee Kirk, formerly of Fairmont, West Virginia finally has his name engraved on the National Law Enforcement Memorial Wall in Washington, D. C.," Huntington's *Herald-Dispatch* reported at the time, "thanks to his son, retired former Superintendent of the West Virginia State Police, Thomas Lee Kirk of Winfield, and his grandson, Kentucky State Trooper Kristopher Kirk of Ashland. Names that appear on the wall belong to men or women who have died in the line of duty."[1]

But his father's legacy left its mark on Thom Kirk long before that.

"I remember being a freshman at East Fairmont High School. It was Career Day in civics class, and we were all asked to write down what our career was going to be, and I wrote down that I wanted to be an undercover narcotics officer for the West Virginia State Police. I must have been around thirteen at the time in the 1960s, and the thing was the WVSP didn't even have an undercover unit at the time."

After graduating from high school and attending college, followed by that tour with the navy during the Vietnam conflict, Thom came home with little knowledge of the law and even less about drug crimes. But he signed up for a cadet class with the West Virginia State Police. He learned over three thousand people had applied for the thirty-four positions that had been posted. The kicker was this: the WVSP had just christened its first undercover drug unit.

The lieutenant who interviewed him frowned on Thom's ambitions nonetheless.

"You were in the navy, right?" the lieutenant said, checking Thom's file. "You were involved in electronics and computers."

"Yes, sir."

"Well, we just started a computer division, too. We're computerizing everything. Why don't you let me put you there?"

Unmoved by the suggestion, Thom stuck to his original plan. He did two years in uniform before claiming a spot that opened up in the undercover unit. The corporal he worked under in the unit was less than enamored with Thom's loner approach and requested he be put back in uniform. That corporal, though, was replaced before the request could be carried out, and his second commanding officer took much more of a liking to Thom's style, seeing something his predecessor hadn't.

The eventually lauded WVSP undercover unit was still in its formative stages back in those days, meaning Thom's first assignment to nail unsuspecting drug dealers came without any backup.

"I remember taping this miniature Panasonic tape recorder, that I'd bought with my own money, to my leg with state police evidence tape. That was my backup, since if the biker gang made me and killed me, I figured somebody would find the tape and be able to identify my killers. By the time I was put in charge of the unit, we were doing things a whole different way."

But not before he faced one of his most precarious situations ever in Welch, West Virginia, a coal town where local drug dealers set up shop every payday and never lacked for business.

"I bought drugs off these two guys for a while. And then all of a sudden, they started avoiding me. That's never a good thing, because it usually means you've been made. I hadn't seen these guys for a while, when one day I was driving out of town and they flagged me down. I stopped and one of them got into the front seat and the other into the back.

"'Can you drop us somewhere?' the guy in the front said.

"'Well,' I told him, 'I'm trying to get out of town, and I'm a little rushed here.'

"'It's okay,' the guy said. 'This won't take long.'

"He tells me to take a left and then a right and now we're getting way off the beaten path. Then I hear something click and feel this jab to my ribs and realize the guy's got a switchblade pressed up hard against my navy pea coat.

"'What the hell?' I said to him.

"'Man, we heard you're a narc, we heard you work for the state.'

"I managed to get my hand into the side pocket where I'd tucked this little automatic pistol my wife had bought me for moments like this. So

I'm driving with my right hand, while my left hand's stuck in the pocket of that pea coat struggling to cock the hammer back.

"'What are you talking about?' I managed, stalling. 'What the hell's wrong with you? You're crazy. Get out of my car!'

"I got the hammer cocked, and the only thing going through my mind is raising my right elbow so I can fire the pistol through my coat without shooting myself. I'd already made the decision to shoot him and was raising that elbow when he starts laughing and folds the knife back up.

"'Hey, man, we got a whole box of these things. Think you can get rid of some of them for me?'

"I was more concerned then with figuring out a way to ease off pressure on the automatic without shooting him anyway."

Of all his storied undercover work, including on the Carl Lee Gallo and Paul Hankish investigations, Thom might well be best known for his infiltration of biker gangs that dealt mostly in crystal meth. The WVSP had developed an informant inside an especially notorious gang called the Sentinels who vouched for Thom and got him into the gang, where his size and moxie paid off right from the start. Building a rock-solid case against the bikers required him to be away from home for long stretches of a time, and all his family members were prohibited from ever telling anyone what he really did.

His son Kris was attending a little three-room schoolhouse at the time that somehow accommodated grades one through six. In second grade, the whole class was asked what their fathers did for a living. Well, because Thom was away so much and Kris wasn't allowed to answer the question truthfully anyway, he did the next best thing...

He told the class that his father was dead.

A few weeks later, Thom attended a school play with his wife. Kris's teacher spotted her in the audience and made it a point to approach after the play.

"Mrs. Kirk," she said, casting Thom a sidelong glance, "it's so nice to see that you're finally dating again!"

"What?" his wife asked, shocked by her statement.

The teacher lowered her voice. "You shouldn't have to live by yourself."

Thom's accomplishments in law enforcement are too numerous to list, but one stands out above all the rest. In 1990, Jack Buckalew, who headed up the West Virginia State Police, ordered the then Sergeant Kirk into his office.

"I want to leave some kind of legacy here," Buckalew began, "and I'm thinking about having a special detective unit for the WVSP to cover narcotics, undercover work, and organized crime. I want to know how many people it's going to take, what it's going to cost, what kind of equipment will be required, and what kind of policies and procedures will have to be put in place. Basically, I want everything and I want it within three months. That way, I can have it written into the state code so after I retire, my successor won't be able to change anything."

And that's how West Virginia's Bureau of Criminal Investigation (BCI) was born. Filling Colonel Buckalew's request, Thom, J. D. Lefler, Jim Powers, and Charles Bedwell accomplished their mandate in all of those three months to the point where the only remaining task was to appoint someone to run the fledgling unit.

"I stressed to the colonel how important it was to get the right personnel in place at the top, starting with the commanding officer," Thom recalls today. "So they put out a notice to everybody that they were forming this new unit and were looking for applicants to run it. Only those with the rank of captain were normally eligible. I was only a sergeant at the time but I said, 'Hell, I'm going to apply anyway,' which meant I'd have to jump over being a lieutenant. They interviewed applicants from all over the country, and I was not their number one prospect. They brought in the guy who was and during the interview he said, 'I'd love the job, but there's someone else you need there.' When they asked him who that was, he said, 'Thom Kirk.' That's how I ended up getting the job, and the first move I made was to appoint that man to be my second in command."

That's also how Thom was promoted from sergeant to captain in a literal minute. Running the newly established Bureau of Criminal Investigations he'd helped build from scratch led to some hijinks, though. Every morning when he'd arrive at the office, an announcement was made over the PA system:

"Captain Kirk is in the building! Captain Kirk is in the building!"

As far as I know, he was never accompanied by Mr. Spock.

Thom ran the BCI for two years, 1991 through 1992, before being appointed superintendent of the West Virginia State Police, where he remained through 1997. Any number of roles followed that, including being a Special Assistant U.S. Attorney, but arguably the most notable being homeland security advisor to Governor Jim Justice from May 2019 through November 2021. Having no intentions of slowing down, today Thom operates Thom Kirk Consulting, which specializes in financial forensics, legal counseling on matters of police operations, and independent investigations among a wide array of offerings geared mostly to servicing police departments.

That's not all. The prosecutor in West Virginia's Putnam County, the county's lead law enforcement officer, was promoted to a cabinet-level position under Governor Justice, and someone threw Thom's name in as a possible interim replacement.

"So they called and asked me to fill the position until their selection process was complete and they found somebody better, or at least younger, to take over," Thom recalls at the age of seventy-three today. "That was a while ago, and I've still got the job."

The Spadafore Brothers

Alfonse Pagano / Alamy Stock Photo

A generic photo of a bookie in action, emblematic of the Spadafores' control of illegal gambling throughout central West Virginia.

CHAPTER 14

Fairmont, West Virginia, 1981

Early in 1981, Anthony Donald Spadafore called Carl Lee Gallo, with whom he and his brothers were in business.

"You know Tommy 'Gun' Banks, right?" Spadafore said.

"Sure, I know him."

"He owes me sixty large for the cocaine and marijuana I fronted him. I'd like your help collecting it."

"Consider it done."

Back in those days, plenty of drug business was conducted over pay phones, and Gallo knew the booth Banks favored near a McDonald's in Fairmont, West Virginia. Gallo was also aware of the times of day Banks placed his calls, so when Tommy Gun stepped into the phone booth one day, Gallo, accompanied by Frank Nicholas and David Lee Stout, stepped out from the side of the building.

Stout removed the receiver from Tommy Banks's hand, and Gallo placed a gun against his head.

"You're going to pay the Spadafore brothers what you owe them, or I'm going to kill you."

"I don't have the money right now, I swear! I explained that to Donald, and now I'm explaining it to you."

"Tell you what," Gallo said as Nicholas yanked Banks out of the phone booth so Gallo could step in.

Gallo placed a call to Anthony Donald Spadafore. "Tommy Gun claims he hasn't got the money. I got him right here. He doesn't cooperate I can dump him down one of my mines. You want to talk to him?"

Spadafore did, so Gallo handed the receiver back to Banks, taking all the length of the pay phone's cord. Banks pleaded his case, and they worked out an agreement. Spadafore gave Banks one more week to make good on the debt, which Tommy Gun did by supplying enough marijuana to have all he owed, and associated interest, zeroed out.

It was in Carl Lee Gallo's best interests to strong-arm Banks, because the bulk of the cocaine he distributed was supplied through the Spadafores via a network sophisticated even for the heyday of coke coming out of Colombia into distribution hubs like Miami and Los Angeles. Prior to going into business with the brothers, Gallo had been traveling to Miami himself to purchase his cocaine. But the Spadafores offered the capacity to cut out the litany of middlemen and each of their various cuts.

The Gallo case itself was like an octopus, spinning off many arms that led to numerous other investigations of criminals we learned about in the process of bringing his gang down. The Spadafore brothers—Anthony, John, and Ralph—were prime examples of that, and we investigated them from 1980 to 1983 for cocaine distribution on a massive, if not unprecedented scale rivaling that of the major cartel players. They had built an international network that stretched all the way to Colombia and especially Peru, where they had contacts in place even as their efforts were being shielded by corrupt lawyers back in the States.

The Spadafore organization smuggled multi-kilo quantities of cocaine into Fairmont, then broke it into smaller consignments for distribution in central West Virginia and Erie, Pennsylvania. Among many other local endeavors, they owned a grocery store where, once the proper code word was spoken, the grocer would pour out grams of cocaine from the middle Bisquick box on the shelf.

The gang originally made their wholesale purchases in Miami but, like Carl Lee Gallo, quickly tired of paying stateside prices and branched out into their own version of international drug smuggling. The lead brother, Anthony Donald (who went by Donald), established a Peruvian connection, reducing the price and increasing supply at the same time. Donald Spadafore's smuggling teams used different private planes to avoid detection. A pilot who was a gang member flew his own aircraft from Lima, Peru, to Stella Maris in the Bahamas, where "vacationers" who doubled as couriers would fly commercial into Fort Lauderdale and then board another of the organization's private planes, which delivered the drugs to an unused, unlit runway of the Morgantown, West Virginia, airport.

The gang approached the drug trade with the same bravado emblematic of their other criminal ventures that had begun with the theft of construction equipment from active building sites. In 1968, Clement Brothers Construction Company was building part of Interstate 79 in Marion County. At the conclusion of the workday on Friday, September 6, 1968, several pieces of heavy equipment were left on the site. On Monday morning, a 977K Caterpillar front-end loader was found to be missing. The machine was reported as stolen, and later that day the police found the bulldozer in the possession of Frank Chisler, a Monongalia County contractor. Chisler told the police that he had sent two of his employees with a lowboy trailer to pick up the machine at the request of two men who had offered to sell it to him. Chisler then identified Anthony Donald Spadafore and his brother John from photographs shown to him. The police then gave Chisler $15,000 in marked currency and instructed him to complete the transaction.

A few days later, the Spadafores arrived at Chisler's office in Daybrook, Monongalia County. When they left the office they were arrested by police, who seized a purported bill of sale and a bag containing the marked currency. The prosecutor had the brothers dead to rights, but only Donald served some time, emerging from behind bars determined to branch out into areas of crime that came with less risk of arrest and prison than stealing construction equipment.

Donald and his two brothers opened illegal gambling halls in Fairmont and elsewhere across northern West Virginia. This time, to keep them insulated from arrest, the brothers bribed both Charles Anderson, the county prosecutor, and Charles Dodd, the county sheriff, through their lawyer James Esposito, who made all the arrangements and delivered the payoffs. And when the brothers' criminal activity ramped up to drug dealing on a huge scale, neither of the "Two Charlies," as they became known, were in a position to do anything about it. The Spadafores had them in their pocket, and they knew it.

The brothers excelled at enlisting potential antagonists in their favor. Those efforts included a young city judge, who obviously should have known better before he was drawn into the Spadafores' drug operation when he agreed to "run some errands" for the brothers in South America, Peru specifically. Those errands included picking up a boatload of drugs for which he was paid $65,000, worth nearly three times that in today's dollars.

Gambling produced a significant windfall for the Spadafores, and with local law enforcement looking the other way, the profits continued to roll in. Since gambling was a cash business, the brothers had a place to park a great portion of the profits from their cocaine operation in the late 1970s. Any way you look at it, Donald, John, and Ralph had come a long way from their days stealing construction equipment under cover of darkness.

The Spadafores' sprawling drug smuggling network stretched all the way to Bogota, Colombia, where they dispatched one of their associates known as "Dr. Bill" to facilitate the release from prison of an expert drug smuggler named Walter Keen. The brothers promptly dispatched Keen to Florida and put him to work on their drug shipments coming in via private plane to Miami and elsewhere. Again, their brash business model was to eliminate the middleman, which in Florida would have been Pablo Escobar and his Medellín cartel.

The Spadafore case was one of the most complex, detailed ones I ever tried. The voluminous indictment told a multilayered story that stretched all the way to Peru. Their source down there was a woman named Carol Olson, who lived and worked in the county and was considered beyond reproach by locals. Besides, especially back in those days, nobody was prone to suspect a woman of such crimes. The network Olson was a part of also included three pilots who rotated shifts to avoid detection and drawing any undue scrutiny. Olson, or someone else in the Spadafore network, would fly the drugs from Peru to the Bahamas, where one of the pilots would be waiting, along with delivery "mules" that included a retired police chief who always traveled with his badge and gun at the ready in case he encountered any difficulties smuggling in the company of his wife. Everything went off without a hitch for years.

Then that plane crashed in Florida. While investigating Gallo, IRS agent Larry Mincks had flown down to dig deeper into the contents since the pilot Peewee Tenant was a known associate of Rudy Zaccagnini, that midlevel drug dealer from Fairmont who was in business with both Gallo and the Spadafores. That aforementioned notebook contained the names of not only Gallo's associates and customers but also associates of the

Spadafores. As was the case with many criminal trees my office sought to dismantle limb by limb, the Gallo and Spadafore investigations occupied neighboring branches.

The Spadafores' primary method of smuggling was to hide the cocaine in souvenir pillows, the kind nobody would think twice about if you rested it behind your head over the duration of an airplane flight. The organization not only dealt large quantities of cocaine but also high-end weed and a boatload of Dilaudid, Percocet, and Quaaludes, thanks to a physician named Charles Edward Fine who wrote the prescriptions in return for the coke he'd become addicted to. That notebook Larry Mincks had brought back to West Virginia also contained the name of Carol Olson, the Spadafores' primary contact operating out of Peru. On August 7, 1985, a grand jury in the Northern District of West Virginia issued a multicount indictment charging Olson and ten others with offenses arising out of their participation in a conspiracy to import and distribute cocaine and other illegal narcotics between 1978 and 1984.

The RICO charges against Olson centered on her role as one of Donald Spadafore's cocaine suppliers. The predicate offenses for the racketeering charges and the overt acts in furtherance of the conspiracy counts consisted of two transactions in 1981 and 1982 in which she sold large quantities of the drug to Spadafore and his associates. The 1981 transaction involved a complex arrangement wherein Spadafore's agents purchased three kilograms of cocaine from Olson in Peru and transported it to the United States via Stella Maris in the Bahamas. The evidence established that in November 1981, Olson received payment for the cocaine from one of Spadafore's associates in Peru and provided the drug to another associate who smuggled it out of the country.

The second overt act supporting the RICO and conspiracy counts involved the 1982 sale of one kilogram of cocaine and its subsequent transport from Florida to the Northern District of West Virginia. The government presented evidence that on April 22, 1982, Donald Spadafore and an associate, Willie Neals, met Olson near Vero Beach, Florida, for the purpose of purchasing cocaine from her. After checking into the hotel where Olson was staying, Spadafore accompanied her to Fort Lauderdale, where she introduced him to one Richard Faiella. Spadafore later testified that Olson then left with Faiella to purchase one kilogram of cocaine and that he had given Olson a sum of money for "part" of the kilogram. The two returned after a number of hours, and Olson and Spadafore drove back to the Vero Beach hotel. At the hotel, Olson produced one kilogram of cocaine, which Spadafore hid in Neals's suitcase. The three then boarded a commercial airline flight to Pittsburgh, Pennsylvania, checking the cocaine-laden suitcase with their other luggage.

On arrival in Pittsburgh, the three became suspicious when the suitcase appeared with one latch open on a separate baggage carousel from that which carried their other luggage. They drove to West Virginia without attempting to claim it. Thereafter, an airline employee noticed the unattended bag and called Neals at his Fairmont, West Virginia, residence. At Neals's request, the airline shipped the case immediately to Fairmont via a local air carrier.

The next day, however, Olson reappeared at the Pittsburgh airport and attempted to claim the bag. She explained to airline employees that when she arrived in Pittsburgh she gave a claim check for the bag to a porter, but the porter failed to deliver it to her car. The employees then asked her whether she owned the bag and whether she could describe it for them. At first, she stated the bag was hers but then responded that it belonged to a traveling companion. She refused to identify the bag or its contents but indicated that she would know it when she saw it. The employees searched for the case but were unable to find it since it had already been shipped to West Virginia.

Olson's demeanor aroused the employees' suspicion, and after she left the airport they requested airline personnel in West Virginia to open the bag—which, it turned out, hadn't left the airport yet—to verify whether its contents coincided with Neals's name on the outside label. The subsequent inspection revealed both the cocaine and an interior bag, which contained various articles belonging to Neals. The Drug Enforcement Administration then attempted a controlled delivery of the suitcase to Neals's residence, but he refused to accept it, saying it was not his. Neither he nor Olson made any further attempts to retrieve the suitcase.

Sometimes what a criminal doesn't do is as incriminating as their actual actions. Olson eluded arrest for a while, but we were able to track her down before she left the country. How, you might ask? Well, we already had Anthony Donald Spadafore dead to rights by that point, and as part of getting us to reduce his sentence, he was serving us up Carol Olson on a silver platter and had agreed to testify at Olson's trial. It didn't stop there either. Donald Spadafore gave us everything we needed on the members and activities of his organization to bring it down lock, stock, and barrel.

On top of that, the gang's lawyer, James Esposito, was going to find himself much in need of a lawyer himself. He had gotten away with storing drugs and money at his personal residence long enough. In addition to delivering the payoff money to the Two Charlies, he acted as a lookout while the Spadafore brothers broke into a police garage hoping to recover cash and cocaine hidden inside an impounded car, only to find that somebody else had gotten there ahead of them.

What kind of man was James Esposito? Well, when the Spadafores planned an arson fire to reap substantial insurance benefits, he advised the brothers to "put a dog and cat in the house and you'll get paid easier." Indeed, who would burn their own pets to death? James Esposito, apparently.

On December 15, 1985, a jury in the Northern District of West Virginia federal court returned a guilty verdict that would send Esposito to jail for ten years. His conviction was the product of the same lengthy investigation that culminated in the indictment of eleven persons on eighty-three counts of federal criminal violations, all of which stemmed from the illegal gambling and narcotics operations organized and supervised by Anthony Donald Spadafore. As part of his plea agreement, Donald also testified against his former lawyer and several other associates. There really is no honor among thieves, or drug dealers in this case.

Anthony Donald Spadafore pled guilty to charges of operating a continuing criminal enterprise, conspiracy to evade income taxes, unlawful possession of an unregistered firearm, and filing a false income tax return. Brother Ralph pled guilty to conspiracy to violate the Racketeer Influenced and Corrupt Organizations Act and for violating income tax laws. Brother John pled guilty to both of those charges, along with some drug-related ones. Ralph's and John's testimony as cooperating witnesses, in return for lighter sentences when they were facing life behind bars, helped us sweep up pretty much the entire roster of their criminal enterprise, including Esposito.

That should have been the end of things, but not so fast, as the aftermath of the case brought the long-simmering clash between me and Judge Robert Maxwell to a boil.

In October 1986, during the pretrial hearing in the James Esposito case, Maxwell fixed his gaze on me from the bench and diverted from the proceedings.

"It is understood," he said hatefully, not bothering to conceal his resentment, "that Mr. Kolibash, as United States Attorney, wrote a letter to the Public Integrity Section of the Department of Justice, reporting bribery allegations apparently against [probation officer] Mr. Ancel and myself. It is understood that this was after the so-called informant, Donnie Spadafore, failed a polygraph test as to the truthfulness of statements that allegedly were made by him to federal marshal Ronald Donell while being transported as a prisoner."

I held my temper, but not my tongue. First off, Maxwell had his facts wrong: Donald Spadafore had actually made those comments before a grand jury, and all I did was follow the proper procedure in filing a report as to that with the Public Integrity Section. If I hadn't, I would have been guilty of violating numerous codes, including one that read in part that "all cases involving Federal Judges pose obvious conflict of interest for the United States Attorney, and should be referred to the Public Integrity Section for investigation."

I looked up and saw Maxwell glaring down at me. That was nothing new. I'd heard rumors that he'd had the chairs set in front of his desk in chambers shaved down so all lawyers who sat before him would have to look up, just as I was now in court. I think that's why he took an instant dislike to one of my Assistant U.S. Attorneys by the name of Bruce Smith. Bruce was all of six foot nine, so he was pretty much eye to eye with the judge in court, and Maxwell hated that.

On this day, though, I wasn't going to let Maxwell's glaring down my way hinder my response in the slightest.

"Your Honor," I began, "it is apparent to the United States that the Court has been misinformed about the chronology of the bribery investigation by some individuals not familiar with the true facts and as evidenced by the allegation that this matter was referred to the Public Integrity Section after Mr. Spadafore failed a polygraph examination concerning these allegations. The problem with that is the matter had been submitted to the Public Integrity Section, in keeping with protocol, five months before Anthony Donald Spadafore signed his plea agreement and nine or ten months before the allegations were discussed with Anthony Donald Spadafore by agents investigating the bribery allegations. Defendant Spadafore neither took, nor failed, a polygraph test at any point prior to the report being filed."

In addition to responding curtly to Maxwell in court, I filed my own response five days later on October 21, 1986, that stated the following in the opening paragraph: "It is the opinion of the United States Attorney's Office that those matters were handled in accordance with appropriate Department of Justice procedures and that nothing was done improperly or with any intention other than to conduct a fair and impartial investigation of the allegations."

Among other things, in reference to this failed polygraph test Maxwell mentioned, I corrected the timeline and stressed there was actually no evidence to suggest such a polygraph had ever been administered, stating that "the Court has received information which is erroneous, taken out of context, or consists of rumors and innuendos. It is also apparent that the motivation of individuals who are supplying the Court with this type of information is to create an antagonistic atmosphere between the Court and the United States Attorney's Office."

I wish I'd been there when he read that and, even more, this:

"Also in the Court's comments, made at the October 16, 1986 hearing, there is a statement that the United States Attorney sought from the Department of Justice a publication described as 'How to Get a Judge.' Again, the source of the remark is not identified. Since there is no such publication in existence in the Department of Justice, this allegation is also obviously erroneous."

I never tried another case before Judge Robert Maxwell, but apparently he wasn't finished with me yet, which was okay because I wasn't finished with him either.

Joseph Vincent Truglio

Ian Atkinson / Alamy Stock Photo

Generic photo of a woman held captive to serve as a prostitute, the practice favored by Truglio's criminal operation.

CHAPTER 15

Wheeling, West Virginia

"We had a section of Wheeling that was marked off by a natural boundary—'south of the creek'—which had a different set of laws," longtime resident Bill Hogan wrote in December 2014 for Weelunk.com about growing up in Wheeling in the 1940s. "It was very heavily populated with saloons which openly offered illegal liquor, gambling, and women. There were houses of prostitution everywhere, even in the alley behind Saint Alphonsus Catholic Church. The houses were accepted as part of the fabric of life. Private homes had small, enameled metal plates with 'Private Residence' attached to their doors so drunks wouldn't pound on the doors at all hours of the night seeking admittance. Whereas the town north of the creek, where the shopping was located, was run according to the laws of the community and was very proper, the south end was 'wide open.'"[1]

"The history of prostitution in Wheeling really is true history, but it is never celebrated as such, despite the fact that many credit the profession for the city's legendary 'Wheeling Feeling' marketing slogan," Steve Novotney adds. "Truth be told, the green-door dates and potential parking lot rendezvous were once as much an attraction to young folks from the tri-state region as were Jamboree USA and the racetrack on Wheeling Island to Canadian tourists. Downtown Wheeling was stoked with steak houses, theaters, and bars, and all of them were infiltrated by 'organization.' It became normal. When most heard that 'Wheeling Feeling' slogan, they immediately thought of hookers."[2]

While many would take issue with that statement, the history of prostitution in Wheeling clearly doesn't stop there.

"Wheeling city officials were without shame in their spurious claims of sincerely attempting to eliminate prostitution," George T. Sidiropolis wrote of the 1950s and 1960s in the Friendly City. "They conducted coordinated periodic raids, arresting a few of the prostitutes only to allow them to return to their beds the following day. The calculated raids served to help silence the critics while reinforcing the belief that law enforcement was committed to cracking down on prostitution. More important to law enforcement, it also reminded pimps, madams, and owners of the imperative to continue their protection payoffs. At times, law enforcement exercised even more, less disruptive procedures. Once during the raid of only four of the twenty-six active whore houses, only eleven women were arrested and taken into custody. They were photographed, fingerprinted, paid a fine and immediately released."[3]

There were allegations that prior to raids on the houses of prostitution, the girls were notified that the raid would occur. That information was provided to us by a former prostitute named Pepsi O'Brien, whom FBI agent Dick Jones and I interviewed. Pepsi was actually a local girl who graduated from Wheeling High School. She stated that she was familiar with some of the police officers who conducted the raids and that they always asked for her during them. When she received advance notice that a particular house was going to be raided, she stayed the night at a different location. Pepsi eventually left the area and moved to New Jersey, where she married a truck driver.

Anyone who thinks prostitution is a victimless crime occurring behind a bevy of green doors with red lights hanging over them never heard the story of Carla Dellerba, aka "Black-Haired Bobbie," a Wheeling "madam" who supposedly committed suicide in 1974. I say supposedly because who kills themselves by stabbing themselves in the chest with a knife three times after stuffing a towel in their mouth? Detectives in Akron, Ohio, where Dellerba lived and died, explained the latter by saying she did that to avoid roiling neighbors with her screams.

Oh, and it also turned out she had a broken neck that was never mentioned in the coroner's report, completed absent an actual autopsy and issued by Dr. Gus Shaheen, who would later become known for corruption, the shoddiness of his work, or some combination of the two.

According to Tim Botos and Shane Hoover, writing in their superb series "The Madam Must Die" for the *Fayetteville Observer*, "She was a 45-year-old prostitute with a half-dozen aliases who ran a brothel in the industrial city of Wheeling, West Virginia, just across the Ohio River. The week before her violent death, she had been arraigned in federal court in Cleveland on a prostitution case. Similar federal charges were pending in Miami for transporting prostitutes over state lines, a new law passed explicitly to give us ammunition to fight prostitution."[4]

Dellerba operated her brothel under the auspices of the infamous Agnes "Aggie" Toomer, who oversaw virtually all the brothels in the city for the Wheeling mob headed by Paul Hankish. The concern among Hankish's mob, especially on Toomer's part because Dellerba could implicate her directly, was that facing years in federal prison would coax Dellerba into coming clean and testifying against her criminal associates. It was actually Agnes Toomer's daughter Joyce Simms who took matters into her own hands by retaining a pair of thugs, Ronald Asher and Ronnie Brice, the latter of whom happened to be her boyfriend, to eliminate the problem. They only followed through on Simms's wishes, though, after Paul Hankish himself, or someone close to him, blessed the operation.

There was plenty of evidence to support that Asher, a convicted murderer, and Brice were, in fact, responsible for the death of Carla Dellerba. But it took years for the truth to be revealed. Tom Burgoyne, accompanied by Jimmy Wright, who was my law enforcement coordinator and a former Wheeling detective, visited Ronnie Brice on his deathbed and interviewed him about the Dellerba murder. Brice admitted that Asher was responsible for breaking Dellerba's neck. He then said that Asher put a washcloth in Dellerba's mouth and stabbed her. Brice died a few days after that admission to Tom and Jimmy, perhaps finding a degree of peace as a result.

My first experience in prosecuting prostitution cases in the Northern District of West Virginia occurred when I was an Assistant United States Attorney and involved none other than Agnes Toomer herself. The case also marked my first encounter with lawyer Thomas Livingston, a bushy-haired street fighter who made a career of representing many of the most prominent crime figures in the tri-state area, including Paul Hankish and his top lieutenants. I met with Tom in an attempt to resolve the matter without going to trial. When those efforts failed, we proceeded to trial and Toomer and her associates were found guilty, though the Fourth Circuit overturned the convictions, finding there was insufficient evidence to support them.

My initial encounter with Joseph Vincent Truglio's prostitution organization similarly occurred when I was an Assistant United States Attorney in the late 1970s. We had indicted an individual named "Bull" on felony possession of a firearm charge. The firearm involved was a sawed-off shotgun that was seized at the King of the Road Health Club. The government's position was that Bull was providing security for what was in reality a brothel, not a gym, given there wasn't one piece of exercise equipment anywhere to be found. The defense's position was that he was merely using the shotgun to scare away wild animals that were around the club, since it was located in a rural area.

The case was scheduled to be tried in December before Judge Robert Merhige on a day when it snowed and snowed. Judge Merhige was known to be a stickler for keeping things moving in the courtroom and detested when any parties scheduled to appear before him arrived late. On this day, though, he didn't make it to the courthouse himself until six o'clock, and his court reporter never made it there at all. He had sent word that all the lawyers, including me, were not to be dismissed, which left us waiting hours for the judge to arrive. We didn't see the point of this, since it was pretty obvious Judge Merhige would have no choice other than to continue the cases until the following morning, despite the backlog it would create.

Just after six in the evening, the bailiff called out, "All rise!"

Judge Merhige entered the courtroom and took his place on the bench.

"Be seated."

To create a record as required in federal court, Judge Merhige had a recording device put into the courtroom to replace his court reporter. That was our first hint maybe these cases weren't going to be continued until the morning at all.

"I know you were all expecting to be sent home, but that is not going to happen," Judge Merhige began. "We are going to try the cases on today's docket starting in order. When there is a break in one case, we are going to start another. Are there any objections?"

No hands were raised.

My case involving Bull and his sawed-off shotgun was the first on the docket, a criminal jury trial. Judge Merhige called the potential jurors, and we started the jury selection process. After the jury was selected, each side presented their case in short order, since many of the facts were not in dispute, and the judge called for a break to prepare the jury instructions. During that break, which came right around ten o'clock in the evening, he started selection of another jury for a civil case that was the second one on the docket.

Judge Merhige instructed our jury and, while they were deliberating, commenced the second trial. Unfortunately, the jury did not find in our favor in the case of the gun charge, and I wonder if they blamed us for being kept in the courthouse for so long. The second civil jury trial ended around midnight. Then the third case on the docket was a tax case involving servers at a local restaurant who were allegedly not declaring their tips. I remember Judge Merhige stating that the lateness of the hour should not pose a problem since restaurant servers were used to working late, in this case four in the morning.

Four hours later, at eight o'clock in the morning, Judge Merhige was still on the bench, beginning the fourth case on the docket.

The case involving the security guard named Bull and the King of the Road Health Club was actually not my first connection with Joseph Truglio. Before I became an Assistant U.S. Attorney, Truglio was indicted in a post office case involving stolen money orders, along with two other defendants. Because of the amount of evidence, all three defendants pleaded guilty. Truglio, though, appealed his case to the Fourth Circuit on the grounds of inadequate representation, as all three defendants were represented by a single lawyer. In his appeal, Truglio claimed the lawyer ignored exculpatory evidence that might have exonerated him, because it weakened the case of the other two. The Fourth Circuit agreed, and the case was sent back to the district court for retrial. Truglio was represented by a new lawyer this time, and we eventually worked out a plea agreement where he pled guilty for time served.

My next encounter with Mr. Truglio came in an investigation that involved his prostitution operation. The King of the Road Health Club had an arrangement where the young women who worked there would be taken to the local doctor on a weekly basis to get checked out. The doctor who was providing the examinations doubled as the county coroner and also provided the prostitutes with certain drugs, thanks to forged prescriptions that were primarily written by his nurse, who happened to be a former madam herself. We prosecuted that doctor for illegal distribution of the drugs, but that was just the start of my office's dealings with the supposed health club.

Based on all my previous experience, along with a detailed investigation conducted by the state police, my office knew about the large-scale prostitution operation being conducted out of King of the Road, headed by Joseph Truglio. The same investigation revealed that an individual named Phillip Pavilack, a known associate of Truglio, worked as a courier at King of the Road, basically a gopher and driver responsible for ferrying women from the club to that doctor, as well as taking care of other needs for them. The prostitutes were basically locked in and not permitted to go anywhere without being accompanied by Mr. Pavilack or some other Truglio associate in what amounted to a virtual slavery ring. Pavilack was responsible for stocking the King of the Road kitchen so the women would have plenty of food to eat, along with assorted sundries to give them less need to ever leave the premises. For five dollars, he'd also make "taxi runs" to and from motels where the women had customers eagerly waiting.

The King of the Road Health Club was actually located in the parking lot of a truck stop, which made it the perfect location to service customers who were away from home for long stretches and didn't need to account for their time. It was a one-story, plain structure that blended in perfectly with its dusty surroundings. I tried to picture operating that kind of business amid the squeal of tractor trailer brakes and hiss of the big engines winding down. The smell of diesel fuel from the exhaust fumes and nearby pumps where truckers gassed up before hitting the road again hung heavy in the air.

We did surveillance on the King of the Road Health Club to confirm our suspicions. Along with information provided by the West Virginia State Police and FBI working in tandem (headed by Thom Kirk and Tom Burgoyne respectively), we developed enough evidence to establish probable cause for a search warrant for that location, as well as a women's exotic attire business Truglio operated in downtown Wheeling.

On the evening we executed the warrant on the club, I was standing outside with members of the WVSP, not far from a state police cruiser with its red lights flashing right in front of the building, when a car pulled into the parking lot. I watched a guy park next to the cruiser and walk right up to us, as if all this activity and overwhelming law enforcement presence was just business as usual at King of the Road.

"They open for business?" he asked.

"They sure are," I told him, stifling a laugh. "You just walk through the door, and there's a gentleman sitting at the table who will give you your membership cards to the club on the spot."

I thought that would be enough to get him to turn around and hightail it out of there. Instead, he thanked me for my help and continued on straight into the building. Instead of getting a membership to the King of the Road Health Club, he was given a subpoena to appear in Elkins, West Virginia, before a federal grand jury.

That same day, a search of Truglio's exotic attire store in Wheeling produced currency, books, records, invoices, and homestyle movies, all involving interstate prostitute operations at the club. The search also turned up eight audio cassettes in a kitchen cupboard.

It turned out that in addition to operating the house of prostitution, Truglio was running a bookmaking operation out of the exotic attire store. He would take bets by telephone, and in order to verify the bets, they were recorded on those cassettes. Some of the recorded calls also involved individuals who were requesting services from Truglio's prostitution operation, including a very prominent businessman in Wheeling with alleged ties to the gangster Paul Hankish. In addition to indicting Truglio on the racketeering charges, the grand jury returned a second indictment charging him with violating the federal wiretap statute. Three of those cassettes were ultimately introduced into evidence and played for the jury, helping us secure a conviction against Truglio and the other defendants in the case on racketeering charges.

Meanwhile, that prominent businessman hired an attorney who approached me and asked if we were going to play the tape at Truglio's trial, noting that this would prove extremely embarrassing to his client. I advised him that we certainly were going to play the tape, as it was the evidence of the wiretap violation, at which point attorney Tom Livingston entered the picture again. After the selection of the jury for the racketeering case, Judge Kidd also asked us to select the jury for the wiretap case, which Tom Livingston and I did. After Truglio's conviction on the racketeering charge, though, Livingston decided that he was not going to pursue a defense in the wiretap case, and Truglio entered a plea of guilty instead. I suspect that Paul Hankish, or some of his associates, exerted some influence on Truglio, leading him to plead guilty to protect the identity of the prominent businessman.

Along with his associates, Truglio was sentenced to hefty prison terms that ended the large-scale prostitution operation taking place at the King of the Road Health Club. Because of the prime location at a truck stop and large number of men accustomed to pulling over for more than just gas, prostitution activity continued, mostly involving the women going from truck cab to truck cab.

A subsequent investigation revealed that some of the lost business had moved to a local "gentlemen's club" called the Desire Lounge, which remains in operation to this day. We obtained a search warrant and conducted a raid with members of the West Virginia State Police, as well as agents of the FBI and IRS.

One of the participating state police officers was none other than Big Bob Cunningham. Big Bob crashed through the glass back door, and I followed him inside. Everyone else entered through the front door and announced that there was a raid being conducted—not that they needed to, since the noise that Big Bob made breaking down the back door was more than enough to let everyone know we were there.

Yet despite all the commotion, the dancers on the stage continued their act. One of the IRS agents, Donnie Benninger, got up there among them and grabbed the microphone.

"Everyone, stay where you are!" he announced. "This is a raid being conducted by state and federal authorities!"

The patrons froze in place, as bystanders are prone to do, but the dancers didn't miss a beat, and Donnie realized he had made his announcement while standing next to a thinly clad dancer who seemed ready to rub up against him until Donnie eased her aside. Nothing, apparently, could stop the show.

The documents we found in that raid indicated that the dancers actually had employment contracts with the operator of the Desire Lounge and that most of them were on a traveling circuit and worked at various gentlemen's clubs throughout the county. Although there probably was some prostitution activity going on at the location, we failed to find any evidence that would support a prosecution. If there was any, it was conducted on an individual basis and not sanctioned by the operators of the Desire Lounge.

Agnes Toomer, who ran the vast majority of Wheeling's brothels for Paul Hankish, meanwhile, remained an elusive target, forever slipping out of our grasp. She was always represented by none other than Tom Livingston, just as he had represented Joseph Vincent Truglio.

One of the unrelated prostitution prosecutions involved Hankish and a henchman of his named Jesse Anderson. Jesse was Black and huge, with the build of a professional football player, which made him the perfect enforcer for Hankish. One summer afternoon I received a call that Jesse had transported one of the prostitutes to a truck stop just across the West Virginia–Pennsylvania line. The truck stop was a known location for prostitution off Interstate 70. We verified the information, and the grand jury returned an indictment against Jesse for interstate transportation of a female for prostitution purposes.

The main witness against Jesse was the prostitute's pimp, a guy named Bobby Mitchell. Mitchell was in federal custody on unrelated charges and initially refused to testify because he was aware of Jesse's reputation. On the Friday before the trial, I went to see Mitchell at the jail in Grafton, West Virginia, where he was in custody at the time. I told Mitchell that we were going to call him as a witness and he had no choice but to tell the jury what had happened. Mitchell agreed to testify on one condition: that we let him wear his pimp outfit, which consisted of a purple-blue velour suit and shoes that had a glass heel with a goldfish enclosed.

On the morning of the trial, Mitchell was transported to Wheeling, along with his pimp outfit, which had been removed from storage. Dave Jividen, a law student who later became our task force coordinator, was my legal intern at the time, and I told Dave to be sure that Mitchell had his requested attire and to be particularly cognizant of his glass-heeled shoes, even though no goldfish were allowed in court. Once he took the stand, after stating his name I asked Bobby to state his profession.

"Pimp," he said, without hesitating in the slightest. "I provide affection and protection."

Ultimately, Mitchell's testimony helped convict Jesse Anderson. After Anderson was found guilty, we approached him about cooperating against Hankish. When Jesse appeared for sentencing before Judge Charles Haden, he explained his refusal to cooperate by telling the judge, "I can come back from prison, but I cannot come back from the grave."

The Jamaicans

Creative Commons via Wikipedia, https://commons.wikimedia.org/wiki/File:Crack-paraphernalia.jpg

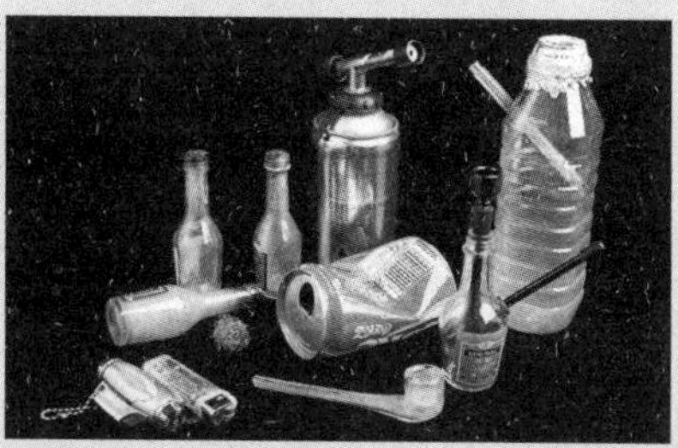

The types of crack paraphernalia used to smoke the drug sold throughout the United States, including West Virginia, by Jamaican posses.

District Court Justice Robert Merhige, who presided over the West Virginia trial in which nearly 100 members of a Jamaican posse were convicted. Merhige would later preside over both the Paul Hankish and Keith Ham (aka Kirtanananda Swami) prosecutions to be covered later in this book. (Reprinted with permission of the Wheeling Newspapers.)

CHAPTER 16

Martinsburg, West Virginia

To outsiders, Martinsburg, West Virginia looked like a charming colonial town set in the Shenandoah Valley. The community of 14,000 appeared to offer a refuge from the grinding problems of big cities. But the truth was quite different. Less than three years ago, Martinsburg was engaged in a life-and-death struggle against drugs, and it was losing. What happened in Martinsburg offers valuable lessons to the hundreds of towns in the United States that are, quite literally, under siege from drug traffickers.[1]

That quote, from a February 1989 edition of *Reader's Digest,* highlighted another of the greatest drug surges my office ever faced. But the roots of that scourge are best exemplified by an event that took place in Florida four years before the *Reader's Digest* article ever appeared.

Colin Fowles may not have been living as a Renaldo- or Messi-like soccer star, but at thirty-three he had carved out a solid career for himself playing for the Florida Strikers. His primary asset, even in his thirties, was speed, and he was christened with the nickname "the Panther" as a result.

Fowles was playing for a local club team in an August 1985 tournament held in Bunche Park located in Opa-locka, Florida. That day, unfortunately, a bullet was exactly what Fowles needed to outrun when members of a Jamaican gang known as the Shower Posse stormed the field and sprayed it with bullets just before halftime of a 0–0 game on a blistering hot day. No motive was ever provided for the shooting, and it remains unclear to this day whether the Jamaican-born Fowles was the intended target and, if so, why.

The incident, in crime annals for that era, was hardly an anomaly. By 1985, the Shower Posse—called that for their proclivity for "showering" crowds with bullets in order to gun down a single target—was spreading violence from coast to coast. While they were far from the only Jamaican gang to do so, they were the most violent, as the citizens of Martinsburg, West Virginia, learned when they showed up in our state around the same time that Colin Fowles was gunned down in Florida.

Like much of West Virginia, the small city had been a factory and mill town. By the 1970s, though, many of those businesses had closed, leaving staid brick buildings vacant and dealing a near death blow to the local economy. Residents, a great number from families that had lived in Martinsburg for generations, fled to where jobs could be had. That exodus did great harm to local businesses, which no longer had the customer base they needed to stay open.

In large part because the exodus of residents had left so many menial jobs vacant, Martinsburg became a favored landing spot for migrant workers from Jamaica. The problem was hundreds of those migrants came not to pick fruit during harvest time or work in the kitchens of local restaurants but to deal drugs. It got to the point that residents couldn't open their windows without hearing gunshots or walk down the street without being approached by drug dealers looking to make a sale and brazenly carrying pistols in plain view, either in holsters or tucked into their waistbands.

"Throughout the United States, law enforcement officials say that Jamaican gangs, known as posses, are the newest and most violent organized crime groups," the *Washington Post* wrote at the time. "Officials say they know of 30 posses nationally..."[2]

"They are known to be involved with over 1,400 drug-related murders since January 1985," Attorney General Dick Thornburgh noted, "as well as kidnapping, robberies, assaults, domestic and international gun trafficking, money laundering and fraud."[3]

The posses were believed to control 40 percent of the United States market for crack, the enhanced form of cocaine, sold out of storefront crack houses normally located in vacant or abandoned buildings. The wooden doors of those buildings were replaced by metal ones that were nearly impregnable and featured both closed-circuit camera security and pit bulls. Those steel doors were outfitted with a small opening through which the drugs were passed to customers. Posse members handling this process always wore gloves so those customers would be unable to identify the color of their skin. These posses might have been brazen, but they weren't stupid.[4]

In the early years of the Jamaican posse crime invasion, successful prosecutions of the actual gangs were few and far between because of the loose organizational structure the posses maintained, unlike, say, the Mafia or the kind of criminal organizations my office was used to prosecuting. While it was relatively easy to scoop up low-level street dealers, those efforts normally led nowhere because they had no worthwhile names to give up.

Reader's Digest titled its article about this new drug criminal paradigm, "Crack Invades the Countryside," in which "an informant had once seen basketball-size chunks of pure cocaine stored in the 'safe houses' in Martinsburg. 'There was so much coke lying around, your eyes stung when you walked in.'"[5]

"The U.S. Bureau of Alcohol, Tobacco, and Firearms has been tracking the posses since their mainland debut in the early 1980s," Laurie Gunst wrote in her groundbreaking study *Born Fi' Dead: A Journey Through the Jamaican Posse Underworld*, "and it now reports that the gangs have killed forty-five hundred people in the United States since then. The gunmen began migrating to America [in 1980].... They brought with them a killer enthusiasm honed by years of warfare with one another and the police, and when they came onto America's mean streets, they were afraid of no one. Their timing was superb: the Jamaican posses quickly proved themselves indispensable to the Colombians, Cubans, and Panamanians who controlled the supply of cocaine and needed street-level dealers to sell the cheap new product called crack."[6]

You might even say America felt like home to them, because they'd taken the name "posse" from the American westerns that featured gunplay galore. They fashioned themselves out of the outlaw gangs of lore, and their role models were drawn from films like *Dirty Harry*, *Scarface*, and the Rambo series, in which violence defines the characters. That helps to explain their brazen practice of wanton violence in real life and lack of remorse for the collateral slaughter of innocents. For these posses, such victims were no different than movie extras to be cut down indiscriminately, even though there was no movie director to bring them back to life by yelling, "Cut!"

The Bureau of Alcohol, Tobacco, and Firearms (ATF) estimated that there were at least forty Jamaican posses with more than thirteen thousand members operating in the United States by the late 1980s.[7] In West Virginia, a few hundred of them had set up their base of operations in Martinsburg.

"With its tidy clapboard houses and neat apple and peach orchards on land George Washington surveyed centuries ago," an article in *Newsweek* said in March 1988, "Martinsburg, West Virginia (population 13,000) seems far from the mean streets patrolled by drug gangs. But over the last three years, an invasion of Jamaican drug dealers has turned the home of the Mountain State Apple Harvest Festival into a mecca for cocaine."[8]

The Jamaican posse that set up shop in Martinsburg, like others scattered across the country as a whole, had a proclivity to engage locals in their efforts, more to expand their business than curry favor, though both could be true. A woman named Mary Hill served as a prime example of how this new wave of dealers upset the figurative apple cart.

"For Mary," that February 1989 article in *Reader's Digest* continues, "the temptation of easy cash for this 'innocent' work finally grew too strong to resist. She had been working two jobs and still couldn't make ends meet—let alone provide luxuries for her kids. *What's the point of turning down that kind of money?* she asked herself. Soon she was a drug courier, moving cocaine and crack from one location to another in The Hill's warren of shabby rooming houses. Once she was enmeshed in this dark, seductive drug world, it was easy to lose what was left of her bearings. Almost inevitably she decided to sample the drug she was carrying."[9]

Mary became both a full-fledged addict and a cautionary tale of the cost extracted from local communities by drugs. And the Jamaicans who set up shop in Martinsburg approached their business with a brashness that suggested they had claimed the town for their own.

"West Virginia had never experienced criminal activity as extensive, open, and notorious as the 'Jamaican problem,'" Tom Mucklow, the Assistant U.S. Attorney from my office who ultimately prosecuted the case, recalled recently. "It was an open-air drug market on The Hill and so brazen that several dealers even tried to sell coke to a U.S. marshal who was driving through the area in a large one-color sedan, black-wall tires, and several antennas attached that was clearly an unmarked cop car. We were not actually quite sure exactly what we had taken on until our first drug-dealer-turned-informant was murdered execution-style just hours after signing what we referred to as a 'pre-indictment plea agreement' which required his cooperation against the major dealers in town."

That Jamaican problem was something we in West Virginia, and the country as a whole, had never seen before. Unlike identifiable criminals, who were subjects of years of investigation, the Jamaican posse members were like ghosts, surfacing only long enough to pursue their murderous ambitions before vanishing again. It was virtually impossible to get informants inside, and since the gangs were entirely decentralized, taking down one seldom yielded any more than that. And it wasn't like Martinsburg was a big city; it wasn't even Wheeling. Martinsburg was a working-class enclave with the smokestacks of mill and factory buildings looking down upon it.

"At first, the drug trade was confined to the town's seedier bars," the *Reader's Digest* article elaborates. "But within months, word had spread to dealers from Florida to New York: Martinsburg boasted a ready market and little serious opposition from police. By 1985, the growing operation pushed into The Hill, an easy walk from city hall. Before long, dealers crowded every corner of the six-block neighborhood, accosting motorists and pedestrians with calls of 'Rock or powder?'—crack or cocaine."[10]

When people equate drug use with personal freedom, a so-called victimless crime regardless of the overall societal effects, I remind them of examples like that. And I also remind them that men like me and Tom Mucklow weren't about to let it stand.

Thanks to Tom, my office obtained sealed federal grand jury indictments against no less than forty-six of the dealers who had claimed Martinsburg as their own. In the cold dark of the early morning of October 16, 1986, more than a hundred law enforcement vehicles packed with more than two hundred federal, state, and local officers cruised along the streets of the city toward their preselected targets. They were part of the largest single coordinated operation ever in West Virginia and were outfitted with the best military hardware available. Planes and helicopters swirled overhead, providing surveillance. Fire engines blocked the streets in the general area of The Hill to prevent any of our targets from escaping or triggering a chase.

In perhaps the most dramatic task force operation conducted during my tenure, the two hundred officers, divided into twenty-five teams, launched their raids in the same coordinated moment. We arrested all our targets without firing a single shot. Ultimately, the total number of arrests swelled to forty-eight and, under Tom's stewardship, forty-seven of them were convicted and sentenced to prison for up to forty years.

The main defendant in the case was Ishmael Wilber Russell, head of the West Side Posse who went by two aliases: Sid Russell and Sid Johnson. His significant other and partner in crime was Cathy T. Riggs Johnson. The case began with the shooting death of Vincent "BB" Jackson. We flipped Jackson, and he had signed a pre-indictment plea agreement through his lawyer, Sherman Lambert. As mentioned, the very night he signed that agreement, Jackson was shot five times in the head execution-style. We knew Russell was behind the hit but lacked the evidence, or witnesses, to definitively prove it before a jury. Both Russell and Cathy Riggs Johnson eventually pled out, as did other members of the posse we scooped up in the raid. There was Bazil Bailey, aka Slave; Kenneth Johnson, aka President; Karl Ludlow Wright, aka Slim Goody; and Kenneth Black, aka Bag-a-Dirt. These colorful, almost juvenile nicknames belied the murderous culture this particular posse had brought to West Virginia.

The Jamaican posses were like snakes, continuing to slither about even after their head was cut off. In West Virginia, with much of their operation decimated, the members of the posse we didn't scoop up relocated sixteen miles down the road in Charles Town. Further investigation confirmed that the gang was part of the infamous Shower Posse. And inspection of the crack they were pushing revealed it to be 90 percent pure, assuring instant addiction and, thus, repeat customers galore. Tom Mucklow picks up things from there.

"They were openly and notoriously selling out of a pool hall and on the corner of a one-way street nearby. In 1988, we staged a second raid."

Some of our efforts were coordinated in a nationwide sweep under Operation Rum Punch 2. On October 14, 1988, the *New York Times* reported, "Police and Federal agents in 20 states have arrested more than

120 suspected members of Jamaican gangs that are said to be responsible for more than 1,400 murders and the large-scale distributing of illegal drugs. The arrests, which began Wednesday night and continued today, were concentrated in Houston, Miami and New York. More than 400 warrants have been issued."[11]

Once again, West Virginia was ahead of the curve that had wound its way into our state. A federal grand jury seated in Elkins returned seventy-eight indictments charging sixty-one individuals with cocaine and marijuana distribution, all of whom were either convicted, deported, or both.

"None of these operations," Tom recalls, summing up what made our efforts different, "would have been possible without the unselfish interagency cooperation with the West Virginia State Police, other local law enforcement, the FBI, and coming in just before the 1986 raid, the DEA."

My office had put away a lot of criminals over the years, many of them violent. But these Jamaican posses were unique in their utter lack of compunction in their actions. Career criminals and bosses often end up staking out their territory not all that far from where they grew up. That was the tradition in West Virginia anyway, where virtually all the kingpins I put away were homegrown. In stark contrast to that, these posses bore no allegiance to the local community and had no concept of anything approaching honor, which made them infinitely more dangerous to both the general public and law enforcement. Their only code was killing.

Again, Tom Mucklow best summed up the impact of taking Martinsburg back from the bad guys and returning the town to its roots and residents.

"There are many 'war stories' that came out of these investigations, but one lasting tribute to our efforts is 606 West King Street here in Martinsburg. That was the address of a small apartment house on King Street, one of Martinsburg's two main streets. It is located just a few blocks from the federal building. On the surface, it was a flophouse rented out to Jamaican orchard workers, but it had also remained a highly active drug distribution center. Over several years there were many Martinsburg police calls to the residence, and the task force made any number of drug purchases from the residents. We finally wrote a letter to the landlord formally advising him of the criminal activity in and about his property and told him that if there was one more transaction involving 606 West King Street, we would seek to forfeit the property and that he could not claim to be an innocent or ignorant owner as a defense. While he was not very happy, he evicted all the tenants, and the flophouse became a thrift shop operated by the adjacent homeless shelter. It remains a thrift shop to this day, and there has been no further criminal activity associated with it. I take pride in that each day I drive past, because it's a symbol of what can happen when everyone works together to clean up a town."

Bradley Thomas

Lee's County Sheriff's Office

A raid in Florida by sheriff's deputies on a boat similar to the one that was part of Bradley Thomas's smuggling operation seized in Fort Lauderdale in 1986.

CHAPTER 17

The Caribbean, 1984

Until May 1986, Bradley Thomas had never been arrested, despite a virtual lifetime of crime. Unfortunately for him, that's when he was nabbed in Fort Lauderdale, Florida, and charged with the attempted murder of two men he perceived as a threat to his criminal empire.

The primary component of Thomas's criminal empire was drugs, and we built our case over a three-year period utilizing the task force approach—composed of both state and federal authorities—we'd already encountered great success employing. In this case, that included the FBI, the Criminal Investigation Division of the IRS out of Youngstown, Ohio, and local officers from the small communities in Belmont County, Ohio, along with the law enforcement officials down in Fort Lauderdale who'd arrested Thomas.

One of the most unique factors about this case was that Brad Thomas's organization imported their cocaine directly from Jamaica without going through a middleman, transporting the coke by boat into southern Florida, where it would be transported to Ohio and West Virginia. During those ocean-bound trips, the biggest challenge they faced were the Cuban authorities who patrolled the waters between Florida and Jamaica. Thomas's people would always have a couple of scantily clad women on board. Their job was to go topless whenever a Cuban patrol boat approached in order to distract the officers and, hopefully, keep them from boarding. Given the corruption in Cuba at the time, my guess is Thomas's organization wasn't afraid of arrest as much as having their cargo of white powder confiscated. I'd also heard of the Cuban authorities disabling the boats at sea and stranding them so the criminal occupants would have to call for help, on top of having lost the shipments they were carrying.

We first learned of the Thomas organization in May 1984 when an FBI informant was contacted by a man named Joseph Olsheski on the pretext of purchasing scales used to portion out amounts of cocaine. Our informant witnessed both Olsheski and another organization member, Matthew Mills, weigh and then package the coke.

"That's a lot of product," the informant said, hoping to gain additional information. "You buying out of Miami?"

"Fuck Miami," Mills said, the temper that had given him a much-deserved reputation for violence surfacing a bit. "We deal direct, out of Jamaica mostly. Keeps things cleaner that way."

"Yeah, dirty is bad for business."

Mills gave the FBI informant, who went by the name of Brooks, a longer look. "Brooks" was an ex-marine who still cut a formidable figure. "You looking for more work?"

"Always."

"Even if it's dirty?"

"Depends," Brooks said, not sure where this was leading.

He found out when Mills set up a meeting for him with Brad Thomas himself at Thomas's office in a building where he ran a sham textile business as a front.

"I heard you were looking for work," Thomas said, after closing the door.

"You hiring?"

"I heard you were a marine, saw some combat."

Brooks remained silent.

"If I needed someone taken out, is that something you could do?"

Brooks nodded.

"Guy ripped me off for eight kilos of coke. I can't let that shit go."

"Guy got a name?"

"Richard Cox. Know him?"

"Nope."

"Interested?"

"Depending on the specifics. And the fee."

"I'm sure we can work something out."

"And I got somebody looking to make a big buy."

That somebody was an FBI agent named Katherine Tang, who worked undercover as well. Brooks introduced Mills and Olsheski to Tang, who then accompanied her to a Thomas organization site known as "the Candy Store," located on Wheeling Island in May 1984. Tang ended up purchasing a half ounce of cocaine. During the buy, it was clear Mills was attracted to Tang and wanted to impress her.

"My friend runs this place."

"Anybody I know?" Tang asked, even though she was well aware of the answer.

"Brad Thomas. The other day he told me I could run this place or oversee security for it."

"He must trust you."

"Like I said, we're friends. I went to Jamaica with him and came back with seven pounds of coke and two hundred of marijuana."

We'd later learn that particular shipment had been delivered to a drop point in Florida to be transported to both Wheeling and the Martins Ferry, Ohio, area.

"Hey," Tang said, making it plain she enjoyed the attention and was flirting with him in return, "can you tell me more about your Jamaican deal?"

Mills explained that Thomas bore a kinship with those murderous Jamaican posses operating out of Martinsburg, not just because the bulk of the cocaine he was putting onto the street came from their homeland but also because he conducted business in a similarly violent manner. Loaded weapons were always maintained on the premises of his organization's safe houses in Wheeling, and heavier weapons were inevitably stashed on board the various boats he owned that cruised the Atlantic from southern Florida to the Caribbean Islands and especially Jamaica.

Anyone who knew Bradley Thomas's history was hardly surprised by this. Born in 1957, he'd been in and out of trouble through much of his youth, running with street gangs known for committing petty crimes. These were not the kind of kids who'd gather outside Wheeling Downs awaiting two-dollar bills from Big Bill Lias; they were more likely to be waiting to snatch those bills, sometimes right out from the kids' pockets. Easy money, and they knew well enough not to make their move until Big Bill had driven off in his Cadillac to avoid facing his wrath. Reaching his formative teenage years coincided with Paul Hankish taking over the

Wheeling mob dominating the rackets through much of West Virginia and eastern Ohio.

Thomas learned his stock and trade at the hand of thugs who turned a blind eye and deaf ear to the old phrase honor among thieves. There was no honor practiced at all among this new generation of criminals, who saw power as something to be seized, not respected. And Thomas learned in these years that all he had to do to avoid running afoul of Hankish was to make sure Hankish, or his underlings, got a cut of whatever minor scores they pulled off, mostly handbag thefts, shoplifting, and selling swiped cigarettes to other kids often younger than themselves. Though I have no data to prove it, I suspect any number of the street punks Bradley Thomas ran with grew up to work for Paul Hankish himself.

In later years, what set his organization apart from others we prosecuted was that it controlled both the importation and distribution of drugs. Its modus operandi was to contact the grower or middleman in the islands, pick up and bring the drugs into the States, and then control the sale of those drugs on the street. His people on those boats spoke in coded language to arrange drop-offs and dockings so the Coast Guard or other authorities who may have been listening in to the communications would have no idea what was going on. While that made catching and making a case against Thomas a major challenge, it also meant if we took him out, the organization would die with him because the layers of insulation precluded a succession plan.

In December 1984, we caught another major break when we arrested Thomas Huntsman, one of Bradley Thomas's dealers, for distribution of cocaine. In return for a plea deal, Huntsman came clean about how he had rented apartments on Thomas's behalf on Wheeling Island to serve as clearinghouses for the cocaine he had brought into the region from the islands and Jamaica by way of Florida.

The next key arrest that led to Thomas's downfall took place in Fort Lauderdale just over a year later in the person of Louis Duarte, an associate who was nabbed on possession charges. Duarte gave up Thomas as well, specifically how the drug shipments were concealed on boats to avoid detection, like behind fake walls even law enforcement officers who boarded would be hard-pressed to find. When Duarte was called as a witness at trial, he appeared in a disguise consisting of fake glasses with a mustache and a ball cap. He also laid his head on the railing of the witness stand. Judge Kidd ordered him to remove the disguise and sit upright.

Duarte's trial testimony was further supplemented by a boat captain named Michael Shepherd, whom Thomas hired to skipper a boat named *Second Wind* from South Florida to Jamaica in November 1986. Suspecting something criminal was afoot, and not wanting to be implicated himself, Shepherd contacted federal authorities, who monitored the voyage every step of the way. Upon reaching Jamaica, Shepherd met with Brad Thomas's uncle William, who had brought 750 pounds of marijuana down from the mountains where it was grown and packed into that hiding place behind a false wall in the boat. As soon as the boat returned to port in Fort Lauderdale, federal agents from the FBI and Customs Service were there to arrest the occupants and secure the drugs.

One of those occupants was Bradley Thomas's uncle William Thomas himself, who was twenty-five years his nephew's senior. William had stepped in when his brother, Bradley's father, died suddenly when Bradley was still a boy. His method of fatherhood was to indoctrinate his nephew into the petty street crimes and drug dealing that had defined much of his adult life. But it was Bradley who built a thriving criminal organization from those humble roots. More ambitious and smarter than his uncle, while still in his twenties he had seen the opportunity provided by the explosion of cocaine distribution nationwide to make money beyond anything William Thomas had envisioned.

The family had lost their home when Bradley's father died of an aneurysm while selling vacuum cleaners door-to-door when his son was only ten. Bradley's mother agreed to let Uncle William take the boy in, where he was encouraged to be a good student, especially in math, while being introduced during his high school years to the small-time capers his uncle was adept at pulling off. Bradley was a freshman in high school when he served as a lookout for his uncle and a few cohorts while they loaded appliances plundered from a warehouse into the back of a truck.

His uncle's association with the Jamaican dealers from which he was obtaining his supplies of drugs became the model his nephew used to expand a street-level business into a drug distribution empire. It was William Thomas who parlayed those existing relationships in Jamaica to broker direct buys of increasing amounts of marijuana and cocaine that local Jamaican crews would bring down from the mountains for shipment on boats like Mike Shepherd's bound for the United States. We were never able to fully calculate the amount of drugs the Thomas organization was responsible for putting out on the streets, but it easily measured into the thousands of pounds of marijuana and in the hundreds of kilos of cocaine distributed out of both Wheeling and the Martins Ferry, Ohio, area.

That gave us more than enough to hit Thomas and four other defendants with both RICO and CCE charges, though the attempted murder charges lodged in Fort Lauderdale didn't stick.

In an article entitled "More Indictments Expected in Bust of Five-State Drug Ring" on July 7, 1987, UPI reported that "a 108-count indictment returned by a federal grand jury at Elkins charges the five imported large volumes of marijuana and cocaine into Florida, then distributed the drugs in West Virginia, Ohio, Pennsylvania, North Carolina, and Florida."[1]

In November 1987, almost a year to the day after that voyage of the *Second Wind,* Bradley Thomas was convicted before Judge Kidd in the U.S. District Court for the Northern District of West Virginia on those charges, along with cocaine conspiracy, income tax evasion, and twenty-five additional substantive charges.

At the trial, Thomas was represented by a slick drug lawyer out of Florida named Joel Hirschhorn. He showed up in Judge Kidd's courtroom on the first day of the trial wearing a Rolex watch, a thousand-dollar suit, and a ring with a diamond the size of a walnut. Out of professional courtesy, I approached Hirschhorn, whom I'd already met at a pretrial hearing.

"Word of advice, Joel," I stated.

He looked at me suspiciously.

"You're in Clarksburg, West Virginia, not Miami, Florida. Take your diamond ring off, leave your Rolex in your pocket, and go down to the nearest department store and buy yourself one of those shiny suits that looks like it's got some mileage on it. Do that and you might have a chance before the jury."

One of the codefendants in that case was Charles "Chucky" West Jr., who was known to have quite a temper and was no stranger to violence. He got that from his father, Charles Sr., who was none too pleased when the testimony of Chucky's sister pretty much nailed the case for us. It came at a price, though, since the FBI's Tom Burgoyne told me she rang up a big room-service bill from partying the night before at the hotel where we'd put her up, and Tom was going to have to foot the cost out of his limited budget.

During her testimony the next day, her father, Charles Sr., caused such a commotion in the courtroom that Judge Kidd had him kicked out. I could tell the apple hadn't fallen too far from the tree when during our closing argument Chucky himself tipped over defense counsel's table and looked like he was ready to make a run at somebody. Fortunately, federal marshals tackled him and started to drag him toward the same door his father had been escorted out of the courtroom through. That door featured a glass panel on it, and when the marshals were wrestling with Chucky to get him through it, the panel shattered, glass flew, and all of a sudden there was blood everywhere. Judge Kidd called for a recess, after which he gave the jury their marching orders so they could begin deliberations.

"I remind you, last but not least, to not let the blood we just cleaned up influence your decision," he finished.

Once the jury returned with guilty verdicts, followed by a hefty prison sentenced imposed by Judge Kidd, the Thomas organization ceased to exist, just as I expected. And, although no one stepped up directly to take over his operation, I was about to take on arguably the most notorious criminal in West Virginia history…

The aforementioned Paul Hankish.

The Task Force:
The FBI—Tom Burgoyne

Bill Kolibash and FBI agent Tom Burgoyne emerging together from downtown Wheeling's federal courthouse. (Reprinted with permission of the Wheeling Newspapers.)

CHAPTER 18

Wheeling, West Virginia

J. Edgar Hoover himself personally assigned Tom Burgoyne to Wheeling to sort through the crime wave that resulted when Paul Hankish had supplanted Big Bill Lias as the area's criminal kingpin. In that capacity, he would ultimately work the Hankish case by my side for years.

Tom came to Wheeling after postings in Miami and Pittsburgh, where he left his mark not only fighting crime but also within the community coaching baseball in both cities. It was winter when he arrived in the Friendly City, but by spring he had met his future wife, Kathy, whom he would marry within a year or so. He came to call Wheeling home after growing up in the Boston area as an excellent baseball player himself. The only thing as important to Tom as getting bad guys off the street was teaching the sport he loved to the city's youth. He became a Little League baseball coach and remained one through all our toils and tribulations in trying to take down Paul Hankish. After we were done, he spurned an offer to take a big job at FBI headquarters in Washington, DC, because he'd fallen in love with the community he'd given so much to.

Mike Young, legendary football coach at Wheeling Central High School, recalls Tom as a man who built lasting relationships with his young players that extended into adulthood.

"Winning championships at Wheeling Central is one thing," Mike said recently. "It's great to get trophies, but living a championship life is the greatest award of all. Tom's faith, his family, and his community involvement—that's your championship life. It's not about money or prominence but gaining the respect of the community thanks to the contributions you make to it and the values you represent."

Mike mentions a young man named DeVaughn Gordon, whom Tom met mowing lawns when he was little more than a scrawny kid. DeVaughn soon began playing Little League ball for Tom, who then helped convince him to attend Wheeling Central instead of the larger public high school. DeVaughn then led the Knights to three state championships, even as Tom was getting him more yard work than he could handle. He went on to play college football and currently serves as the associate strength and conditioning coach at the University of Pittsburgh.

"Tom Burgoyne was always a man that practiced what he preached," DeVaughn says today. "He treated everyone with respect. He practiced kindness and humility, and I can honestly say that I've never seen him have a bad day. No matter what he was going through, his character was unwavering, and that is something that has always stuck with me. I just hope to be able to pay forward everything he has taught me, like the greatest lesson is respect for others regardless of who they are. I truly believe he tried to see the good in everyone, which I'm sure is a very hard thing to do when you work in law enforcement your whole life. He was very empathetic, and I believe that is why he was a great leader and relationship builder."

DeVaughn revels in talking about how his relationship with Tom has helped him develop comparable relationships with the athletes he works with at the University of Pittsburgh.

"Although I'm not coming into these athletes' lives at the age that Tom came into mine, I'm placed in their lives at a crucial part of their development into becoming a man. That is a responsibility that I do not take lightly. Not only do I want these young men to succeed as football players, I want them to become great husbands, fathers, and pillars of their community, because that is the most important responsibility!"

Even as he holds his relationship with Tom Burgoyne close to his heart.

"The memories will stick with me forever," DeVaughn reflects. "They come to mind at athletic events, academic events, graduation ceremonies, et cetera. The best memories are the Saturdays in the summer from middle school through high school, the SWEAT program. We would load up the old sheriff truck with our lawn equipment and would go from yard to yard all day. It was something that I always looked forward to."

Mike Young recalls another young man named Travis McBride, who was having trouble landing a job after recovering from drug addiction. He contacted Tom for help, but Tom wanted to meet with him first. The last time they'd met, Travis had been under the influence of a lot of drugs and thought Tom was there to arrest him, so he was understandably intimidated. At the meeting, Tom asked that he to come to Wheeling Central to talk to the students about drug addiction.

"That helped me more than the kids I was addressing," Travis recalls. "How I told them it doesn't matter where you came from, addiction can definitely find you. It doesn't matter if you're rich or poor, Black or white, gay or straight. Tom gave me the opportunity to express to other people in the community that that's not who I am anymore and that I just needed a little bit of help."

And then Tom helped Travis find a job.

"Tom led by example," Mike Young says with a smile. "Because he was a sheriff, and an FBI agent before that, he knew both sides of the street, which gave him great credibility when it came to encouraging young people to avoid behaviors that were not acceptable. He could build rapport with anyone and was adept at getting kids who were straying headed back in the right direction."

William Ihlenfeld, who currently sits in the same chair I did as U.S. Attorney for the Northern District of West Virginia, put it this way in a taped message when Tom was presented with Wheeling's Youth Services System Good Samaritan Award in 2021: "He was tough when he had to be tough, but he also understood that you have to be compassionate to help those who maybe stumbled early in life and needed a second chance. He was going to help them avoid becoming the target of one of his investigations."

Tom was just as good getting in someone's face when they needed it as he was giving them a hug when they needed that instead. He could flip a switch between being the compassionate role model and hard-edged lawman. He always said he'd never met a stranger, because a stranger was just a person you hadn't struck up a conversation with yet. He supported the community relentlessly, always with the greater good for the most people in mind. For Tom, the "i" in "life" was definitely lowercase.

I genuinely believe that his embrace of the principle of teamwork helped our multijurisdictional task forces thrive, while the notion was floundering elsewhere in the country. So often in those days, members of different law enforcement bodies would get involved in pissing contests over credit and authority, becoming rivals instead of allies. But representing the FBI, Tom served as an example for others to emulate, from the IRS to the West Virginia State Police to local law enforcement officers in Ohio and Pennsylvania, as well as West Virginia, in applying the same attitude to his professional life as he did his personal life.

"While serving as a volunteer assistant athletic director at Wheeling Central," Mike Young recalls, "he'd say to a boy who played baseball or a girl who played softball, 'I'll be at the ballfield at three o'clock. Meet me there for some extra hitting practice.' When the player arrived, Tom never bothered to teach them how to bunt; in his mind, it was all about hitting home runs, and that's where he taught young people to train their sights by swinging for the fences, in life as well as in baseball."

But don't let the image fool you of Tom gregariously cheering his young charges on while they ran the bases or stepped up to bat; he was also a tough-as-nails crime fighter who gave no quarter to anyone, including a chief Hankish enforcer named Jimmy Griffin, who was also rumored to be one of the gangster's hit men. He told me once that in his early days in Wheeling he spotted Griffin in the street and approached, telling the alleged killer that he was going to get him. Years later, when we visited the dying Griffin in prison in search of a deathbed confession, the former feared enforcer, now gaunt and sallow, said to us, "Remember when you said it was your job to get me?" Tom told him he did. "Well," Griffin resumed. "I guess you got me." But Griffin still refused to divulge any of his dealings with Hankish to us.

Tom didn't get that deathbed confession, but I was with him when he visited a suspect in the hospital who'd just come out of surgery. The guy was still a little loopy from the anesthesia, so he looked at Tom with this wide-eyed, grateful stare.

"Thanks for stopping by, Father," the suspect said, mistaking Tom for his priest.

"It's my pleasure. Is there anything you'd like to tell me?"

And, right then and there, the guy confessed to the crime we were pretty certain he'd committed.

Tom retired from the FBI in 1996 after thirty-one years with the Bureau and then served two terms as sheriff of West Virginia's Ohio County, during which he became even more proactive with Wheeling's Youth.

"While sheriff, Burgoyne started a program called SWEAT, which stands for Support Wheeling's Effort Assisting Teens," the *Worcester Telegram & Gazette* newspaper reported in July 2021 on the occasion of his receiving that Youth Services System Good Samaritan Award. "It started with a handful of sixth-grade boys, whom he picked up every Saturday morning and took to mow lawns in Woodsdale and other neighborhoods 'out the pike.' Afterward, he'd distribute their pay and take them to Dairy Queen. He helped them open savings accounts with their earnings."[1]

"Every Saturday, we would round up kids and we would go out and cut grass and do lawn work," Tom told the *Times West Virginian* in September 2023. "[My wife] Kathy would bring us sandwiches wherever we were. It kept a lot of kids off the streets and away from the drug dealers. We showed them the benefits of hard work."

"Well, I'm really excited about this," he said the night he was honored. "I've been with Youth Services in some way, shape, or form for about twenty-five years, and it's been very meaningful for me, but it's been a pleasure. Youth Services does a great job. They do so much for the people in the Ohio Valley, from Hancock County all the way down to Wetzel County."

"If I had to pick one word to describe you, it would be relentless," Tom Burgoyne Jr. added about his dad in the tribute video played that evening. "From trying to sell you a raffle ticket to making sure his grandchildren give him a call after every sporting event, that's the best way to describe my dad. He never quits, and he just keeps on going."

One of his daughters, Beth, recalls Tom driving her to school every day. And every day before she got out he'd point to a sticker on the dashboard that read ATTITUDE and remind her to do her best. For Tom, attitude was everything.

"He believed in people more than they believed in themselves," recalled his son-in-law Joe Amico.

"He's a jack-of-all-trades," Terra Crews, Director of Development for YSS, noted. "He is a man of kindness and grace and fairness, and we are so honored to be able to have him here tonight and all of these people who have been impacted by him in some way in this community."

Of course, there were plenty of people not in attendance that evening who'd been impacted by Tom Burgoyne in a different way, like those who failed to heed the warning sign he posted in the windows of stores throughout his jurisdiction as a sheriff.

Mike Young had a newspaper route as a boy, and he recalls picking up his daily delivery bundle one day with a picture poking out of a smoldering husk of a car in which Paul Hankish had lost his legs and very nearly his life.

"I was in sixth grade at the time," Mike recalls, "and years later the same guy who got blown up was pushing drugs and prostitution and running numbers. Hankish was a particular obsession for Tom because of the way he used and hurt people."

One night, Tom was dining with his wife at Ernie's Esquire Supper Club in Wheeling when a waitress appeared at the table toting a refill of what Tom was already drinking.

In Wheeling, if you had an important business meeting, milestone birthday, or anniversary, you went to Ernie's Esquire. Perched along a hillside on Route 88, the supper club's expansive windows and abundant natural lighting set it apart from the dimly lit ambiance of the traditional mahogany-style steak house. It maintained an air of luxury and exclusivity and played host to a myriad of socialites, politicians, and businessmen. The club's allure and prominence also drew in the likes of Hankish and his henchmen, who reveled in showcasing their wealth, power, and status and the ability to network with influential individuals, both inside and outside the law.

"Mr. Burgoyne," she said, setting the drink down before him, "the gentlemen at the bar send this over."

Tom cocked his gaze in that direction and spotted Paul Hankish in the company of some of his cronies.

"Here you go," he told the server, handing the drink back, not about to be beholden to Hankish in any way, shape, or form.

Tom told me on numerous occasions that the Hankish investigation was the biggest of his career and also the most challenging.

"I mean, this guy had no legs, and that meant he had to rely on someone else to be there to do almost everything for him. And yet he ruled the rackets across multiple states with an iron fist. He knew how to play people. He knew how to scare people. And he knew how to play up to the right people. It's too bad he ended up a criminal, because he was smart enough to be a CEO for some big company."

We'd long had a tradition where the night before Wheeling Central football games, Tom, myself, and head coach Mike Young would go out for dinner at a local restaurant called Abbey's. In the offseason we'd find other reasons to get together, like a New Year's Day party to watch college football. I knew Tom was battling cancer, and one day in 2023 we got to talking about his latest prognosis. The experimental drug he was taking hadn't proven to be very effective, and if the next couple of treatments didn't take, he told me things didn't look good at all.

"Bill, it looks like I'm up against the one opponent I can't beat."

Tom died just a few weeks later. I'm going to miss those pregame dinners with him and Coach Mike Young.

"The one thing I think of when I think of Tom Burgoyne, it's not the FBI guy, it's not the sheriff," local radio talk show host Howard Monroe told WTRF at the time. "It's not the great stories he would tell; it's what a great guy he was, what a great human being he was. He cared so much about other people."[2]

But it was indeed Tom Burgoyne, the FBI guy, who took on Paul Hankish and wasn't about to stop until we put Hankish behind bars.

The Boss:
Paul "No Legs" Hankish

Crime boss Paul Hankish arrives with his lawyer Jack Doherty, for his 1990 trial. (Reprinted with permission of the Wheeling Newspapers.)

Bill Kolibash (center) outside the courthouse with the other members of his Hankish trial team, John Reed and Marty Sheehan.

CHAPTER 19

Wheeling, West Virginia

On the morning of January 17, 1964, a violent explosion ripped through a normally quiet Wheeling neighborhood at 336 Richmond Avenue near the intersection with Fourth Street. Dynamite had been rigged to the engine block of a new Studebaker belonging to a then up-and-coming and ambitious gangster by the name of Paul Hankish. Hankish had run afoul of none other than Big Bill Lias by making noise about moving in on Big Bill's territory. The explosion blew one of Hankish's legs clean off and left the other hanging by sinews.

Both front doors were blown off, and the entire front of the car, including the windshield and firewall, was blown from the frame. The hood, front fenders, grille, and radiator were scattered for hundreds of feet. Two large pieces, which had been parts of the fender, were found across the street at 339 Richland Avenue 150 feet from the blast. Windows were reportedly blown out along the entire block from the concussion.[1]

A neighbor named Harold Bauers rushed to the scene, where the car's carcass continued to belch smoke and flames, to find Hankish covered in blood but still conscious and lucid.

"That fucking Bill Lias," Bauers heard Hankish say, before rushing off to call for help.[2]

Later that same day, according to police officers who interviewed him at the hospital, Hankish said, "Fuck that fat pig," without getting any more specific.

The fire department arrived to find Hankish still conscious, lucid, and screaming.

"Get me out of here! Get me out of here before I burn to death! Hurry! I'm on fire here!"

He actually wasn't, not yet anyway, and Hankish was extracted from the vehicle and rushed to the nearest hospital. Surgeons there quickly determined there was no way to effectively save his second leg, so they amputated, leading to the nickname that would follow Hankish through his entire career as the most infamous and notorious criminal in West Virginia history.

No Legs.

He'd been in prison twice already before my office put him away for good, having blazed a steady rise through the West Virginia and Pittsburgh mobs that was actually abetted by his initial two stays in prison before I came onto the scene. Hankish was born in Wheeling in 1931, and that's where he spent his formative years learning his trade as a street thug hanging out in the city's infamous Tenderloin District, where he had his first encounters with the forces of Big Bill Lias in the 1950s.

He had grown up poor. His father, Peter, had been born in Beirut, Lebanon, a steelworker who would ultimately succumb to pancreatic cancer at the age of sixty-five, a decade or so after he and his wife separated around the time Paul entered elementary school in Wheeling. His mother moved to Detroit, and young Paul went with her for a time before returning to Wheeling to live with his dying father. He passed when Paul was fifteen, and after the funeral, he caught a bus for Texas, where he worked menial restaurant jobs for cash paid under the table. At the age of seventeen, he returned to Wheeling and worked as a bartender before bouncing around from one job to another, including Wheeling Downs racetrack as a money runner and ticket seller for Big Bill Lias.[3]

Hankish's first brush with the law came in the middle of that decade when police connected him to a well-known, supposedly secret gambling establishment, and he scored enough success there to climb the underworld ladder. That rise included hiring outside muscle to force out a numbers runner in order to take over his territory in 1959. An armed robbery beef later that year temporarily waylaid his ascent, and he ended up doing a year in prison. In true career criminal fashion, Hankish saw that stay behind bars as a learning experience. He cozied up to hard-core gangsters culled from the Five Families of the New York mob. That was unusual in itself because Hankish was Lebanese by birth, which didn't exactly endear him to made men in the Italian Mafia. It helped that his mother was Italian, but attitude and the criminal mindset he'd developed in his formative years led him to emerge from prison even more determined to muscle in on bigger territory, specifically the whole of the Wheeling underworld that ultimately ran him afoul of Big Bill Lias.[4]

Hankish wasn't about to forget the man who had cost him his legs. With Big Bill vanquished and his grip on power solidified, Hankish called on his New York criminal contacts, through the Gambino crime family, to bring in a top hit man named Raymond Freda. Freda was from New Jersey and allegedly had twenty-three kills credited to him. Freda staked out Big Bill's downtown Wheeling home for four days, intending to gun him down as soon as he stepped outside. However, the security around Lias's residence was so intense that Freda was not able to penetrate it to carry out the hit and ultimately gave up, letting the once seminal crime boss fade into obscurity.

Whereas Big Bill ran his operation with a combination of community ingratiation and involvement, Hankish was part of a new breed of gangster for whom violence and intimidation were synonymous with tradecraft. He didn't give out turkeys at Thanksgiving, dollar bills to kids, or gifts for the downtrodden around Christmas. If people weren't scared of him, Hankish figured, he was doing something wrong, and that went especially for anyone associated with him, from his numbers runners to his enforcers from out of state (mostly New Jersey, thanks to the mob connections he'd made while inside prison) to the storefronts where he did business.

"That was the thing with Hankish. No talking, or he would take action," Tom Burgoyne noted. "And he did when people did talk, and people knew it. It was a pretty vicious atmosphere back in those days."[5]

So vicious that when Big Bill caught wind of the fact that Hankish had every intention of muscling in on his vast criminal territory, he had no choice but to order the bombing.

"Someone definitely wanted him dead," Burgoyne elaborates. "You don't do what these people did to just take his legs. Whoever really did it wanted his life to end."[6]

Surviving the bombing birthed a legend and built a mystique around Hankish that he was indestructible. Indeed, if the most powerful gangster of his era couldn't stop No Legs from continuing his ascent to criminal kingpin and mob boss, then who could? He ended up being fitted with prosthetic legs, rudimentary back in those days, and walked with silver canes clipped onto his arms in an awkward gait that made many of those who didn't know him think his disability was the result of childhood polio, not uncommon at all in those days.

"By the time I arrived to Wheeling in 1967, Paul Hankish was up and running, and he was in control of the number sheets and sports betting rackets, and he had taken over the prostitution, and he was into stolen property big-time," Burgoyne recalls. "And by that time Bill Lias was pretty much out of it. The only time I ever heard the Lias name, it was when people were talking about past activities. When I got here, it was all about Paul Hankish, and that was because he survived. Surviving the bombing gave him instant credibility, and not just with the people in and around Wheeling. It gave him credibility all over the East Coast, and that allowed him to get involved with a lot of activity."[7]

As Big Bill dropped out of the picture, Hankish's control over the Wheeling underworld sharpened in focus. Unlike Lias, though, Hankish had his sights set on the Upper Ohio Valley and much of the East Coast to expand his criminal empire. Whereas his predecessor saw himself as a man of the people and thus steadfastly avoided any business pertaining to drugs, Hankish embraced the dealing of pills, marijuana, and the cocaine he ultimately became hooked on himself. He also targeted the prostitution trade, putting the aforementioned Agnes Toomer in place to oversee that part of his business. Local establishments were no longer immune to being robbed, sometimes at gunpoint, and, not so strangely, there were never any witnesses around who could identify the perpetrators. And, even if they were brave enough to talk, they held their tongues out of fear one of the cops or sheriff's deputies they were talking to might be on the take, one of any number of law enforcement officials Hankish regularly paid bribes to or wiped out gambling debts for from his establishments.

"Hankish developed a personal brigade of criminal talent which ranged from shoplifters to contract killers," George T. Sidiropolis wrote in *Murder Never Dies: Crime and Corruption in the Friendly City*. "Many of his soldiers possessed diverse talents that contributed to the racketeering trade which strengthened his empire.... Understanding that information was power, he put in place an efficient intelligence system. His database held the identity and details of cheating spouses and closet gays to a collection of secretly filmed whore house episodes of prominent Wheeling officials."[8]

In that respect, Hankish was way ahead of his time and a harbinger, as well, of a new era of gangster in which the old norms and traditions were fading away. More Michael Corleone, in that respect, than Vito. I remember somebody telling me the story of local Wheeling businessmen coming to Hankish for help running a casino night to benefit a local organization that supported disabled children. Hankish was more than happy to lend them a hand, including hosting the event in one of his clubs. What the organizers didn't know was that pretty much every game that night was rigged, from craps to roulette to blackjack—not that they cared, because Hankish's underhanded efforts pocketed them a big fat check for $25,000. The organizers never learned that Hankish had kept an equal amount of cash for himself.

Hankish was also masterful in playing a different kind of game with the Pittsburgh mob that technically oversaw organized crime in Wheeling, in full awareness that someday he would usurp their power as well. He was already well entrenched running the Wheeling rackets when Big Bill Lias finally died in 1971. But he still bore a grudge against the man he blamed for costing him his legs and decided to deliver one last payback. At the funeral, he ordered associates to steal the prayer cards and logbook so that Big Bill's family would have no record of who had come to pay their last respects. As far as posterity was concerned, no one had showed up at all, and the man who defined Wheeling for so long was left with that final ignominy.

Hankish, though, never lost the taste for more run-of-the-mill crimes like robberies and truck hijackings. Getting implicated in one of the latter ended up sending him back to prison in 1974, when a pair of associates, John Bruno and Jackie Longfellow, stole a tractor trailer rig loaded with 1,456 cases of Stroh's beer. The shipment was in transit from Detroit to a liquor distributor in Huntington, West Virginia. Hankish agreed to buy the beer from Bruno for $1.50 a case and asked Bruno to bring it from Huntington to Wheeling, West Virginia. Longfellow drove the rig to Wheeling, where he was met by Bruno and another Hankish associate named James Matthews. Following their directions, Longfellow crossed the line into Ohio, but the truck broke down on a steep hill. The beer was unloaded into rented trucks and taken back to Wheeling. Following their arrest, Bruno and Longfellow ultimately implicated Hankish.

That apparent setback to his criminal hegemony again turned out to be anything but.

While in prison in the 1970s, Hankish cozied up even closer to associates of the New York crime families with which he was developing closer and closer ties with an eye on gaining their support in taking over the Midwest rackets stretching all the way to Chicago. No longer, in Hankish's mind, would he be reporting to Pittsburgh, because Pittsburgh would be reporting to him. He was one of those crime bosses who grew only more powerful behind bars. Upon his release from prison in 1980, he was spotted in the company of the heads of the Five Families at a wedding in New York and, later, at a gathering in Miami. Hankish had bought a second home just outside Miami, a condominium that reputedly became a quasi-hangout for celebrities, and became a major narcotics supplier to the vast swath of territory he expected New York to deed him in pursuit of expanding his criminal empire.

Having his legs blown off may have cemented his legend, but it also left him physically vulnerable and unable to intimidate rivals and those with whom he did business, though he more than made up for this by ruling the Wheeling underworld like an emperor. In large part, that was thanks to the fierce loyalty of a pair of feared enforcers, starting with Jimmy Griffin.

"He was a stone-cold killer, and he was a bad person his entire life—even back in high school," Tom Burgoyne recalls. "He was a guy who would just punch people in the face for no reason at all. He was the enforcer. He was one of those types of guys."[9]

Hankish's second enforcer and bodyguard was Jesse Anderson, who inspired just as much fear on the street as Griffin. He oversaw the Black community for Hankish, cementing it as Hankish's territory and making sure everyone knew that to keep out the competition. He also became known as the boss's chief collector of debts, especially proficient in paying visits to customers who were late in their payments. He almost never left their homes or establishments without what he came for, or if he did, the debtor would be left in considerably worse shape for it. In the book *The Godfather,* Mario Puzo makes the point that Vito Corleone never would have attained such power if he didn't have the fearsome Luca Brasi watching his back. Well, in that respect Paul Hankish had two Luca Brasis watching his back.

He ran the Wheeling underworld with apparent impunity, until our task force came along and joined forces with other law enforcement agencies stretching from Texas to Rhode Island and down to Florida to finally take him on. We even got the Coast Guard involved because they patrol the Ohio River, along which we believed the Hankish organization was moving a portion of its drugs.

You might call that pulling out all the stops, and for good reason.

CHAPTER 20

Wheeling, West Virginia

On the night of April 19, 1978, Mattie Pike was dutifully practicing her gymnastic routine in Washington, Pennsylvania. The ten-year-old had shown great promise, and Melvin Pike, her loving and proud father, stood nearby preparing to purchase a gift for her as he awaited the completion of the session. It was at that moment that Mattie Pike's life changed forever, as a man wearing a ski mask entered the studio and trained a shotgun on Melvin Pike. The fatal shots were fired before Pike, a long-reputed hoodlum, could successfully draw a pistol in his own defense. Young Mattie, who would never again participate in gymnastics, did not then realize that the death of her father was related to an event she had experienced but one week before when someone had followed Mattie and her dad as they drove from their home in Uniontown to the Warbutton Gymnastics Studio in Washington. Nor did she realize, as the government will prove in the present case, that the death of her father was the result of efforts initiated by a criminal enterprise based in Wheeling, West Virginia, to secure an expanded territory for its illegal gambling interests. That such a bloody, horrid crime arose from what was purportedly a "victimless crime" such as gambling is a parallel which will repeatedly appear as the evidence of the activities of the Hankish Organization is presented.

The evidence will track the activities of this enterprise from the 1950s to the present date. This organization, which is led by Paul Nathaniel Hankish, supplanted an earlier Wheeling-based crime group led by William Lias [deceased]. While the group was originally formed to provide services related to illegal gambling and the need for protection associated with such ventures, the evidence will show it has evolved and expanded to encompass narcotics trafficking, extortion, prostitution, pornography, arson, and the fencing of stolen property—both petty and substantial. The focus of the enterprise has been to secure profits in the vice industry on an ongoing basis, to preserve the assets derived from such activity, and to maintain a degree of continuity of operation, notwithstanding occasional interruptions of the operation by the prosecution of its members.

* * *

That's how I began my opening statement in the 1990 trial of Paul Hankish, a man I knew had made serious efforts to have me killed. Unlike his predecessor Big Bill Lias, as well as the vast bulk of the other criminals I put away, Hankish harbored national aspirations that could be traced back to that thirty-two-month stretch he did at the federal prison in Lewisburg on that hijacking beef, where he began to cozy up to associates of the infamous Five Families of crime based out of New York, including the king of them all at the time, Vito Genovese. And that wasn't all he took from prison upon his release.

"When Paul was doing time in Lewisburg," an anonymous associate reputedly told George Sidiropolis, "he was intrigued by the ongoing success of a number of his fellow inmates, some of whom had trouble reading the newspaper. They were visited without limitations by gorgeous women arriving in Mercedes Benz automobiles, dressed to the nines and covered with gold and diamonds. They routinely dropped off rubber banded rolls of hundred-dollar bills for their husbands and lovers, a large part of which was used to bribe prison officials. When he finally realized these guys were dealing in drugs and he discovered the magnitude of the illegal drug profit, he made up his mind that when he left prison, he would get in the drug trade."[1]

Drugs were never what Hankish wanted to be defined by, but the network he started building upon his release from prison made him a criminal figure on par with the heads of those Five Families out of New York he had cozied up to and who were eager to do business with him.

* * *

From my opening statement in the 1990 trial of Paul Hankish:

> *In addition to being the leading organizer and manager of the enterprise, one of the functions undertaken by Hankish was to act as a liaison with other organized crime groups. This had the purpose of facilitating the expansion of the group's criminal activities. The evidence will show that Hankish developed a close association with Joseph "Demus" Covello and other high-level members of the Gambino and Genovese crime families in New York and New Jersey, and affiliated crime groups in Western Pennsylvania, such as those headed by John LaRocca and Gabriel "Kelly" Mannarino [both deceased], and in Youngstown, Ohio, headed by Joseph Naples. The government will show that Covello, Mannarino, and Naples were selected by Hankish to be the godfathers for his three children and that his affiliation with these individuals and their subordinates was often inextricably intertwined with the criminal events that have been charged against the defendants.*
>
> *One of the more subtle but nonetheless important techniques employed by the members to advance the enterprise's affairs was to ingratiate themselves with persons who were otherwise involved in legitimate activities and then to compromise those persons in some fashion. Indeed, the government will prove that Hankish was a master manipulator, not only of individuals outside the enterprise but also those individuals associated with him in crime. The evidence will also establish that in order to promote the organization's affairs, its members often corrupted or made claims of corrupting individuals in the business community, the legal profession, and law enforcement. Hankish exploited Wheeling's reputation as a "wide open" town to foster his illegal commerce with other groups across the nation.*

* * *

Hankish's illicit drug activity wasn't limited to pills, in the form of Quaaludes, or the current taste of the day in cocaine. He also made vast amounts of money dealing heroin with the help of Wilfred Michaels, a Pittsburgh-based participant in a nationwide conspiracy to import heroin from the Far East in the body bags of American servicemen who were killed in action during the waning days of the Vietnam War. Michaels would travel to West Virginia himself to deliver multiple kilos to Hankish, who would then set up distribution through channels he'd built thanks to his association with the Five Families.

Hankish, though, would much prefer to be remembered more for his gambling and stolen goods operations than being associated with the massive profits he made off drugs that supercharged all his activities and made him a major nationwide underworld figure. His stolen goods operation was especially notable for its ambition and sophistication, thanks in large part to the participation of bold figures like Skinner Dorn. A few times a year, Skinner would go out to California in the company of a few of Agnes Toomer's most attractive ladies of the night and visit a high-end department store. They had developed a surefire plan where the women would distract the salesclerks long enough for Skinner to pretty much rob the store blind, stuffing the shoplifted items in a jacket tailored to accommodate any number of these items.

Once, these items somehow included a piece of Waterford crystal that was so big and bulky we could never figure out how he got it out of the store. The Hankish mob funneled the stolen goods to Ronnie Brice, who'd later be implicated in the murder of Carla Dellerba but was then running Ron's Value Center just a few blocks from where Dellerba had operated her Water Street brothel under Agnes Toomer. Brice sold most of the goods Skinner Dorn had fleeced from those California department stores, but a selection of the accumulated wares was always kept off the sales floor to eventually be plucked around Christmas time by the Hankish gang's top-ranking operatives, where the goods would be laid out in a room inside Hankish's home to plume as gifts for girlfriends and wives.

Those operatives included a very well-known attorney who walked out one day with, of all things, that piece of Waterford crystal. We were watching the place at the time with an eye toward busting the shoplifting ring and followed the lawyer to a local mall, where picking him up for receiving stolen property would make for nice payback against the criminal organization that employed him. But we somehow lost the lawyer in the maze of the crowded parking lot, and I'm sure whoever he gave that crystal to was happy to receive it.

Skinner Dorn estimates that the value of property pilfered from the likes of Neiman Marcus, Saks, Bloomingdale's, and Tiffany's to be between $5 and $7 million in total back in the mid-1980s, which means as much as $20 million in today's dollars. As enduring and successful as it was, though, Hankish's stolen goods operation pales in comparison with where he made his first mark and continued to expand throughout his criminal career...

Gambling.

* * *

From my opening statement in the 1990 trial of Paul Hankish:

> *While Hankish was in prison, James Griffin, now serving a life sentence in Pennsylvania for murder, assisted Hankish in the gambling operation with Pee Wee George. By the time Hankish was released from prison, the evidence will show that both [Charles R. "Buddy"] Jacovetty and Griffin had emerged as principal figures in the organization. In addition to activities in the Wheeling area, which was the organization's home base, the evidence will show that Griffin was engaged as a personal aide to Hankish, who acted as an enforcer with needed ties to criminals in Western Pennsylvania.*
>
> *Sometime in 1976, Jacovetty and Griffin recruited Gerald Walls to assist them in expanding their bookmaking and sports parlay operation to Fayette County, Pennsylvania. Walls was trusted because he and Griffin had served time together in a penitentiary. Within a short period, Walls and his Pennsylvania partner were distributing ten thousand parlay sheets a week on behalf of the organization, which was on average worth approximately $30,000. Walls was also laying off between $50,000 and $100,000 per week in straight-wagering activity to the organization.*
>
> *In 1977, Walls was introduced to Theodore Tsoras, who the evidence will show had some years before been recruited by Hankish as his handicapper and chief contact with other bookmakers on a national level. Tsoras had previously been successful in his wagering activities on behalf of Hankish, having broken at least one individual who mistakenly attempted to gamble with them.*
>
> *Acting on the instruction of Tsoras, Walls began directly making large bets with outside bookmakers. These were "steam" bets, based on special inside information. Consequently, these bets were overwhelmingly successful and generated a significant amount of revenue. When Melvin*

Pike, who was believed to be associated with the Gabriel "Kelly" Mannarino crime family, found out about this "steam" action, the scheme was thwarted. As Hankish was an ally of Mannarino, the "steaming" had taken place in a territory thought to be controlled by Mannarino, and the revenue from Fayette County had become important to the Wheeling gambling organization, Hankish, Jacovetty, Tsoras, Griffin, and Walls met in Washington, Pennsylvania, and concluded that something had to be done to stop Pike's interference and prevent Mannarino from learning of their action. The prospect of violence was contemplated at that gathering. A subsequent meeting between Hankish, Griffin, and Walls led to Hankish sanctioning a plot undertaken with some Fayette County businessmen to have Pike murdered and to have Hankish's people pick up all the gambling activity in that area. Pursuant to the plot, Pike was murdered, as described earlier, by a hired gunman recruited for the task by James Griffin.

* * *

Hankish's empire was built on illegal gambling. Illegal gambling was the bedrock of his organization, upon which everything else was built. Sure, the distribution of cocaine and heroin were profitable enterprises, but those involved multiple layers with each taking its share of the pie. While Hankish's might have been the biggest slice, with gambling the whole pie belonged to him.

Profits gleaned from the backroom gambling halls he controlled were put into legitimate businesses Hankish either owned or invested in, expanding the drug empire he was building with a national profile. The illicit gambling trade's biggest moneymaker was wagering on professional and college football, but Hankish's people also took bets on horse races, a holdover from the old days when Big Bill Lias built an empire with Wheeling Downs as its foundation.

"A good example of how the Hankish organization's gambling apparatus worked is the story of Gerald 'Snooky' Walls," Paul Hodos wrote in *Steel City Mafia: Blood, Betrayal and Pittsburgh's Last Don*. "Walls was a Hankish affiliated bookie who took sports bets at his two bars in Uniontown in Fayette County starting in the fall of 1977. He made $1,800 a week at first and eventually $130,000 a week after only a few months."[2]

You don't have to be a math whiz to figure the profits a hundred bookies like Snooky Walls could reap for the Hankish organization. More profits meant more drugs on the streets, and the additional dollars helped fuel Hankish's desired expansion as he became, unquestionably, one of the most successful and powerful crime figures anywhere in the country.

Which brings us back to Melvin Pike, where my opening statement in the 1990 Hankish trial began. Pike was a thug, plain and simple, neither a stranger to violence, strong-arming, nor theft. He was implicated in no less than three murders, including that of his wife in 1965. He was acquitted in one case, a grand jury declined to indict in another, and as for his wife, I'm not sure Pike was ever seriously investigated.

It was Snooky Walls, though, who told us, as part of his plea agreement, that Pike's favored modus operandi was to steal heavy equipment from coal fields and then "sell" it back to the companies for upward of $15,000. Kind of like kidnapping for ransom, only with machines instead of people. Ironically enough, Walls admitted to us that Pike had taught him the organized crime ropes, almost like some kind of dark mentor. That didn't stop Pike from encroaching on his gambling territory on behalf of the rival Mannarino gang out of Pittsburgh, something Walls explained to Hankish when called onto the carpet about his suddenly dwindling profits. On top of that, there was the fact that Pike had somehow gotten wise to Hankish using inside sources to bet on sure things in the sports industry. That allowed Hankish's people to lay off bets with Mannarino's. Wagering on sure things had the added benefit of bleeding cash from his rival's stash.

That knowledge was enough to make Pike a target all by itself. The job was given to Jimmy Griffin, who hired a hit man named Robert "the Codfish" Bricker to take Pike out.

"According to Pike's daughter," Paul Hodos wrote, "Pike had detected people following him as he took her to her gymnastics class on April 17, 1978, in Canton Township. On April 19, Pike took her to class again. Pike was armed with a .38 pistol. Pike, despite his odious reputation, apparently loved his daughter deeply and had five keychain pictures of her on his keys that day. Pike's daughter was doing a routine on the balance beam, attentive Pike watching, when Bricker, clad in a blue hooded sweatshirt, blue jeans and a ski mask, shot her father three times with a shotgun at close range in front of her."[3]

Paul Hankish might never have wanted to be defined by the drug dealing part of his criminal enterprise, but competition continued to erode the profits from his gambling operation, leaving him little choice other than to expand that side of his business. The organized crime contacts out of Miami and South American contacts he had fostered were willing and able to make the supply available to meet his demand. By 1981, he was responsible for supplying at least half the drugs that made their way into the greater Wheeling area. Worse, he broke the cardinal rule of the drug trade by getting hooked himself on one of his primary products: cocaine. He developed a big habit, as much as five grams per week from one source alone. And the rash judgment and poor decision-making that resulted became one of the primary factors that led to his ultimate downfall.

* * *

From my opening statement in the 1990 trial of Paul Hankish:

> *The Pennsylvania State Police also conducted a wiretap investigation of a Western Pennsylvania–based gambler named Frank P. Unis Jr. On November 24, 1988, they intercepted a call from Unis to Hankish at Figaretti's Restaurant in Wheeling. During the cryptic conversation which followed, they were overheard to discuss, among other things, gambling line information, particularly the "over" and "under" figures with respect to that day's football games. Fred Hullett, a.k.a. the Colonel, an auctioneer and jewelry salesman from Miami, Florida, will testify that Hankish informed him that Unis was his gambling partner and that he placed layoff bets for Unis at Hankish's request. Hullett will also testify that he received envelopes in Florida containing substantial amounts of cash, primarily representing gambling proceeds, from a number of sources. Hullett received these envelopes on Hankish's behalf from approximately 1983 to 1988 and turned them over to either him or to people whom he designated.*
>
> *Evidence obtained during the undercover investigation conducted by the government showed that Buddy Jacovetty and Charles G. Joseph, a.k.a.*

Chuckie, played important roles in the Hankish gambling organization. Joseph Wojcik and his son, Jeffrey Wojcik, operated a Wheeling bar which had substantial gambling activity, a large portion of which was "layed off" on Jacovetty. They also paid Jacovetty $3,000 for protection from a county law enforcement official. Donald Richard Clark and Donald Musilli, a.k.a. Moose, will testify concerning their participation in the gambling organization. That evidence will include testimony showing layoff bets to both Jacovetty and Joseph. Other evidence will show that Hankish steered bettors to Joseph and that Joseph was involved for a number of years in the receipt of large-scale sports bets by telephone from both soldiers and customers of the organization. Both documentary evidence and witness testimony will show that Joseph was also involved with Hankish in the stolen property conspiracy and that, indeed, Joseph would sometime settle gambling debts in exchange for stolen property.

* * *

Meanwhile, a lot of that "documentary evidence" was obtained thanks to the work of Thom Kirk from the West Virginia State Police and both Larry Mincks and Jeff Sandy from the IRS. Thom worked undercover on the Hankish investigation, which is a story in itself. A great portion of that work was done inside Ernie's Esquire, the high-end steakhouse that served as a kind of social headquarters for Hankish where he could enjoy the fruits of his riches. Thom would be wired up, while Jeff and Larry would be outside in a van listening in and recording the conversation.

"I knew I had to do something to stand out, to show I was somebody important," Thom recalls. "There were no cell phones back in the '80s—beepers were the big thing then, as much a status symbol as a work tool. You carried it with you and whenever you got a phone call, it went off with the number displayed in small numerals, so you could find a phone and call the person. Well, we didn't have money in the budget to actually buy a beeper, so for my disguise, I found this old garage door opener that didn't work and fancied it up to look like a beeper. My undercover guise was a psychologist from Washington, Pennsylvania. I'd go into Ernie's Esquire, take a seat at the bar, and lay my fake beeper down in front of me. That made people think I had a lot of money. As a psychologist, I told people I couldn't go out to relax at home because people would recognize me and want to talk about their problems. That explained why I came to Wheeling to relax. I remember there was a lady tending bar and the first night I went in, I left her a twenty-dollar tip, which was a big deal back in those days. From that point on, as soon as I sat down at the bar, she had my drink ready for me.

"That vantage point gave me the opportunity to sit there and observe Hankish coming and going and who he was meeting and speaking with. It got to be like walking into the *Cheers* bar. I'd take a seat at the bar, lay my fake beeper in front of me, and people would come up and say, 'Hey, Doc, how you doing?' One day I was sitting there, watching and listening to Hankish, who was seated just a few stools down, and hoping my transmitter was working so Larry and Jeff could hear the same thing I was. At one point, I went over to this old-fashioned jukebox, put in a quarter, and picked the theme from *Miami Vice*, a big television show at the time, which seemed appropriate enough. I went back to the bar, and Hankish came up and sat in the stool next to me."

"'Did you play that fucking song?' he asked me, snarling. 'Because the only person I know would play a song like that would be a fucking cop.'

"I turned to face him and nodded. 'You know, I agree with you. I hit the button by mistake and I looked around for a reject button but there wasn't one there, so I guess I wasted a quarter.'

"He sat there and looked at me for what seemed like a long time, then started laughing and went back to his seat. But then I could see him asking other people who I was. From that point on, we talked from time to time, but we never talked work. I just wanted to be close enough to Hankish to hear what he was saying to other people, and that's what I did on a regular basis. Sometimes we'd get word he was headed over to the club and I'd have to change into nice clothes in a hurry to make sure I claimed my regular spot at the bar, which was close enough to his to hear and see everything that went on. That gave us a whole lot of intelligence on Paul Hankish, and it also gave me the opportunity to personally observe how people treated him, mostly with fear or deference or sometimes both. He acted as if he owned the place, which he kind of did."

Back in those days, we didn't have a sophisticated way technologically to follow the comings and goings of our targets. The best we could do was put a camera up on a telephone pole across from Hankish's house and another at his headquarters. Not that he didn't know it was there, since on at least one occasion he turned toward the camera and shot us the bird.

"It was nothing like what we've got today," Thom Kirk recalls. "It was pretty much like putting an eight-track recorder inside a transformer. We didn't have motion sensors or anything like that. The closest we could come was having the camera snap a picture every four seconds or so. Since we also didn't have the technology to transmit the pictures, every day either Larry Minx or Jeff Sandy would have to climb that pole to switch out the tapes. More and more, what they saw when they looked at them was anybody who showed up at Hankish's house shooting us the bird, too."

A good portion of the case was made in Florida, thanks to us expanding our task force to include plainclothes vice cops out of Hallandale and Fort Lauderdale. These guys, all of them to a man built like football players, didn't work undercover the way Thom Kirk did. They were more about keeping an eye on organized crime in an area that had become a hotbed for drug activity, under the head of their intelligence unit John Morissette, who worked closely with Larry Mincks. Hankish was spending a good portion of the year, particularly the cold-weather months, down at a condo he'd bought there that became a central gathering point for athletes and celebrities interested in mixing with each other and enjoying Hankish's always plentiful stash of cocaine. While those vice squad cops were watching Hankish for drug activity, they noticed him taking calls on a pay phone at one high-end club in particular. On at least two occasions, one of the vice cops overheard Hankish's side of a conversation that clearly had nothing to do with drugs.

And everything to do with gambling.

Hankish relied on his network of bookies in Parkersburg, Fairmont, Morgantown, and Clarksburg for the bulk of the bets he took, but he always took the wagers exceeding $10,000 himself, and that's what he was doing when the vice cops caught him on the phone.

"This guy's not only into drugs," the vice cops reported. "He's taking layoffs, huge layoffs."

After reporting their suspicions, they continued to stick close to Hankish, which included putting a tail on him. That two-man tail, comprised of a rotating pair of those vice cops, followed him back to his condominium one night. Hankish managed to extract himself from the car that had brought him home, but he was so drunk that his wheelchair began rolling downhill.

It had just started to really pick up speed when the vice cops who'd been sitting on Hankish caught up with the chair and brought it to a halt so fast that the wheelchair tipped over and Hankish fell hard to the concrete. They got Hankish resettled in his chair, but along the way, a small brown notebook slipped out of his jacket.

Unbeknownst to Hankish, one of the officers tucked that notebook into his pocket and passed it along to Larry Mincks for good reason: it listed a slew of Hankish's biggest gambling customers, high rollers who helped enable his lifestyle, including their names and the bets they'd placed directly with him. And that gave us witnesses who helped brand Hankish as the gambling kingpin that he was. If anyone had any doubt about that, we served up a smorgasbord of witnesses whose testimony more than proved Hankish's status as the organized crime figure in charge of the bulk of illegal gambling throughout West Virginia and the Ohio Valley, stretching into both Pennsylvania and Ohio.

In all, our investigation went on for three years. And, on December 20, 1987, we raided all of Hankish's gambling halls, confiscating records and gaming devices and then shutting them down. No arrests were made that day, but they were coming. In the meantime, we got word that Hankish had tried to put a hit out on me and Tom Burgoyne, but Jesse Anderson had refused to carry out the order because that would have been certain to bring the wrath of God down upon the entire organization.

I'm not sure if that led to Anderson's falling-out with Hankish, but it may have contributed. Even with that, it turned out Jesse wasn't long for this world. Hankish sent him down to Meigs County, Ohio, to rip off this big marijuana dealer because he'd gotten word that the guy had close to a million dollars in cash stuffed in Kroger shopping bags. But it turned out the marijuana dealer was just as big and tough as Anderson, and they ended up getting into a knock-down, drag-out brawl. Anderson always carried a nine-shot .22-caliber pistol, and somehow amid the struggle, the dealer managed to rip it away from him. He shot Jesse Anderson twice in areas vital enough for even a .22 to do the job, marking the end of Anderson's reign as one of Hankish's chief enforcers. Hankish may have been somewhat on the outs with Jesse, but he had no idea the dealer was capable of turning the tables on him. It was all about that million dollars, not a convenient way to lose Anderson.

Eleven high-level members of Hankish's organization were snatched up in raids, indicted on a total of 218 criminal counts. We had them dead to rights on both RICO and Continuing Criminal Enterprise charges that had been made possible by the likes of Snooky Walls agreeing to testify against his former cohorts in return for reduced sentences. Snooky was vital to making our case because he laid out Hankish's entire gambling operation, how it all got started and how it operated. It was almost like all roads our investigation traveled on led back to Snooky. He knew where all the bodies were buried, figuratively anyway, and we knew how important his testimony was going to be in laying out an overview of the gambling component that was central to Hankish's organization.

We also turned a man named Lee Burgess, who was in the mining repair business in Bridgeport, Ohio, after indicting him on tax evasion charges because he kept two sets of books. Hankish had brought Burgess into his organization because he thought Burgess could help get involved in union activity up and down the East Coast the way the Five Families had for decades. Not only did we turn Burgess, we also turned his girlfriend Bea Davis, who worked at Ernie's Esquire and agreed to wear a wire for us in the investigation.

The problem was, well, she was a very well-endowed woman, so much so that the wire we did our best to hide ended up burning her breasts. We made a deal that she'd do no jail time in return for her cooperation, but my old friend Judge Robert Maxwell sent her to prison for a stretch anyway. That left Burgess with cold feet, so we let him plead guilty in Florida instead, where he ended up getting two five-year sentences to run consecutively. It turned out that we worked harder to get the guy out of jail than we did putting him in, but ultimately we got his sentenced reduced to eighteen months.

Hankish turned himself in to federal marshals in Miami, Florida, in the most undramatic way possible without a camera anywhere in sight. Here we were, the U.S. Attorney's Office for the Northern District of West Virginia, a state much of the rest of the country looked down on, and we had just made a rock-solid case against one of the country's largest criminal organizations.

We had basically shut down organized crime in Wheeling. But whether that lasted would depend on how the pending trial of Paul Hankish went.

CHAPTER 21

Wheeling, West Virginia

The trial of Paul Hankish began on July 18, 1990, at the U.S. District Court in Wheeling, West Virginia, before Judge Robert R. Merhige Jr. It lasted seven days, during which time between sixty and seventy witnesses were called to testify.

But it was the testimony of only six or so of those witnesses in particular that was primarily responsible for the case's ultimate outcome, starting with Charles Kellington, who was forty at the time and hailed from Pittsburgh, where he was well acquainted with Snooky Walls, another of our key witnesses.

Kellington, as you're about see, was involved in a plot to murder Snooky, which explained why he ultimately turned on Hankish and cooperated with my office.

* * *

"How long have you been a resident of the Pittsburgh, Pennsylvania, area?" I asked Kellington at the outset of his testimony.

"All my life, except for when I was in the army."

"During that time period, did you know an individual by the name of Gerald Snooky Walls?"

"Yes, sir."

"How did you meet Mr. Walls?"

"Through an acquaintance, Jimmy Griffin."

"Did you ever, or did you know what type of business Mr. Walls was involved in?"

"Yes, sir."

"What was that, Mr. Kellington?"

"He owned a bar, and the first time I met him he was involved in a gambling operation."

"Did you ever become involved in Mr. Walls's gambling operation?"

"Yes, sir. For a short period. Maybe a month."

"What type of activity did you perform in the gambling business?"

"I picked up slips, football pools, stuff like that."

"When you say slips, do you mean the football parlay cards and things like that?"

"Yes, sir."

"And, Mr. Kellington, during the time period that I mentioned, the late '70s, did you know an individual by the name of Robert Bricker?"

"Yes, sir."

"Did you also know an individual by the name of William Prosdocimo?"

"Yes, sir."

"Were you aware what type of a business or occupation Mr. Prosdocimo was involved in?"

"Yes, sir, drugs."

"During, it would be the summer of 1979, did you become involved in a drug transaction with Mr. Prosdocimo and Mr. Bricker?"

"Yes, sir."

"Were you involved in a marijuana and Quaalude transaction?"

"Yes, sir. It was a rip-off. To steal the stuff instead of buy it."

"Can you tell us how you became involved in that?"

"It came about, Bricker wanted Eggy [William Prosdocimo] to get some marijuana from Snooky or whatever we could get—cocaine, pills, whatever. He was supposed to bring them to a certain spot. And we were supposed to take the dope, plus kill him."

"And did you know a particular time or place when the rip-off was to have occurred?"

"I got a phone call seven o'clock one evening, and Snooky was bringing the stuff, and I was to meet Eggy at his house, him and Bricker."

"When you arrived at the house, were you armed with any type of weapon?"

"Yes. I believe I had a .357."

"Can you tell us whether or not Mr. Bricker had any weapon?"

"Yes, sir. He had a .22 with a silencer."

"Mr. Kellington, were there any plans as to how the rip-off was to occur that evening?"

"Eggy—Mr. Prosdocimo—was supposed to get [Snooky] to come to the house, pull the car in the garage, and we were supposed to take him down."

"And did Mr. Walls show up at the house?"

"No, he didn't. Eggy got a phone call to go meet him, and then Eggy called us at the house that [Snooky] wouldn't come to the house to the meeting. That the meeting would be set for downtown at an after-hours club called Butchy's."

"When you arrived at Butchy's, who was present that you knew?"

"Snooky was there, Stretch, Butchy himself, a few other people, a bartender…"

"What was your role supposed to be at Butchy's? What were you supposed to do?"

"Keep Snooky in there while Bricker located Snooky's car."

"And what was the reason Bricker was going to locate the car?"

"He was going to take the drugs out of it, I suppose."

"Okay, Mr. Kellington. And can you describe what happened down at Butchy's?"

"Well, Snooky started getting a little impatient. I started a little argument with him to keep him in there. I don't know if he got suspicious or what. He turns to Stretch and told Stretch to go to the car to check the car. Well, when Stretch went to check the car, he got killed."

"All right. And how were you notified that Stretch had gotten killed?"

"Bricker called me on the phone from across the street from the parking lot where the car was."

"And as a result of that phone conversation, did you leave Butchy's?"

"Yes."

"And where did you go?"

"I went up the street to the red light. Bricker was in Stretch's Cadillac on the street at the red light."

"Could you describe what happened from that point on?"

"Well, we went to the north side, unloaded the drugs, talked about what he was going to do with the car. He was going to take it downtown and throw the piece in the river. Leave the keys in the car and hope somebody would steal it."

"You unloaded the drugs. Where were they taken?"

"We took them from his car to my Jeep."

"And did you know what type of drugs were unloaded?"

"Marijuana."

"And then what happened to the marijuana?"

"I took it to Hazelwood, gave it to Chucky Bonosor, and he in turn sold it."

"Did you share in any of the proceeds from the sale of the marijuana?"

"Yes, sir."

"Do you know if anybody else shared in those proceeds?"

"Yes, sir: Jimmy Griffin, Mr. Prosdocimo, and Bricker."

It was time for me to drop the hammer, having reached the most vital point of my questioning.

"Do you know an individual by the name of Paul Hankish?"

"I know the name. I seen him around. I never talked to him or anything."

"And where did you see him?"

"I seen him one time on Court Place."

"And did you see anybody else up there at that time that you knew?"

"There was a lot of people. I don't know names."

"What was going on, Mr. Kellington?"

"A meeting of some kind."

"Did you go inside to attend the meeting?"

"No, sir."

"This meeting, and the individual you recall as Paul Hankish, is that person in the courtroom?"

Once Kellington identified Paul Hankish, the stage was set for my next witness.

* * *

Next, to pick up where Kellington had left off, I called William "Eggy" Prosdocimo, who had to be transported by federal marshals from the prison where he was currently residing in Pittsburgh. I focused my questions on the same time period, the late 1970s, that had been reflected in Kellington's testimony.

"Did you have an occasion to meet a Mr. Paul Hankish during the time period?"

"Yes. At a restaurant that was opening up. Orsini's."

"Now, when you met with Mr. Hankish at this Orsini's Restaurant, was this a business meeting or social meeting?"

"It was a business meeting."

"All right. What was the business purpose of this meeting?"

"Mr. Sal Williams wasn't paying money."

"To who?"

"Mr. Hankish."

"And was it during this time period that you worked for Mr. Williams?"

"It was, probably from '78 to '80."

"Now, Mr. Prosdocimo, were you always dealing in drugs during the time you were involved in Mr. Williams's gambling operation?"

"Yes, sir."

"What type of drugs were you dealing?"

"Dilaudid and cocaine."

"Where was the drug dealing being carried out?"

"I would pick up drugs from Fort Lauderdale, Florida, and bring them up here to Pittsburgh. And I would receive drugs from Las Vegas and bring them to Pittsburgh."

"Had you any drug dealings with or know an individual by the name of Gerald Snooky Walls?"

"Yes, sir."

"And did you attempt to set up this type of a deal with Mr. Walls?"

"Yes, sir."

"And at whose directive or insistence?"

"Mr. Bricker, Mr. Griffin, and Mr. Hankish."

"Can you tell us whether you were concerned about that type of deal, what your concerns were, if any?"

"Well, from the beginning, sir, it was supposed to be a drug buy. Mr. Bricker approached me and asked if I could order some drugs for Mr. Walls. And I said I possibly could. And he asked if I would do that for him. I said yes. I don't see any problem with that."

"All right. Did you make the approach to Mr. Walls?"

"Yes, sir. I called him."

"Can you tell us whether or not you ever found out or determined at a later time it was going to be more than a drug deal?"

"They was looking to rob somebody. That was my next impression."

"Mr. Prosdocimo, did you ever receive a call from Mr. Griffin?"

"Yes, he called me a day later and verified that Mr. Bricker was okay to go ahead and help him put this together."

"Did you ever meet personally with Mr. Bricker when you were trying to arrange this deal?"

"Yes. In front of my deli. They came by in a car."

"You say 'they.' Who do you mean?"

"Mr. Hankish. Mr. Griffin."

"And did you have any discussions with Mr. Hankish about the transaction?"

"Yes, sir. I had discussions with both of them."

"Tell us the discussions that you had with Mr. Hankish."

"It moved from a drug buy to a drug rip-off, and then it moved to murder. They wanted to kill him."

"Kill who, Mr. Prosdocimo?"

"Mr. Walls."

"And you say 'they,' who are you talking about?"

"Mr. Bricker, Mr. Griffin, Mr. Hankish."

"Did they give you a reason they wanted to kill Walls?"

"It finally came out that Mr. Walls turned his back on them for something that happened in Fayette County."

"Do you know what this something was?"

"They killed a man, Mr. Melvin Pike, so Mr. Snooky Walls could take over the gambling, the action up there."

"Now, did they tell you, did Mr. Hankish tell you where he wanted Mr. Walls killed? Any particular location?"

"That is where the problem was, sir. They wanted him to be killed in my house."

"What was your response to that?"

"I was totally against it."

"And did you express these concerns to Mr. Hankish?"

"Yes. That was why Mr. Griffin and Mr. Hankish came [to my deli]. I got in the car. And I asked them if I could get out of this. I didn't want to go through with this because it started, like I said, as a drug buy. And then to a drug rip-off which, you know, started getting me a little nervous. And then when it went to murder, I had no reason to be involved. It could have been a very bad scene. I was a major drug dealer, and narcotics agents were constantly surveilling my house. So there were a lot of reasons not to have anything done in my house."

Judge Merhige chimed in at this point. "The primary reason was you were afraid you might get caught?"

"Caught, and I was afraid that after they killed him they would kill me, too."

I jumped back in. "Did you attempt to find an alternate location?"

"Mr. Griffin and Mr. Hankish said that would be okay. But the places I showed Mr. Bricker were not adequate for him, not to his liking. And he pursued the issue of having it done at my house because Snooky would be very hard to lure just anywhere. So it would have to be a setting where Snooky felt comfortable. And they explained that time was running out. That Mr. Walls had become a suspect in the murder of Melvin Pike, so they were concerned about that. So they wanted to grab him."

"And you say 'they,' you're talking about who?"

"Mr. Griffin, Mr. Hankish, Mr. Bricker."

"Was there any particular request directed to Mr. Hankish at this time?"

"Yes. I told him I still didn't want to do it in my house. He said, 'You are in too far, you have no choice. You have to do this.'"

"And what was your response?"

"I had no choice. I knew the capabilities of these people."

"Mr. Prosdocimo, did you get a call from Mr. Walls when he returned to Pennsylvania?"

"He said he had so much marijuana and Quaaludes he was bringing in."

"At that time did you designate a place for the delivery?"

"I told him I would meet him up by my store. From there we would go down to my house and do the deal."

"And do you know whether or not Mr. Walls had anybody with him at that time?"

"At that time, that point in time, I did not know. Just when he showed up that night."

"And was anyone with Mr. Bricker?"

"During that period Charles Kellington came into play. I don't know how or why or who got him, but he started coming around, and he became part of this for some reason."

"Do you know whether or not they had any weapons, either Mr. Bricker or Mr. Kellington?"

"They both had weapons that evening at my house."

"Would you describe for the court what would happen or what occurred at your house, Mr. Prosdocimo?"

"I took [Bricker and Kellington] to my house, and they stayed there because I had to get back to the store. They told me to keep my car out of the garage, let Snooky Walls bring his car in, and then shut the garage door. I would be the first one through, and they would throw down on Mr. Walls and take it from there."

"When you say 'throw down' on Mr. Walls, what do you mean by that?"

"Put guns on him."

"Did Mr. Walls show up?"

"Yes, sir. He showed up around eleven o'clock, somewhere around there. He said, 'I got the stuff. It's right here around the corner.' And he parked around the corner from my store."

"Was there another individual there at the time?"

"Yes. There was a gentleman driving, sitting in the driver's seat."

"What was his name?"

"[Walls] just said, this is Stretch."

"Is that the first time you met Stretch?"

"First time."

"Okay. What were the arrangements made to do the deal? Did you ask him to come to your house?"

"I asked him a couple times to come to my house."

"And what was his response?"

"He refused. He knew there was something wrong. He wouldn't come."

"Was an alternative location then selected?"

"Yes. He would be down at Butchy's for a while. He said he had to see someone down there."

"And what did you do when Mr. Walls refused to come to your house?"

"I drove back to my house and told Mr. Bricker and Mr. Kellington that he will not come. I can't get him down there. He went down to Market Square, down to Butchy's."

"What did Mr. Kellington or Mr. Bricker do?"

"Mr. Bricker said it was a real fast plan between him and Mr. Kellington, that he told Mr. Kellington to go into the bar and keep him there. I told them there was another gentleman with him, a guy named Stretch. And Mr. Bricker said, 'I know who that is.' He asked what kind of car they were in, and I explained the car. And he told Mr. Kellington to go into Butchy's and keep them busy drinking, keep them there as long as you can until he could find the car and secure the drugs first. And then he would come back and we would wait for them to come to the car and kill him."

"This is Walls?"

"Mr. Walls would come back to the car."

"What time did you get downtown, Mr. Prosdocimo?"

"Oh, I believe around probably half an hour after they left my house, sir."

"Where did you go when you went downtown? This is downtown Pittsburgh, right?"

"Yes. I went to the after-hours club called Butchy's."

"Was anybody there at Butchy's?"

"Well, I was standing out front talking to Butchy and Thomas Sacko. And they said there was a murder a block away. I was under the impression that it might have been Mr. Walls. So I was talking to them about who it was, and they said they didn't know. And there was a lot of police coming around and rushing to the scene."

"All right. Did you see Mr. Bricker or Mr. Kellington down there that night?"

"I seen Mr. Bricker. He was coming over and told me something about Stretch—the guy is gone. And I said, 'What do you mean?' He said, 'I shot him.'"

"Now, Mr. Prosdocimo, when you next saw the drugs, the marijuana and Quaaludes, whose vehicle where they in?"

"Mr. Kellington's Jeep."

"You said the split was a four-way split. Could you tell us whether or not you made any payment or witnessed any payment of the drug proceeds to Mr. Hankish?"

"Yes, sir."

"What was that?"

"I made the payment to Mr. Griffin and Mr. Hankish."

"After Stretch was shot, did you have any contact with Mr. Hankish, either personally or by telephone, in addition to the time you made the payment?"

"Yes, sir. There was a phone call made by Mr. Bricker to Mr. Griffin, and Mr. Griffin was upset."

"Did you get on the phone and talk to Mr. Griffin?"

"Yes, sir."

"All right. Did you talk about the Walls murder?"

"Yes, sir. He was very upset. He wanted to know what was wrong, why we shot the wrong guy."

"Did you hear or did you talk with Mr. Hankish on this phone call?"

"Mr. Hankish was right there, too. And he was very upset."

"Could you hear on the phone conversation the talk from Mr. Hankish?"

"Yes, sir."

"What did you hear from Mr. Hankish?"

"He wanted me to bring him down, to go find him and bring him down."

"Bring who down?"

"Mr. Walls to Mr. Griffin's place, and they were going to kill him on the pool table."

* * *

The testimony of Charles Kellington and William Prosdocimo had given my office just about everything we needed to convict Paul Hankish of conspiracy to commit murder. The rest was supplied by the testimony of his intended victim: Gerald "Snooky" Walls. It's a rare opportunity when a prosecutor gets to put such a man on the stand, made even more striking by the fact that Snooky Walls would be just yards apart from the man who had ordered his death.

I started my direct examination of Walls by backtracking a bit to another murder, that of Melvin Pike, which I had begun my opening statement by describing.

"What was Melvin Pike's occupation in the Uniontown area?"

"He was a tough guy. He worked for—"

"Objection!" barked Hankish's defense counsel, my frequent adversary Tom Livingston.

"Objection sustained," said Judge Merhige. "Unless that is an occupation. In your view, Mr. Walls, is it?"

"Melvin Pike's occupation was tough guy."

"You mean he practiced the occupation of being a tough guy," Judge Merhige picked up.

"He practiced. He refined it also. It was his reputation, plus his occupation. He worked for people that—he got paid for that."

I jumped back in. "Then he was known as an enforcer?"

"He was an enforcer."

"And did you have any particular problems of that nature with Mr. Pike before 1977?"

"Before I engaged in gambling, yes, I did. I bought a bar, and he thought I went around him. He was offended by that, and my bar was blown up."

"Can you tell us whether or not during this time period Mr. Pike started to cause some problems with your bets being cut down and betters in the Uniontown area getting concerned?"

"Yes, in several areas."

"Can you tell us what these areas were, Mr. Walls?"

"The chief one was I was in trouble with my people, the Wheeling people, because I couldn't explain why that was happening. And we had what we call a damage-control meeting on this."

"Who was present at that meeting?"

"Myself, James Griffin, Teddy Tsoras, Paul Hankish, and I believe Buddy Jacovetty."

"Had you ever met an individual named Paul Hankish before that meeting?"

"I either met him once before that or it was after that. That was one of the first meetings I had with Mr. Hankish."

"What did you discuss at this meeting?"

"Which way our business is going with the gambling. It was dropping on my end. And I had to explain why it was dropping. And the explanation was, I am having trouble with Melvin Pike."

"And can you tell us, Mr. Walls, whether or not there was any consensus or any decision made as to what to do about the Pike situation at that meeting?"

"Well, it was discussed that night, and we decided something had to be done somewhere along the line to bring this gambling back up."

"Okay. Let's go to another meeting and direct your attention to that night at Mr. Hankish's house. How was that meeting arranged?"

"By James Griffin. I was taken there for the purpose of discussing Melvin Pike."

"And did you advise Mr. Hankish of what the problem was with Pike or discuss that further with the gambling situation?"

"We discussed everything fully and in detail. It came to a point at the time something had to be done or we are out of business."

"Was a decision made at that meeting, Mr. Walls?"

"Yes, sir."

"Was there any decision as to what had to be done to Mr. Pike?"

"Yes, sir."

"What was that?"

"Have him killed."

I led Snooky Walls through a blow-by-blow iteration of the chronology of what followed, getting to the part where Snooky refused to perform the hit on Pike himself out of fear of spurring retaliation on the part of Pike's partners. As a result, he testified, Jimmy Griffin hired Bobby "the Codfish" Bricker to handle it. I was getting to some of the most important testimony of the trial. And for that brief period, it was Judge Merhige who posed the questions.

"What part, if any, did Mr. Hankish play in this? And how was he kept advised of what was going on?"

"By Jimmy Griffin, Your Honor."

"Well," Judge Merhige continued, "that is because Mr. Griffin told you. What do you know of your own knowledge?"

"I know that I was directed to Mr. Hankish's house, and he had to okay the hit or we didn't do it."

In the wake of Melvin Pike's murder, Snooky Walls developed a genuine distaste for the gambling side of the business, in large part because he no longer felt safe in the Pittsburgh area. So much so that he relocated his family to Florida, meaning gambling revenue in the territory he was responsible for suffered measurably. And that drew the ire of Paul Hankish, who didn't appreciate losing one of his top earners.

"They wanted me to come back up, and I didn't want to come back up," he testified. "I was given the assurance that no heat would be on me on the Pike case, and it was just the opposite, the heat was on me. And nobody was doing anything to take it off."

"Were you concerned then about your own safety?" I asked him.

"I knew it was a matter of time before I got clipped."

"All right. Did you also during the time period meet an individual by the name of William Prosdocimo?"

"I met him in the Pittsburgh area through Jimmy Griffin."

"What was his business?"

"Narcotics."

"And did you eventually become engaged in some narcotics transactions with Prosdocimo?"

"We trafficked in cocaine and—well, wait a minute, also marijuana and Quaaludes."

At this point, I took Snooky through the chronology of the night he was supposed to be killed.

"What was your concern or understanding what would happen that night?" I asked him.

"I knew that the blanket of protection had been pulled off me by my crime group. Nobody makes a move on you unless it is okay by whoever you are with. That is my speculation. That is my feeling."

"You had a couple small [drug] dealings with Mr. Prosdocimo, you say?"

"This is after I left the gambling area and went to Florida. With Prosdocimo, I did one or two small buys, and he requested one day he needed a hundred pounds of reefer, which is marijuana, and he wanted fifty thousand in Quaaludes. So I said, 'Cash or credit?' He says, 'Cash.' I said, 'I will be right back.' I was calling from the road in southern Florida. And when I came back, we set a meet."

"Did you, in fact, have drugs with you?"

"Yes, we had, I think it was 188 pounds. That is all I could secure. And the Quaaludes. And somewhere or another I got him at his house. And he said he would be right down."

"Where were you when you first saw him?"

"He was over at Squirrel Hill. I said, 'Hey, what took you so long?' And he says, 'Come on, follow me [to my house].' And I said, 'Well, do you have the money?' And he says, 'Well, no.' I says, 'Oh, wait a minute, where is the cash?'"

"Did you show him the drugs?"

"It was in the trunk, garbage bags of it. I showed it to him and I said, 'It's all here. Where is the cash?' He said, 'You have to follow me.' So I says no. I says, 'You know, you have got an hour to come up with the cash. I will be down at Market Square' to a bar there we called Butchy's because that was the doorman's name, Butch Tibbits."

Not following Prosdocimo back to his house was the reason why Snooky Wells was alive to testify against Paul Hankish. The fact that Prosdocimo didn't have any money to buy the drugs he ordered had confirmed in Snooky's mind that something was definitely wrong, which explains why the plan to kill him fell apart, after which Bricker ended up killing Stretch, Snooky's driver, instead. It was also enough to get Snooky to agree to testify in open court in return for a reduced sentence after we indicted him on multiple charges. And, thanks to his testimony, we had now implicated Paul Hankish in the murders of both Melvin Pike and

Stretch DeStefano. The evidence might have been circumstantial, but it was overwhelming, especially when considering the rest of what we had on Hankish.

CHAPTER 22

Wheeling, West Virginia

Some cases are built on the quantity of both witness testimony and evidence that's to a large degree circumstantial. Other cases are built on the quality of that testimony, mainly from eyewitnesses who could put the accused at a particular place and time doing exactly what they were accused of. Our case against Paul Hankish had equal measures of quantity and quality. He had opted for a bench trial without a jury and pled not guilty, but the deeper the trial dug into his dealings, the more that plea began to disintegrate.

The Hankish organization, and thus the trial, didn't center around a single crime the gang's kingpin was accused of. Instead, we made the case based on an overwhelming preponderance of criminal activity that could bring the court to only one conclusion: that in addition to conspiracy to commit murder, our RICO charges had Hankish on gambling and drug charges, as well as receiving stolen goods, which we learned all about from none other than Skinner Dorn.

* * *

"Would you state your full name, sir?"

"Robert James Dorn Jr."

"Do you have a nickname?"

"Skinner."

"Mr. Dorn, how old are you?"

"Forty-one."

"Mr. Dorn, are you testifying, or have you testified before the grand jury, and are you testifying here today under a judicial use of immunity order?" I asked, referring to a practice where nothing Skinner testified to could be used against him in any future proceedings.

"Yes, sir."

"Mr. Dorn, do you know Paul Nathaniel Hankish?"

"Yes, sir."

"How long have you known him?"

"Well, probably around twenty years. We started doing business in '85, around that area."

"What type of business was that?"

"Selling stolen property."

"And what kind of property were you selling to Paul Hankish?"

"Well, clothes, crystal, about anything, purses, anything."

"And were there any other individuals, Mr. Dorn, involved with you at that time in selling stolen property to Paul Hankish?"

"What do you mean, shopping with me or—"

"Shoplifting with you?"

"I took different girls out."

"You say you went out. Where did you go?"

"About every state in the United States."

"And what kind of stores did you hit?"

"Neiman Marcus, Saks Fifth Avenue, Bloomingdale's, Tiffany's, Gump's, Nordstrom, all over the country."

"And what was the value of some of these individual items of crystal that you would steal?"

"Well, I have gotten a thousand dollars apiece. Twenty-five thousand dollars apiece, and then we got, you know, like two-thousand-dollar pieces. Usually five hundred and up at every store."

"Who did you take that stolen property to after you stole it?"

"To Paul."

"How many trips were made, approximately, outside the area of West Virginia to go steal things and bring them back?"

"Well, at least five hundred trips. I don't know how many. A thousand of them."

"What is the dollar value of the stolen property that you have stolen or sold to Paul Hankish over the years?"

"I estimate myself, between five to seven million."

"Was it ever spoken in front of him that these are stolen goods?"

"Paul told all of his associates that I was a booster, so he had to know."

* * *

Among other witnesses, William Sundel was able to detail for us the illegal gambling activity that Hankish supervised directly and what might happen if one of Hankish's "customers" failed to make good on a debt in due course.

"Did you discuss gambling activity with Mr. Hankish, Mr. Sundel?"

"Well, yes, we did. Mr. Hankish was an avid sports fan, and so was I. We got along very well together."

"And as a result of those discussions, did you come to become engaged in any type of gambling activity with Mr. Hankish?"

"Yes, I started betting with Mr. Hankish."

"What type of arrangement did you have?"

"Mr. Hankish and I agreed that we would exchange winnings and losings at the fifty-thousand-dollar figure."

"You say you started betting. Can you describe how the betting relationship went?"

"Well, I was just a sports bettor, and Mr. Hankish would call me with the lines on all the games for that day, and maybe half an hour later call me back and I would place my bets."

"How much were you betting?"

"Well, my betting progressed. At first I bet a thousand dollars a game, eventually would up betting two, three, four, five thousand a game. I can remember betting the Super Bowl for ten thousand a game."

"Was that mostly on football, or on other sports activity, Mr. Sundel?"

"I bet football, basketball, and baseball with Mr. Hankish."

"And how many games would you play on a given weekend, given Saturday during football season?"

"Well, it would differ. Sometimes five, sometimes eight, sometimes as many as fifteen college football games. The games start at one. Mr. Hankish would call me again at four, and night games would start at seven or eight."

"And did you ever have to pay Mr. Hankish?"

"Yes, sir."

"On how many occasions?"

"Between seven and nine times."

"And did there come a time, Mr. Sundel, when you stopped taking Mr. Hankish's calls?"

"Yes."

"And what time period would that have been?"

"Late September of 1985."

"Could you tell us what your reason was?"

"I owed Mr. Hankish somewhere between forty and fifty thousand, and I didn't want to bet with him anymore. And I wanted Mr. Hankish—Mr. Ippolito owed me two hundred twenty-six thousand. I wanted Mr. Hankish to deduct the forty to fifty thousand that I owed him from the money that Mr. Ippolito owed me, because Mr. Hankish was holding some of Mr. Ippolito's money."

"And how did Mr. Hankish receive that news?"

"Not very well. He told me to pay up while I still could."

"And did you?"

"No."

"After you stopped taking Mr. Hankish's phone calls, did you have a meeting or see Mr. Hankish?"

"Mr. Hankish came to a building that I owned in Newport, Rhode Island."

"Was anybody with him?"

"Two gentlemen."

Here I asked the court's permission to allow the witness to draw a rough schematic of his office to provide a clear sense of where the next events took place.

"Now, Mr. Sundel," I resumed, after he had completed his drawing, "what was the name of your business?"

"The name of my business was Dirthy Property Company Incorporated."

"All right. Now, when you say Mr. Hankish on the occasion that he came to Rhode Island, where did—where were you when you first saw him?"

"I was sitting at my desk. Mr. Hankish came in in his wheelchair through the door with two other gentlemen: one was Jesse Anderson. The other gentleman was big, over six feet. I really don't know the other gentleman's name. They came into my office with guns."

"Did they all have guns?"

"I believe two of them."

"Who were the two that had the guns?"

"Jesse Anderson and the other gentleman."

"Did Paul have a firearm?"

"Not when he came in the office, no."

"And then what happened when the three individuals came into your office?"

"I said hello to Mr. Hankish. And when I saw the guns, I said, 'What are you doing?' And I says, 'Paul, there are people in here that has nothing to do with our business, including a customer.' The customer was allowed to leave."

"What happened to you, Mr. Sundel?"

"The gentleman, the other gentleman that I am not sure of his name grabbed me by the neck and started banging my head into the walls. He dragged me into the hallway and just kept banging. And I said, 'Paul, this is crazy. What are you doing? You know we have been friends for a long time. If it is over the money, I don't understand why you don't deduct it from Mr. Ippolito's money.' I says, 'The money I will pay you. We don't have to see each other anymore. Let me just pay you.'"

"Did Mr. Hankish permit you to do that?"

"The amount of money was such a small amount of money for the dealings I had with Mr. Hankish. Mr. Hankish had been a friend of mine, visited me at least two or three times in Newport, stayed with my family, ate with my family. I thought we were friends. I didn't understand what this was all about. I went back into my office and went to this cabinet where I had a gun. So I took the gun and I found some bullets. I went behind my desk, and I started putting bullets into the gun. Just as I was putting the bullets into the gun, the door flew open. Mr. Hankish came into my office in his wheelchair, had a gun pointed at my head. Told me whatever was in my hand, drop it on the floor."

"What happened to your gun, Mr. Sundel?"

"I dropped it on the floor. Somehow or another, for the next five or ten or fifteen minutes, Mr. Hankish calmed down, and I kept saying, 'Paul, this is ridiculous, you know.' There was a black bag alongside of Mr. Hankish's wheelchair. He put that on the floor. The bag contained a stun gun, a set of handcuffs, some tape, and a camera."

"Did you say you were going to pay him the money?"

"Mr. Hankish sent the big gentleman outside through a door that led outside in my office. I told him to have Mr. Anderson, Jesse Anderson, leave. I said, 'No need for these people here. We can work this out.' Mr. Hankish became much more mellow, reasonable, and said I could pay him within a week or two, ten or twenty thousand at a time. And that he was going to leave."

"Did he, in fact, did Mr. Hankish in fact leave?"

"Yes, he did."

"And did you pay him the money?"

"Yes, I did, sir."

* * *

Paul Hankish actually hired a local Wheeling contractor named B. J. Thomas to go to Rhode Island and repair the damage that was done by his enforcers at Mr. Sundel's office. When we interviewed Mr. Thomas, he stated that the holes in the drywall that he was asked to repair looked like someone had used Mr. Sundel's head as a stud finder. Sundel helped us make the gambling, assault, and extortion parts of our case. But the real centerpiece, in addition to the murders in which Paul Hankish was implicated, was the drug dealing. And we were able to demonstrate that Hankish didn't just oversee the selling of vast amounts of mostly cocaine and Quaaludes, he was also a user of cocaine, thanks to witnesses like John Belot.

Belot was a prominent businessman in eastern Ohio, running a very successful concrete company. He was introduced to Paul Hankish by a local attorney at a picnic-like function that Belot provided for friends and business clients. As their relationship developed, Hankish provided Belot with a small amount of cocaine, which Belot said he used to enhance his speaking ability at a business seminar. Belot testified that he never purchased cocaine from Hankish but was provided with a portion of cocaine that he would process for Hankish to remove certain impurities and enhance its purity. After Belot processed the cocaine, which he called "washing," he would retain a certain amount for his personal use and return the "washed" cocaine back to Hankish. Like the cherry on top of a sundae, Belot also gave up Hankish for marriage infidelity, which, along with the drug use, seemed to embarrass him more than any other evidence we presented.

"Mr. Belot," I began in my redirect examination, "did one of those double dates you arranged for yourself and Mr. Hankish occur in Morgantown at the Ramada Inn?"

"Yes."

"Who was there?"

"Debbie DePolo and her sister."

"Who else?"

"Myself and Paul Hankish."

"And what is the sister's name?"

"Donna."

"And was there any cocaine present on that occasion?"

"I had cocaine."

"Did Mr. Hankish have any cocaine?"

"I left my bottle in the other room that he was in."

Once again, Judge Merhige interjected. "I take it all the cocaine that you ever had you got from Mr. Hankish. Is that what your testimony is?"

"Except for an ounce and a half that I got from Columbus at one time from Tom Dillon."

"I want to direct our attention to the summer of 1986," I picked up, after Judge Merhige nodded my way. "Do you recall going there and having dinner with Mr. Hankish?"

"Yes. A few times."

"Two times," I specified. "All right. And did you have a girlfriend with you on that occasion?"

"Yes."

"What was her name?"

"Debbie DePolo."

"When you had dinner on that occasion, was there any other person there at that dinner beside you, Ms. DePolo, and Mr. Hankish?"

"I don't remember having dinner when she was there. I remember being at the Esquire when she was there."

"Was there anybody else there at the table with you?"

"Originally, no. Jay Byrum came in later."

"Did he join you at the table?"

"Yes."

"He was the individual from the Wheeling area?"

"Yes."

"Did you do any cocaine that night?"

"I did, yes."

"All right. Do you know if anybody else did any cocaine?"

"Debbie said that she and Jay did some in the car on the way down to the Eagle Inn."

"How about the Esquire Club?"

"I didn't see anybody doing any, no."

"Did you—is that cocaine that you brought yourself?" Judge Merhige interjected.

"No."

Judge Merhige leaned closer to him in the witness box. "Where did you get it, Mr. Belot?"

"The same cocaine that I had been talking about."

"I see," said the judge. "Part of what you say you got from Mr. Hankish."

"All right," I picked up again. "Did you go down to the Eagle Inn that night?"

"Yes."

"All right. Who all went down there?"

"Paul and myself and then Jay Byrum and Debbie came in later," Belot testified.

"Is the Eagle Inn a bar here in Wheeling?"

"Yes."

"Did you do any cocaine down at the Eagle Inn? On that occasion? On that night?"

"Yes, I did."

"Where did that cocaine come from?"

"From my pocket."

"Do you know whether Mr. Hankish did any cocaine?"

"No, but I heard that he did."

"How about Mr. Byrum or Ms. DePolo?"

"She took cocaine from me. What she did with it, I don't know. She went in the restroom. I didn't go in the restroom with her."

"The cocaine she took from you is the same source that we are talking about, is that correct?"

"Yes, and she said she got some from Paul's pocket, too."

When the group left Ernie's Esquire supper club, they headed to the Eagle Inn. The Eagle Inn was nestled in a shopping plaza on National Road. It featured a busy mahogany bar with hustling bartenders sliding drinks into patrons' waiting hands. Among those patrons, divorced housewives masked by layers of makeup mingled with local businessmen amid the haze of cigarette smoke. The Eagle Inn was also known as a place where secrets stayed secret, helping to explain why Wheeling's underworld elite called it home.

To supplement John Belot's testimony, next I called Debbie DePolo to the stand.

"Ms. DePolo, you previously testified that [your sister] Donna asked you to do something. As a result of the request, what did you do?"

"I fixed her up with Paul, and John [Belot] brought Paul to the Ramada Inn in Morgantown, and the four of us went out, and we had adjoining rooms and spent the night."

"You say there were two rooms?"

"Yes."

"And did you see any cocaine in either of the rooms that night?"

"Yes."

"How much?"

"We had seventy-five grams."

"And did anything happen to a portion of that cocaine that night?"

"Well, we also had some compacts with cocaine in them, and my sister knocked her glass over and it broke into the compact. And she wanted to continue to use that particular cocaine, and Paul told her not to be worried, there was plenty more where that came from."

* * *

Looking over at the defense table at that point, I could tell Paul Hankish was humiliated. Not only were we making a case against him for his crimes as a mob kingpin, we were demonstrating he had cheated on his wife and was a cocaine user, if not addict, himself. We produced more witnesses who had given or sold cocaine to Hankish for his personal use, some of them dealers who moved cocaine and Quaaludes for him in bulk. He was near the breaking point, and it would be the testimony of Donald Clark, one of the dealers who sold for Hankish, that pushed him over the edge.

"Were you selling kilos of cocaine to an undercover FBI agent?"

"Correct."

"Do you recall what day that was?"

"November 21, 1986."

"Were you taken into custody at that time?"

"Yes, I was."

"You were detained pending trial?"

"Yes."

"Pled guilty and you have been in custody since, is that correct?"

"Correct."

"Have you entered the Witness Protection Program?"

"Yes, I have."

"When was your son born?"

"November 1 of 1984."

"In connection with that, did you try to do anything to earn extra money?"

"When I got involved in the drug business, that is how it started. Back when my wife was pregnant with my son, I thought I would make extra money. And that is what started my involvement in the drug business, which led to my arrest over a two-year period."

"How did you finance your first drug deal, Mr. Clark?"

"This was back when I was running my car lot on Sixteenth Street. I got to be pretty good friends with Mr. Buddy Jacovetty," Clark said, referring to one of Paul Hankish's top associates. "And through the course of time as we became acquainted, I made arrangements with him to start putting money together for me to borrow, and that led into, you know, pretty much whatever I wanted to do."

"Okay. Where were you obtaining cocaine with these funds?"

"Back then, what I did was I ended up doing business with Mr. Bobby Zeal. I purchased cocaine through him through a Florida connection."

"Did there come a time when that connection stopped?"

"In 1985 when Mr. Zeal was arrested by the government."

"Did you seek out another source of supply?"

"Yes."

"What was that?"

"Through Mr. Jacovetty and Mr. Hankish."

"How did the first deal come about?"

"The first deal came about, it was the summer of 1985. Mr. Jacovetty came to my car lot, and he said that Paul gave him some cocaine for me to look at. And it was like six ounces but could have been four. And he said, 'Take this because I don't want it. You take it and let me know in half an hour whether you want it or not.'"

"What decision did you make with respect to this particular cocaine?"

"Well, the first time that I purchased it, it was cut. And I told Buddy I would be interested in doing business but told him to pass on the message that I would be willing to pay more money to have it not cut."

"Okay, Mr. Clark, did you have occasion to get more?"

"Yes, I did. The next time I purchased it, Mr. Jesse Anderson brought it by the lot. He brought me four ounces. And I told him I only wanted a couple. He said, 'Paul says two means four.'"

"Did you ever have a relationship with Matthew Bartnicki?"

"Yes, I did. One time when Jesse came by the lot, I think I bought a half pound of cocaine from him. And what I used to do is I used to go to Matt Bartnicki's house to weigh up the product, and about an hour after I got the product from Jesse I was at Matt's house weighing it, and Jesse Anderson came by the house and said that Paul was in the car and wanted to speak to me. So I went out and got into the car, and there was a question about the amount of cocaine that was given to me earlier by Anderson. They were questioning whether there was a mistake made, thinking they might have given me more. And I told [Paul] that I'd already weighed it and it was the right amount. And he seemed to be, seemed to be pretty edgy and weird at the time. And he told me that he thought that I should check it again, because he felt that he gave me more than what was there.

"So I went back in the house and I reweighed it. It was the right amount. I came back out to the car and told him the weight checks out the way it was supposed to, the eight ounces. He seemed to get rather upset, like he thought I was lying. And I says, 'I have no reason to lie to you.' He says, 'What I want you to do is this. I want you to give me a gram of cocaine, and I want you to meet me at Western Sizzling Steak House in half an hour,' but I didn't know what to expect. And when I pulled into the parking lot, Jesse came to the car and told me that Paul had found the mistake, so I was off the hook. I gave Jesse the package with the gram of cocaine and drove off."

During the course of the Hankish investigation, we were also investigating Matthew Bartnicki's drug activities. As part of the investigation, we obtained a court order permitting the FBI to place a bug in Bartnicki's residence. Finding an appropriate time during which the agents could enter any residence to plant surveillance devices always proved a challenging situation. It was during the summer, and we knew that Bartnicki would usually spend time on his boat on the Ohio River, especially on the weekend. Through surveillance, we were able to verify Bartnicki was doing just that on this particular day, and the agents were able to proceed with placing the bug in his residence. However, before the completion of the operation, we learned that he had been stopped on the Ohio River by the local police for certain violations of pleasure boat protocol and was ordered to return to the shore. Agents were in the middle of the operation and needed additional time to complete the placing of the bug.

So, in order to delay Bartnicki's return to his residence, agents deflated the tires on his vehicle. Meanwhile, one of the neighbors noticed the strange activity occurring at Bartnicki's residence, which left Bartnicki suspicious enough to avoid saying anything incriminating the bug otherwise would have picked up, producing nothing we were able to use at trial.

"Did you ever have any meetings with Mr. Hankish at the Eagle Inn?" I asked, continuing my examination of Donald Clark.

"We snorted cocaine in the bathroom. And then he questioned me wanting to know why my sales were down. He said that previously my sales were a lot higher, and all of a sudden he was wondering what the problem was."

"What in fact was the problem, Mr. Clark?"

"Well, the fact was the problem was that I reestablished my connection in Florida, and I was getting kilos brought in on the side. Also, I was buying off of Mr. Hankish. And at the time I was more or less selling from both sources."

"Did you ever have occasion to have Mr. Jacovetty again deliver cocaine to you at your car lot?"

"Yes. Mr. Jacovetty and Mr. Hankish at one time pulled up in the alley of my car lot. I was in the auto sales office, and he came up to the door. And I opened the door, and he said, 'I just threw a package underneath the building.' So I went out with him. I was talking to him, and he started to walk down over to get back in the car. And Paul yelled to me to come to the window. He told me to go back up and pick up the package. He wanted me to take possession of it. So I did. I reached under the building and grabbed the package, a brown paper bag. And I took possession of it, and that was good enough for them. They drove off."

* * *

Clark's testimony before the jury had been vital to us being able to make the case that Paul Hankish was a major wholesaler of cocaine, as well as a user. It also ended the case. At the conclusion of Clark's testimony in open court, Hankish changed his plea to guilty. He'd seen enough, heard enough, had enough and knew he was going away. The only question was for how long.

"Hankish, 58, reputed head of organized crime in northern West Virginia, southeastern Ohio and western Pennsylvania," the *Pittsburgh Post-Gazette* reported, "pleaded guilty in late July to racketeering, gambling and drug charges. He faces up to 77 years in prison and $980,000 in fines at his sentencing in October."[1]

In October 1990, Hankish was formally convicted of violating RICO laws and eight counts of gambling, drug distribution, and tax fraud. He was sentenced to thirty-three and a half years but had served only six when he passed away in 1998.

But the apple, as they say, doesn't fall far from the tree. In November 2007, Paul's son Chris Hankish was charged with conspiracy for his involvement in a bookmaking operation headed by former video poker kingpin John "Duffy" Conley. He pleaded guilty and was sentenced in June 2008 to serve three years in prison but died unexpectedly at his home in Scott Township, Pennsylvania, three months later in September at the age of forty-six while the case was still under appeal. "Unexpectedly" often means suicide, something I never bothered confirming for Chris Hankish, because I knew what had ultimately killed him was the world he'd grown up in and was ultimately seduced by.

At least he didn't die in prison like his father.

John Richard Carlucci

Wikipedia Commons, https://commons.wikimedia.org/wiki/File:Crystal_Meth.jpg

Crystal meth, the source of Carlucci's criminal empire.

CHAPTER 23

Clarksburg, West Virginia

"You clearly don't know who you're talking to, so let me clue you in. I am not in danger, Skyler. I am the danger. A guy opens his door and gets shot, and you think that of me? No! I am the one who knocks!"

Those words were spoken by Walter White, brilliantly played by Bryan Cranston, to his wife Skyler, portrayed with equal brilliance by Anna Gunn, in the sixth season of the television series *Breaking Bad*. The show featured Cranston's character, a frustrated high school chemistry teacher, becoming a methamphetamine cook and distributor in order to provide for his family after he learns he's dying of lung cancer. Airing between 2008 and 2013, *Breaking Bad* introduced millions of viewers to all things crystal meth, often romanticizing both the process and the colorful thugs with whom Walter White interacted.

When meth came to West Virginia in 1979, there was nothing romantic about it. And of all the drug scourges I witnessed and battled, this ranked with the worst. In large part, that's because meth is often addicting from the very first time a user tries it. Over time, the brain develops tolerance to the drug, and the user needs to take higher and higher doses to achieve the same pleasurable effects. That leads to more crime, and one thing that *Breaking Bad* got right was the violence that pervades meth at all levels of usage and distribution.

Why such an explosion of both in this particular decade, though? Well, in the 1980s, the United States began to tighten regulations around the sale and use of the ephedrine, a pharmaceutical precursor used to make crystal meth. As a result, illegal meth labs turned to an easier-to-obtain precursor—pseudoephedrine—a chemical found in many cold medicines. Not only that, the resulting drug proved to be nearly twice as potent. And if that wasn't bad enough, unlike more sophisticated drugs, meth could be manufactured pretty much with ingredients commonly found beneath a typical home's kitchen sink.

In years past, meth had been viewed as a low-rent drug. Manufactured and distributed mostly by warring biker gangs, crystal meth had found favor with the likes of the Hells Angels, Banditos, Pagans, and Outlaws. It was referred to as "crank" because of the manner in which it was often transported by these bikers—in the crankcases of their motorcycles. As the drug's popularity grew, the gangs took to kidnapping each other's cooks to increase their manufacturing volume and claim new territory. The internecine biker battles that resulted became one of law enforcement's best weapons to holding the line against the kind of distribution levels of a drug like cocaine, which reached the point where it saturated society. Then, in the 1980s, the manufacture and distribution of crystal meth continued along the lines of the biker gangs that had spawned it, but in the form of criminal organizations that set up shop in territories they defended with a ferocity that would have made the bikers proud.

In West Virginia, that organization was run by John Richard Carlucci out of a sprawling, farm-like miner's camp outside Clarksburg. The Dawson Mine Camp was the kind of place where nobody talks to outsiders and everyone looks out for each other. The residents in the small cabins and mobile homes of the mine camp were more scared of Carlucci than beholden to him, and with good reason: his capacity for violence knew few bounds. His criminal record dated back to 1968 for breaking and entering. In 1971, he violated the federal Gun Control Act. In 1974, he received and transported stolen property. A year later he was charged with delivery of a controlled substance. And in 1978 he was charged with submitting a false statement to obtain a firearm.

None of those offenses, though, compared to Carlucci's violent reign as head of the largest methamphetamine distribution network in the state during the era of the drug's heyday. Take a pair of murders one of our main witnesses was present for that ultimately helped us arrest and convict Carlucci. By the time of those murders in 1982, we had arrested a number, as many as two dozen, of Carlucci's associates who had made deals to cooperate with us in return for lighter sentences, providing they gave us actionable intelligence and testimony on Carlucci. He knew we were closing in and summoned a Clarksburg couple who used and dealt for him, Gary and Marian Schaffer, believing they were our chief informants.

They weren't, but Carlucci lured them to his house on August 29, 1982, and shot them to death anyway. He then burned their bodies in barrels and later dumped the barrels containing their ashes down a strip mine that he'd purchased to launder the incoming cash from his meth operation. His girlfriend Sandra Fominko was actually in the next room when he shot the Schaffers, but our eyewitness to their murders was an underling of Carlucci's named Sid McGinnis. They had grown up together in the same mining community, and ultimately McGinnis became his right-hand man and errand boy. He did whatever needed to be done, from delivering drugs to picking up money, and it was McGinnis who helped Carlucci dispose of the bodies. Then Carlucci ordered McGinnis to drive the Schaffers' car to a regional airport nearby and leave it there to provide the impression they'd fled when, in fact, their remains had never left Harrison County, West Virginia.

Carlucci also burned down his mobile home in the Dawson Mine Camp in an attempt to erase all trace of his connection to the Schaffers' murders and the meth trade. From that mobile home, secluded away at the end of the Dawson Mine Road, he had cut and packaged for distribution hundreds of pounds of methamphetamine. Then he took off for Ohio with Fominko and her two young children in tow, the younger she had with Carlucci and the older with another man prior to meeting him.

Carlucci also maintained a network of underlings who were all meth addicts themselves, which meant he could control every aspect of their lives and he did, to the point of taking the guys' wives or girlfriends for himself. His primary supplier was a fugitive from the Philadelphia area named Freddie Gebhart, who was living in Harrison County under the alias of Joseph McDermott. McDermott would routinely return to Philly in the dead of night, where he had significant ties to organized crime and large-scale meth suppliers; he would return to Harrison County with multipound quantities of methamphetamine and always called on Carlucci first so he'd have first dibs on the drugs.

What made us take serious notice of Carlucci's operation, and the cost of meth on society in general, was a rash of burglaries, armed robberies, and petty street crimes committed by meth addicts desperate for cash in order to buy their next fix. For all the criminal chaos it wreaked, cocaine had always been perceived as a lifestyle drug that did not necessarily spur waves of crime beyond its sale and distribution. And marijuana, to a great extent, was the preferred drug on college campuses and could seldom be linked to violent crime. Meth represented the first time rampant drug use had reached rural West Virginia, somewhat rightfully perceived as the drug of choice for those who felt weed was too mellow and cocaine too expensive. The kind of crystal meth users who made up the bulk of Carlucci's customer base were so consumed by the drug, most of them could never hold a job. Yet the addictive nature of the drug meant that they needed to use more and more of it to get high. So where were they going to get the money they needed to buy it from the network of Carlucci's street dealers?

"It led to an unprecedented crime wave," recalls Lowell "L. J." Maxey, the West Virginia state trooper who arrested Carl Lee Gallo and then later joined the DEA. "Hundreds of crimes, including armed robberies, burglaries, break-ins, muggings, shoplifting, and just general street crime. The final straw came when one of Carlucci's meth dealers, and user himself, named Carl Rebrook shot and robbed a Clarksburg bar owner and a week later shot and killed Archie Smith, the owner of a small mom-and-pop convenience store just outside Clarksburg. After the robbery, Smith chased Rebrook out of the store with a weapon of his own, but unfortunately, Rebrook shot and killed him and left him lying in a ditch. However, Rebrook returned to the body and stole Smith's weapon. I was first on scene and became responsible for the investigation. A few weeks later, I flipped the guy who Rebrook sold Smith's weapon to and arrested Rebrook. He was detained without bail, convicted of first-degree murder without mercy, and is still serving his sentence. But he never gave anyone up."

Our task force snatched up every customer and dealer of Carlucci's we could find. Joseph McDermott, Carlucci's chief supplier, finally became the victim of a routine traffic stop by the Bridgeport, West Virginia, Police Department. Sergeant Jim Hotsinpiller called Lowell Maxey after seizing what he suspected was drugs. Maxey responded, and the seizure turned out to be a pound of pure methamphetamine. We charged McDermott federally, and he was held without bail after his true identity could not be verified. Afraid McDermott would cooperate with the government, Carlucci actually tried to facilitate his escape from jail. When that attempt got no farther than the parking lot, he circled the wagons, murdered Gary and Marian Schaffer, and then disappeared with Sandra Fominko and the kids.

Fearing for their safety, Sandra ultimately got away from Carlucci and returned to West Virginia with her young children. Upon learning she was back in the state, L. J. Maxey and his partner Trooper Gary Cooper approached her at her parents' home south of Clarksburg. They laid out their case against Carlucci in detail to Fominko, including her culpability in the massive conspiracy. They said it was time for her to choose sides between the man who was threatening her and law enforcement, who could keep her and her children safe. A few days later, she chose to cooperate and was able to provide vital intelligence on Carlucci's operation, because she knew it inside and out from being around Carlucci all the time as his de facto common-law wife.

"We got her settled in an apartment in Parkersburg with round-the-clock protection," Larry Mincks, who was assigned to keep her safe until the trial, remembers. "She was terrified that if he found her, Carlucci would stop at nothing to kill her, and she was right—that was the kind of criminal he was. This went on for, oh, at least six months and probably longer until the trial finally got underway. I had to leave my house to go buy groceries, clothes, and the like. One weekend, she called me and said her kids were very sick with the flu, so I arranged for a doctor friend of mine to make a house call, and he ended up giving them a prescription. Of course, I couldn't give him their real names, so he used the kids' first names and my last name on the bottle. My wife must've spotted the prescription paperwork and came to the conclusion that I was having an affair, because I couldn't tell her what I was up to.

"In the end, Fominko made for a very compelling witness at the trial, and her testimony was pivotal to putting Carlucci away. Afterward, she and her kids were placed in the Witness Protection Program. I never saw her again, and my wife was just fine with that."

Doing what passed as phone taps in those days was extremely vital to making the case.

"There were a few cell phones around then, but not many, so dealers had to conduct business over landlines," Larry continues. "We'd sit on the homes of suspects and if we detected a lot of activity going in and out, we'd get a warrant to have the phone company put a pin register on the line. That allowed us to track all the calls going in and out, and we were able to accumulate the numbers of the suspect's customers as well as supplier. The idea was always to work our way up the ladder, starting with the lowest rung."

And that ladder yielded those twenty-four members of his organization whose sworn testimony before a grand jury led to the arrest and conviction of Carlucci, who'd first come onto our radar during our investigation into Carl Lee Gallo. The thing about a lot of the investigations we had ongoing over the course of this time was that they were running parallel to each other. We weren't just climbing a ladder, we were climbing a tree, and each branch represented a different target we needed to saw off at the base.

Carlucci was just about the boldest, most brazen of any of the kingpins we took down over the years, to the point that he actually called L. J.'s house while he was on the lam in Ohio and after he knew we had Sandra Fominko and her children in protective custody. L. J. was out for a run when his wife answered the phone.

"Is Lowell Maxey there?" he asked her.

"No, he's out for a run."

"Well, this is John Carlucci."

"Shut up, Cooper," she said to him, believing it was her husband's state police partner. "That's not funny."

And then L. J.'s wife realized it wasn't Cooper at all.

"Who is this?"

"John Carlucci. Tell your husband I'm gonna call him back."

L. J. picks up the story from there. "I was walking up the hill to my house cooling down from the run. My wife was on the front porch frantic, almost yelling for me to hurry up that John Carlucci had just called for me and was going to call back. It was obvious she wasn't joking. I wasn't back in the house more than five minutes when the phone rang and, sure enough, it was him. 'I know you have Sandy,' Carlucci said. 'I know you've talked to her, but I'd be careful if I were you. You're never gonna get me.' He was trying to intimidate me, which I think he realized pretty quickly wasn't going to work. I told him I wasn't looking for him yet, but when I started looking for him, I'd find him. Our conversation lasted around ten minutes. I told him enough about what we had to really get into his head—that's just something I like to do, especially when I have a solid case. We got him indicted pretty quickly after that. He had abandoned the Ohio home where he'd lived with Sandra Fominko, but with information we provided, law enforcement there tracked him down not long afterward, and U.S. marshals brought him back to West Virginia to stand trial."

Carlucci was convicted in August 1986 of forty-five drug and racketeering counts stemming from his operation of an interstate methamphetamine ring. The counts included Continuing Criminal Enterprise, Racketeer Influenced and Corrupt Organizations, and RICO conspiracy violations. He was also convicted of violating federal income tax laws. His conviction under the federal RICO statute included as predicate crimes the murders of Gary and Marian Schaffer. He was sentenced to thirty years and lifetime supervised release.

The U.S. Attorney polled the jury at the trial's close to see if they would have convicted Carlucci on the murders alone. Murder isn't a federal crime, so the thought was to gauge the likelihood that state authorities could have put Carlucci away for even longer, potentially for life, but the results were mixed, so the state never charged him.

Too bad. For some criminals, no sentence is long enough.

The Task Force:
The DEA—Lowell Maxey

DEA Agent Lowell "L. J." Maxey pictured today.

CHAPTER 24

Clarksburg, West Virginia

Lowell "L. J." Maxey might not have been born to be a crime fighter the way Thom Kirk and Larry Mincks were, but his infatuation with law enforcement nonetheless started at a very young age.

"It goes back to watching television on one of the two channels we had in southern West Virginia back then," he recalls. "Shows like *Highway Patrol, Dragnet,* and even *Sky King.*"

Dragnet chronicled the kind of hard-nosed investigator he was destined to become. *Sky King* followed a rancher who doubled as an airplane pilot who used those particular skills to catch criminals, essentially a western with the hero flying a plane instead of riding a horse. And *Highway Patrol,* of course, centered on the efforts of a crime-fighting organization very much like the West Virginia State Police, home of modern-day gunslingers, where L. J. hung the first of his two hats. In other words, he became the living embodiment of the heroes he watched on TV as a young boy.

L. J. grew up in a small town in southern West Virginia called Peterstown and went to Peterstown High School, where his graduating class numbered all of eighty-eight. His father worked at a Celanese fiber plant, and his mother was a stay-at-home mom for the first sixteen years of his life. She was one of fifteen siblings, so L. J. had no shortage of cousins and company growing up.

"If you had to compare Peterstown to anything, it would be Mayberry from *The Andy Griffith Show,*" L. J. remembers. "After high school, I spent two years at a small community college in Roanoke, Virginia, and then got my bachelor's degree at Eastern Kentucky University in Richmond, Kentucky."

That was May 1974, and driving home from the graduation ceremony, L. J. literally stopped at the West Virginia State Police Academy in Institute, West Virginia, to pick up an application. He reported to the academy on a Sunday night and woke up his first morning of training on his twenty-second birthday, September 10, 1974. After the academy, he was assigned in uniform to the Clarksburg, West Virginia, area, met his wife through one of his state police supervisors, and started a family.

"I had this desire to be a sworn law enforcement officer to do my part to keep my state and the community safe," L. J. says today.

Just like his fictional television heroes.

"It was a career that appealed to me in large part because no day was ever the same as the day before. I could never imagine myself in a job where you sit behind a desk all day doing the same thing over and over. Thom Kirk and I were in the academy together. We stood across the hall from each other every morning as our rooms were inspected. I can't tell you what an experience it was to develop relationships with fellow officers and people that had a desire to do the exact the same thing as me. And I will tell you this: the day I resigned from the West Virginia State Police in February 1987, I cried."

He resigned to take a special agent position with the Drug Enforcement Administration, but his twelve-plus years with the WVSP more than prepared him to take on the kind of bad guys he'd chase for the rest of his professional career.

Always a fitness nut, especially running, L. J. was out jogging in his neighborhood late one evening when a suspicious car passed him. "I saw it hit its brakes and make a U-turn. It came back toward me real slow, and a guy rolled down the window. It was Thom Kirk and another officer named Ricky Brown. They were both working drugs at the time throughout northern West Virginia. Right there on the side of the street, Thom kind of laid out what they were up to and what was unfolding with regards to undercover drug work and wanted to know if I wanted to be a part of it, working directly under Captain Joe Trupo. So I said, 'You know Cooper [L. J.'s partner, Trooper Gary Cooper] and I are a team. We have to come as a team.' Thom had already anticipated that, as I believe Captain Trupo had also, when he gave Thom the okay to approach me. Thom said he didn't think that would be a problem, and the rest is history."

Almost immediately, L. J. knew he'd made the right decision.

"I just felt comfortable at the time that the right people were being brought together to achieve what leadership at every level, state and federal, wanted to accomplish."

Even before he became a formal part of the whole task force concept that was just ramping up, L. J. found himself working with the likes of Tom Burgoyne and Larry Mincks, as well as Thom Kirk, on cases like the one that nailed John Richard Carlucci. Not just because of the direct damage kingpins like Carlucci were doing to the community, but also the indirect damage.

"There was a rash of burglaries and breaking and entering; homes and businesses, more than two hundred of them over just a couple years, along with sixty or so safe jobs and an armed robbery almost every week."

A crime wave that was the direct result of the dramatic rise in methamphetamine use during L. J.'s tenure with the WSVP. He actually worked a plethora of those cases specifically for Captain Trupo as a plainclothes investigator before being approached by Thom Kirk and Ricky Brown while on that late-night jog through his suburban Clarksburg neighborhood. He was still working for Captain Trupo, only now in the capacity of an undercover drug investigator assigned to the task force, where he'd be able to focus his efforts on the root cause of the crime ravaging the community.

As L. J. and Cooper cleared many of those crimes, the eventual cooperation of the defendants helped put the nails in Carlucci's coffin. They described in great detail their meth purchases from Carlucci with money they'd stolen from local merchants throughout northern West Virginia, Pennsylvania, and Ohio. The multijurisdictional task forces we pioneered were expanded to include local law enforcement in those other states as well, since networks like Carlucci's were operating across state lines. Prior to the task force concept, these local municipalities were never in communication with each other about the common crime problems they were facing and the common criminals at the root of them. Disparate groups united now in common cause became the best weapon to battle organizations like Carlucci's (remember, he was arrested in Ohio, not West Virginia), forming relationships that persevered through the years and opened the door to the kind of communication that could keep criminal kingpins at bay.

Carl Lee Gallo was one of those kingpins as well, and L. J. and Thom Kirk turning him over to Captain Joe Trupo's charge to be taken into federal court in Clarksburg didn't sit well with L. J.'s wife.

"My wife was, like, 'Why? Trupo didn't arrest him.' I told her, that's part of my job. I work undercover. I got my satisfaction from putting handcuffs on Gallo and then turning him over to my captain to handle the rest. When you're undercover, the last thing you want to do is go before the cameras. It was Captain Trupo who gave me the opportunity to be a part of bringing all these people to justice. Anything I needed, anytime I called him, I got what I asked for... I believe he trusted my judgment."

In February 1987, L. J. accepted a special agent position with the DEA that took him to Rochester, New York, in Monroe County, where his task force experience smoothed the transition since that was the way the DEA worked in Rochester, with a nearly a fifty-man task force. His first case brought him up against a large-scale cocaine trafficker who was found to be hiding over $1 million in cash in the rafters of his garage. That was followed by an even bigger case L. J. helped make thanks to securing the first-ever wiretap under the Chemical Diversion and Trafficking Act Congress enacted in 1988. That case fleshed out a massive conspiracy operating out of a warehouse across the street from Eastman Kodak corporate headquarters, within view of L. J.'s sixth-floor DEA office in the downtown Rochester Federal Building. Massive quantities of the primary ingredients needed to cook crystal meth, including hydroiodic acid and L-ephedrine HCL, were being brought in and stockpiled in Rochester as a way station to a facility in Southern California from which they were distributed mostly to outlaw biker gangs who cooked and sold the meth. Controlled deliveries of those chemicals were made by DEA agents in California, and ultimately surveillance followed them to clandestine labs all throughout Southern California, most being operated by outlaw motorcycle gangs. Ultimately, nearly two dozen people were indicted in New York (including the Rochester resident at the head of the conspiracy) and California, and simultaneous arrest and search warrants were executed in both states, thanks to disparate agencies working cooperatively with each other, a notion L. J. was already well familiar with.

Then he got a call that opened the next phase of his life.

"I had put down the Charleston, West Virginia Resident Office of the DEA through the Office of Preference in DEA headquarters that handled agent transfers. There wasn't a DEA office in Clarksburg, so I thought Charleston would at least put me back in West Virginia. One evening, around six o'clock, I got a call from my office in Rochester telling me that Agent Placement wanted me to give them a call. I called the guy who left the message, and he asked me if I was still interested in going to West Virginia. It turned out he had no clue that was where I was from and told me they had just opened a small office in northern West Virginia and asked me if I'd heard of the place. 'The city's called Clarksburg,' he said. 'Would you be interested in going there?'"

L. J. was, and he spent the rest of his career with the DEA back home in northern West Virginia, an area he knew like the back of his hand.

"I came back and started working cases, you know, picked up the same relationships, and developed new ones with people that weren't around when I left. I worked the same way with the DEA as I had with the state police. At the time, West Virginia was the number two or three state in the country for both indoor and outdoor cultivation of marijuana, and I was appointed as the DEA coordinator for that, which was a big responsibility. Part of my job, like the DEA coordinator in each state, was to write an operational plan each year that funded the eradication effort that was primarily conducted through a Letter of Agreement with the West Virginia State Police. So here I was, getting funding for my former department for those operations, to be coordinated with the state police coordinator who was a longtime friend from my state police days. I came back home and enjoyed every second of that stage of my career."

The rest of that career, though, included a detour along the way.

"Shortly after 9/11, I along with fifty other DEA agents from across the country were recruited and chosen to go over to Afghanistan and Pakistan for intelligence operations. This would have been early 2002, and we coordinated several operations throughout that area with our Islamabad and Karachi DEA offices, supporting the guys that were over in Afghanistan, who were working out of a couple of bases over there. So, when I think about it, my career with the West Virginia State Police helped prepare me for developing relationships even with cops in Pakistan. That

West Virginia State Police experience laid the groundwork for all I was able to achieve, regardless of where I was or who I was working with. That's why my years with the WVSP were the most rewarding time in my career."

L. J. retired from the DEA in 2009, but he hasn't slowed down a bit.

"A month after retirement, I started conducting contract background investigations for the FBI, for their new hires, here at CJIS [Criminal Justice Information Services] Division in Clarksburg, where all the Automated Fingerprint Identification System [AFIS], UCR [Uniform Crime Reporting], National Crime Information Center [NCIC], National Instant Criminal Background Check System [NICS)], and more are located. And in that capacity, I actually had to conduct a background investigation on my old friend Jeff Sandy from the IRS Criminal Investigation Division when he was appointed to Governor Jim Justice's cabinet as the public safety secretary. I also ended up interviewing Thom Kirk, because Jeff had appointed Thom as his deputy secretary."

The DEA, though, remains close to his heart for good reason: his son is a DEA special agent down in the drug hotbed of southern Florida.

"I don't worry as much as my wife, because he was a field agent for over ten years and was on the Special Response Team, but now he's in kind of a supervisory position. He is the senior special agent in Technical Operations and heads the DEA Marine Unit out of Fort Lauderdale and Miami. He tracks cell phones, installs covert cameras, and other things of that nature, so he's still involved in cases. And he does go out on surveillance missions on land, in the air, and on the water throughout the Caribbean. There comes a point in time when you're going to have to get out of your car and go knock on or hit a door, and you've got to be completely focused on what's behind that door. I don't worry about my son, because I know that's his mindset, too. He was a uniformed cop in Montgomery County, Maryland, before joining DEA, and he tells me he works with a lot of state and local cops who he has developed relationships with. When I go down and visit him, he's doing things the same way I did. There are tons of agents, local cops, and DEA task force cops calling him all the time for his advice on technical equipment issues and arranging water and aerial surveillances.

"He's like me in another way, too. I was never one of those guys, like a lot of cops, who go out and celebrate a big arrest. I went home when I could; I enjoyed my home life. A lot of cops use this profession as an excuse not to go home. I enjoyed going home, I enjoyed being home."

L. J. has seven grandchildren from his son and daughter, ranging in age from eighteen months to sixteen years. Though the scourge of drugs he spent his career fighting hasn't touched them, drugs haven't spared his greater family, thanks specifically to opioids.

"One of my cousins, his father was my mother's youngest brother; it was his only son. He was probably in his thirties, and he's got a nearly six-figure job working for General Electric in southern West Virginia. This would have been around 2007. He was raised in a very stable family and a home where there was not even alcohol. His wife had a common surgery and was prescribed opioids for post-op pain. They both got hooked on pain pills and ended up trafficking, going to Ohio to pick up pills to bring back to deal in southern West Virginia. He had a room set up in his basement where he sold and eventually began to shoot up opioids. My aunt and uncle, his parents, were completely oblivious as to what was going on. One of the troopers that I had worked with in the state police, who was heading the regional task force in southern West Virginia, eventually got search warrants for his home. My cousin lost his job, both he and his wife went to jail, and he had two preteen girls that went to live with their grandparents until their parents got out of jail. In 2007, a nearly six-figure job in southern West Virginia was hard to come by, and he blew it all."

And what does L. J. tell the new generation of West Virginia state troopers and local cops he comes across from time to time?

"That it's going to be unlike anything you'll ever experience. The work is just nonstop, and I loved every second of it. There are cops who love to hang stuff all over the place about their career, news clippings and the like. I'm not one of them. That's all stashed away. I just loved the work, and as I anticipated early on, no day was like the day before. Here's the perfect thing to put on my gravestone when that time comes:

> *"He always enjoyed what he was doing; he loved going to work and he loved coming home."*

The Swami

Creative Commons via Wikipedia, https://en.wikipedia.org/wiki/File:Kirtanananda_Swami_-_1982.jpg

Keith Ham, aka "Kirtanananda Swami," pictured in his heyday in 1982 as the leader of the Hare Krishna sect in Marshall County, West Virginia.

Tom Westfall, the so-called "Krishna Cop," who attracted national attention first as a sheriff's deputy and then as a homicide detective whose work led to Keith Ham's ultimate arrest and incarceration after he began working directly with Bill Kolibash in the U.S. Attorney's Office.

CHAPTER 25

Marshall County, West Virginia

"*Almost heaven, West Virginia,*" John Denver's hit song "Take Me Home, Country Roads" begins.

But for twenty years within the rustic hill country of Marshall County, it was anything but heaven. In fact, it resembled something much closer to hell. And in this case hell went by the name of New Vrindaban.

New Vrindaban was located along the southern spur of the Appalachian Mountains at the base of West Virginia's northern panhandle. It was hard to imagine then, just as it is hard now, a more beautiful place—quiet, serene, and peaceful in a landscape shaded in such a vibrant shade of green that it appears God himself created it with His personal paintbrush. In the summer months rich with humidity and autumn months of crisp mountain temperatures, a dewy mist rises through the balsam fir, red spruce, and sugar maple trees, making it look from above as if the ground rich in rhododendrons, azaleas, and mountain laurels is smoking. Thrushes, wrens, and warblers greet the sunrise with a song, accompanied by a chorus of clacks from woodpeckers chipping away at tree bark as hawks cruise the sky peering down in search of their next meal.

The founding of the Hare Krishna community of New Vrindaban in Marshall County brought with it a new predator to the scene his followers knew as Kirtanananda, the group's guru or swami, known in Krishna circles by his full name, Kirtanananda Swami Bhaktipada. Law enforcement, though, knew him by his given name…

Keith Ham.

Ham was a direct disciple of Srila Prabhupada, leader of the modern-day Hare Krishnas originally based in India, who was responsible for bringing the movement to America in 1966 under the auspices of what was then known as the International Society for Krishna Consciousness. The religion centers on the belief that every living thing has a soul, and as a result, followers don't eat meat. They also don't believe in getting intoxicated, drinking coffee, gambling, or sex outside of marriage, and typically adopt a philosophy of nonmaterialism. Prabhupada capitalized on the hippy and counterculture movements, already in full swing in America, to find young people looking for a new way to view the world, as well as their place within it. His goal was nothing less than to create heaven on earth, with him accepting the mantle of nothing less than God on earth.

The son of a Baptist minister, Ham joined the movement in 1966. A year later, he became Prabhupada's first disciple to be initiated into the Vaishnava order of renunciation centered around a lifelong vow of celibacy, an honor that brought with it being renamed Kirtanananda and being granted the role of swami. But his rapid ascent was equaled by a precipitous decline triggered by his traveling to New York in 1967, against Prabhupada's wishes, to assert his own vision for the movement. The price for that was akin to excommunication, as Kirtanananda was banned from preaching, effectively removing him as a person of influence among the Krishnas.

Searching for redemption, in March 1968 Ham spearheaded the effort to lease 132 lush acres of land located in Marshall County's hill country at the base of the Appalachian Mountains. To further curry favor and remain in Prabhupada's good graces, in 1977 Ham began construction of what would become known as the Palace of Gold to serve as a residence for Prabhupada, who had blessed the effort. Kirtanananda's vision was behind the construction a multilayered temple of marble, teakwood, and, of course, gold so the palace would glisten in the sunshine atop a majestic hilltop that was the highest point of the property. The gold, though, was not solid gold at all but gold leaf, which was nothing more than thin sheets pressed from gold laid over the wood and hardened mud bricks that comprised the temple's structure. So the entire Palace of Gold was an illusion, a harbinger of what was to come and a metaphor for the rot at the moral center of the movement under the leadership of Kirtanananda, formerly Keith Ham.

Krishna consciousness, and the international movement as a whole under its spiritual leader Prabhupada, owed its roots in America to the turbulent times of the 1960s, when a combination of civil rights unrest, the Vietnam War, and the assassination of President John F. Kennedy left many searching for an alternative. A means to escape society might be a better way to put it, while renouncing the very materialism many believed was at the root of the tumult. Members willing to embrace the Krishna tenets were given a new name symbolic of their new identity and commitment to their new way of life.

Tom Westfall visited the Krishna community early in his career as a deputy sheriff of Marshall County in 1972.

"Newly initiated Krishna devotees were told that it was going to be this pastoral landscape, like a spiritual Shangri-La. But when they got there, they found out it was really just a slum with some residents living in lean-tos or old cars. The houses, shacks really, looked ready to fall apart, and there was a farm building that looked like the only structure that could withstand a stiff wind. So life was pretty difficult there."

Life had been pretty difficult for Westfall as well. His parents' bitter divorce meant neither of them was willing to cosign a college student loan for him, so he joined the army and became a military policeman. Assigned to Okinawa during the toughest years of the Vietnam War, he found himself part of the largest military police detachment in the world, thanks to the number of American troops stationed there. And he also found he had a talent for building databases, rare in those computerless days to say the least.

"I started using pushpins on a wall map to determine, on an island with a thousand bars, where the drugs were, where the hottest areas of crime were. I just had a knack that when I looked at something, I could see things nobody else could see."

And Tom brought that talent to his work as a deputy in the Marshall County Sheriff's Office, pretty much from his first day on the job.

"Because I was from the area, I knew about the farm. So when I became a deputy, I paid a visit there just to see what was going on. I'd ask people where they were from, what they were doing. It was small back then, in 1972, only about fifty people, but I got a sense right from the start something wasn't right."

Tom recalls his first proof of that long before the Swami was on law enforcement's radar.

"Where you from?" he asked a devotee he met that day on the farm.

"New York."

"How do you like it here?"

"Well, I'm going to ask you a favor, sir."

"What's that?"

"Get me the hell out of here."

"So he ran up to this little shed he was living in," Tom picks up from there, "grabbed his stuff, and jumped in my car. I took him down to the sheriff's station so he could call somebody to send him money so he could come home. And that started happening more and more as the farm grew, and it grew pretty quickly. And I let it be known when I was driving through and just talking that I'd help anybody the same way I helped that kid. Parents started calling me, asking if I could find their child. I kept collecting information and came to the realization that something had to be really wrong with this place if so many people needed my help to get away. A few of them told me they'd come here to get away from the material world, money and all that, but they'd be sent places, all over the country, to collect cash. 'What the heck was that about?' I asked myself. I'd even park my cruiser just off this public road next to Eddy's Grocery Store that everybody used to get from one side of the farm to the other, so those people knew where to find me if they needed help getting out. Word spread pretty fast about me. I don't think that made the Swami very happy."

A would-be follower, who arrived at New Vrindaban around that same time, concurred in the brilliant documentary *Krishnas: Gurus. Karma. Murder*.

"They were trying to convince me to come and stay with them. They kept saying you never know what something's like until you come live it. And so I promised that I would stay for six months, and they promised that if I didn't like it after six months, I could leave. New Vrindaban had this aura of some kind of mystique. Part of me was scared to death, but part of me was kind of excited. I brought what little I had into my living quarters, which happened to be above the cows in the barn. And the first thing I had to do was learn how to wash the walls with cow urine. That was a pretty stinky job, but it was believed that the cow urine was antiseptic and so that's how we're going to keep things clean. The food was a shock—this brown gooey substance served on a piece of wax paper. And it was very, very cold. We took our showers outside but were only allowed about a gallon of hot water a day. You would traipse across the snow into this little enclosure, pour your hot water over your head, while your feet were freezing to the boards underneath you. There were families living in very small rooms with no heat, so children were going to bed in snow-suits and mittens. There were times when I really, really wanted to leave, but I had made this promise to stay for six months. And by the end of that six months, I was brainwashed. I was there, I was in, and I stayed for eleven years."[1]

Tom Westfall had an answering machine in his office. And many days when he went into work for his afternoon shift that began at three thirty, he'd press the button and a voice would say something to the effect of, "I'm such and such and I want to get out of here. And I've got a bunch of stuff I want to tell you…"

When he was able to make contact with the caller, Tom would tell them to get down to Route 250 near Curry Ridge and he'd meet them there to help them get away. He also recalls the first time he met the Swami himself.

"He was living in the top of a barn. He probably had maybe eighty or ninety followers at the time. And I had an inquiry from California about somebody missing. So I went out early in the morning and knocked on his door. He answered and told me he didn't know the kid I was looking for, said she wasn't there. I was trying to read his face to see if he was lying, and right before I left I noticed this boy, fourteen or so, standing behind him. There was something about the whole scene that creeped me out, and I left believing something was really wrong with this place."

This was around the same time that cults like the Family under Charles Manson and the Children of God under David Berg were both blazing trails dipped in blood and pain, as well as riddled with crime.

"As the community grew," Tom Westfall continues, "I started building a database of who was there. Before long, I began collecting information from police all over the country to see if I could find out more about how these folks were collecting the cash a few of them had told me about. One of the people that caught my attention early on at the farm was a man named Thomas Drescher. He had served in Vietnam, had two Purple

Hearts, and was no stranger to violence. Drescher had a criminal record long before he ever came to New Vrindaban, and almost all his crimes involved violence. He was clearly a very unusual person to be on a Hare Krishna farm."

And it wasn't just Drescher who brought violence to the community. One day, a report came over the radio that shots had been fired on the farm.

"I lived close by and knew there were only two ways in and out, so I blocked one and radioed the West Virginia State Police where I was. They were on the other end, and none of us saw any armed group fleeing the premises after what we thought might have been a gunfight. Myself, two other deputies, and the state police drove onto the farm and tried to make sense of what had happened. There were three or four devotees who had suffered minor injuries. It was pretty clear no armed gang had stormed the property and there'd been no gunfight. But when the media showed up, Keith Ham told a completely different story about the place being invaded by a motorcycle gang and how he risked his life to fight to protect his people while the bullets were flying from machine guns. And he would continue to tell that story for years to come, making himself into the hero who stood up to a motorcycle gang to defend the Krishna religion."

It turned out the commotion came courtesy of a father showing up with a friend in search of his daughter. The father had a shotgun with him, and at some point, a scuffle broke out and the shotgun went off. That was it. Neither Tom Westfall, nor the West Virginia State Police, had spotted a biker gang fleeing the property because they'd never been there in the first place. The man and his friend raced off the property without finding his daughter.

"The county tried to prosecute them," Tom recalls. "But the local prosecutor could not proceed with the case because Kirtanananda made sure the people who were injured, or witnessed what had happened, were gone when investigators came back to ask questions."

When the legend becomes fact, as they say, print the legend. Under Ham's stewardship, New Vrindaban became a fortified, armed encampment. And as the mythology around the Swami solidified, his followers found themselves even more worshipful and beholden to him. At the same time, the Krishna community became more withdrawn, insular, and independent from the rest of the rural stretches that surrounded it.

"[Kirtanananda's] devotees carried him on a jeweled palanquin, knelt when he passed," the *New York Times* wrote in a review of John Hubner and Lindsey Gruson's 1988 book *Monkey on a Stick*, "and, while he barked orders, they worked 14-hour days without pay to build him a temple of marble, onyx and 24-karat gold leaf. They also built an arsenal of illegal weapons to defend the community from attack by karmis (meat-eating barbarians—i.e., anyone who was not a member of the movement)."[2]

The death of the Krishna movement's spiritual leader, Srila Prabhupada, further entrenched Ham in his position of leadership while providing license for him to act without any accountability. Gone was the oversight and conscience supplied by Ham's mentor, the man he emulated and saw himself becoming, something he was now free to do. In the wake of Prabhupada's passing, a council of ten gurus, including Kirtanananda Swami, was given control of a sprawling international organization that preached a dogma Ham no longer saw any need to follow. The philosophy of practice what you preach no longer applied to him at all, his sociopathic personality unleashed to pursue his own whims and ambitions at New Vrindaban's expense. The Palace of Gold, originally intended to be a home for Prabhupada, became a testament to Ham's own power to be utilized, like everything else, toward pursuit of his own self-aggrandizement. With Prabhupada's passing, Ham became God on earth, free to pronounce judgment on anyone who dared oppose him. And when retribution or punishment was required, he had just the man for the job in Thomas Drescher.

Drescher was already a bully of the highest order, and Ham enlisted him to become his personal enforcer. The vast majority of New Vrindaban residents cowered before both men. They would kneel or bow when their leader Kirtanananda passed or was carried by and would avoid Drescher at all costs out of fear of doing anything that might upset him.

"This man was a stone-cold killer and a psychopath," Tom recalls, "one of those guys who took pleasure in hurting people. He was from upstate New York, and I got his file from the cops up there and it was one violent crime after another. They even, unofficially, opened Drescher's juvenile record for me, and some of what they told me gave me goose bumps."

By all rights, Ham was doing everything he could to alienate himself from his flock. He preached modesty and the shunning of materialism, yet he was driven around in a Cadillac limousine and toured the grounds of the community always shadowed by his personal Praetorian guard just in case that nonexistent motorcycle gang came back with their machine guns. Add to that the fact that rumors were swirling that Kirtanananda Swami, who'd taken a vow of celibacy before his mentor Prabhupada, was being sexually active, and with men instead of women.

That conduct caught the attention of an up-till-then reasonably loyal community member named Charles St. Denis (aka Charkradara, or Chaka for short). A child of a broken family, St. Denis migrated to the Krishna community as a teenager. He was the kind of man Keith Ham normally used to suit his purposes, until St. Denis disrespected the faith by refusing to cut his hair, don robes, or give up alcohol and marijuana.

"I ran into Charles once in a convenience store when he was buying a case of Molson Ale," Tom Westfall recalls. "I said, 'Is that for the Lord?' And he said, 'It is tonight.' Charles made an enemy of the Swami, and there was more than one incident where Swami would talk to him about his conduct. He called out St. Denis for not following the rules—not shaving his head and for drinking beer and smoking marijuana. And at one point when he did that, Charles St. Denis called him a hypocrite in front of a whole bunch of followers."[3]

According to Tom, St. Denis called Ham onto the carpet to face truths no one else had ever dared raise. Where did all the money the community members were raising go, beyond the Swami's Cadillac limousine? If he'd splurged on that, what else had he splurged on? It was a classic case of the pot calling the kettle black, and Charles St. Denis wasn't going to take it anymore, especially with rumors floating around about Ham having sex with men while preaching celibacy.

The strife and rivalry between them spilled out into the open. Not only was St. Denis challenging Keith Ham, he was doing so in public. That meant one of them had to go, and it sure wasn't going to be Kirtananda Swami.

Meanwhile, Dan Reid, a Kirtananda loyalist and bookkeeper for New Vrindaban, had his own beef with Charles St. Denis, since St. Denis had had sex with Reid's wife. One night, on the Swami's orders, Reid and Drescher devised a plan where Reid would contact St. Denis on the pretext of moving on from the past and becoming friends again. They'd drink some beer, smoke some weed, and bury the hatchet so to speak. St. Denis left that evening in his Chevy Blazer for the short to drive to Reid's home, and that was the last time anyone in New Vrindaban, including his wife and son, ever saw him again. We'd later learn that Thomas Drescher had shot St. Denis in cold blood eleven times before brutally stabbing him. Somehow St. Denis clung to life while Drescher dammed up a creek, dug a watery grave, and buried him alive.[4]

Keith Ham's metamorphosis into Kirtanananda Swami was now as complete as the Palace of Gold perched on that hilltop. He had gone fully down a road from which there was no return. The murder of Charles St. Denis by Thomas Drescher on his orders was heinous and brutal, ordered by a man whose authority was absolute and who didn't believe he could be held accountable by anyone. And yet that murder wasn't even the most desperate one committed under his reign.

It was only the first.

CHAPTER 26

Marshall County, West Virginia

The second murder was that of Steve Bryant, a man who committed himself to bringing down Kirtanananda Swami at all costs, which turned out to be his life.

Well before that, word spread that Charles St. Denis had up and left New Vrindaban, leaving his wife and son behind. Those in the community who felt differently were almost surely afraid to voice their opinions, lest they suffer the same fate. They were in the thralls of a leader who now ruled with fear instead of love and respect, as diametrically opposed to Krishna teachings as it got. The one exception was St. Denis's wife, who reached out to Tom Westfall at the Marshall County Sheriff's Office.

"His wife called me one day," Westfall recounts. "She was crying and she said, 'Sergeant Westfall, Chaka is gone. Something's happened to him. I'm afraid that Thomas Drescher may have done something to my husband.' And I believed her. Thomas Drescher could be a pretty imposing, scary kind of guy. He took to the role of being a bully, and he liked it and so did the Swami. He enjoyed having him as, like, his personal protection."[1]

St. Denis's Chevy Blazer was found parked down the street from a friend's home in Bridgeport, Ohio, across the Ohio River from New Vrindaban. But the friend insisted St. Denis had neither called him nor come to his house. Tom Westfall and a forensics team responded but found no evidence of any sign of struggle or any trace of blood. And, according to Tom, St. Denis's wife, Debra, filed a report with the West Virginia State Police instead of the Marshall County Sheriff's Office, because the Swami had warned his followers not to talk to Tom under any circumstances. In any case, the Swami was already on the WVSP's radar, and the disappearance led them to increase their investigative efforts.

"I went out to the farm over the next few days to talk to residents of New Vrindaban," Tom says of the aftermath of the disappearance of Charles St. Denis. "To a man and woman, they'd look me in the eye, look away, and say, 'No, we think he probably just left here. He went to California, he's away. He's on some trip or something.' When I approached Dan Reid, his face was completely white. He was sweating and wringing his hands.

"'Where's Chaka?' I asked him.

"'I don't have any idea,' he said. 'I don't know.'

"Finally, I found Kirtanananda himself.

"'Hear anything about Charles St. Denis?' I asked him.

"'He's gone to California. Everybody knows that.'

"Well, I didn't, and I didn't believe him for a second. 'He never left here, Swami,' I said to Kirtanananda. 'He never left here.'

"I think there was an undercurrent of people who did believe that Charles St. Denis had been killed by the Swami. I came to believe that he was probably killed and that Thomas Drescher had something to do with it. But nobody was really listening, because we didn't have a body."[2]

Meanwhile, Keith Ham continued his goal of turning New Vrindaban into a kind of spiritual Disney World, from the Palace of Gold at the top of the hill all the way down. It got to the point where the community had tens of thousands of people coming every year on tourist buses to see this city on a hill. Of course, all of them paid an admission charge for the tour, as low as ten dollars and as high as twenty, depending on whether they got a group rate. Even the money raised from that, though, wasn't enough to satisfy the Swami's insatiable appetite for both expansion and more power, which were intrinsically connected. The bigger and grander New Vrindaban became, the more his place would be cemented in Krishna culture and the less anyone would dare oppose him.

For years, decades even, all of us had grown familiar with the sight of Krishnas in their traditional garb collecting money at airports. It wasn't panhandling, but it came pretty close. The term for this was *sankirtan*, which meant "devotional fundraising." Normally, when they'd approach you they'd ask if you wanted a copy of their book, essentially the Krishna bible, which they called the Bhagavad Gita. Then they would ask for a donation, whether you took the book or not. They were selling millions of books, but in the case of New Vrindaban, nobody knew exactly how many except for Kirtanananda. Those proceeds, even coupled with the funds gleaned from tourists, wasn't enough, so Ham had come up with a new scam.

He sent his devotees, almost all of them young women, across the country in vans. They were told to scrap the Krishna garb and instead approach people wearing regular clothes. Their instructions were to ask for money for well-known charities like Meals on Wheels, Vietnam veteran associations, schools, and churches. According to Tom Westfall, they called this "the Pick" after a term used by traveling carnivals that used to stay in one place only until locals got wise to the fact they were being taken advantage of or outright pickpocketed.

One of the most popular "Picks" the Krishnas would use had one of the young women approaching a mark at a football tailgate at a major game, usually in the Midwest, and saying, "I'm giving you a ticket… for having too much fun." They were impersonating parking lot security officers, and it was a conversation starter that very often led to the marks purchasing some souvenirs. It was the classic Krishna fundraising gimmick.

Except those souvenirs were counterfeit. The Swami would manufacture major college memorabilia like baseball caps and bumper stickers from schools like Ohio State, Michigan, and Notre Dame. Then he'd dispatch those teams of female followers from New Vrindaban out to stadiums on college football weekends, and they'd walk through the parking lot before and after the games, claiming the proceeds from the merchandise they were selling was going to a charity like Save the Children. The devotees even had official-looking name tags fraudulently identifying them as members of the various charities. It was like a traveling road show in that these women would make stops at smaller venues along the way, where they'd sell more generic merchandise branded with Disney or Charlie Brown characters. (Charles Schultz himself was very upset when he found out that his Charlie Brown characters were among those being peddled.) They frequented concerts, the Indianapolis 500, and the Kentucky Derby to name just a few of their favorite targets.

"Nearly all the vans were registered to a post office box in Moundsville, West Virginia, in Marshall County, so I started getting these calls from cops all over the Midwest where these Big Ten schools were located," says Tom. "And they all wanted to know, 'Who the hell are these people?' I kept building out my database of where the Krishnas were going and what they were targeting. This one police department Des Moines, Iowa, put my name, phone number, and teletype address up on a bulletin board. And the chief said, 'You get anything to do with a Krishna, and I don't give a shit where they're from, call this guy.' And that's how I became the 'Krishna Cop.' Calls would come into the sheriff's department, and whoever answered would take down the information. That gave us a really good notion of where the vans the Swami would dispatch were at any given time. He might have fifty or sixty of them on the road at once, and they'd stay out for months at a time. The women would live like rats, staying in these low-rent motels. They were lucky if they got to take a shower. And when they finally returned, they'd pour all the cash they'd collected on top of Kirtanananda, literally showering him with money."

Many of these young women had come to New Vrindaban to escape the kind of material tasks they were being required to perform on the road. That's when the Swami invented this convoluted religious-like tenet he called the "Doctrine of the Unknown Benefactor." He would tell the devotees they were helping these people spiritually by taking their money, because the movement was doing good things with it.

Following that money was virtually impossible, because it was all cash. And the Swami was smart enough to never make a single deposit in excess of $10,000, because that would have attracted attention from the banks and IRS. Our investigation revealed that there was a room dedicated to nothing but piles of money, and this scam became New Vrindaban's primary means of fundraising, solidifying Keith Ham's hold on power as, potentially, the most powerful guru in the world after Prabhupada's passing. He ran his community like a Mafia don, exuding an aura of power and authority, his rule solely based on intimidation and fear. Meanwhile, behind closed doors, Kirtanananda indulged in whatever whims suited his desires. His appetite for money and power proved insatiable, along with something else…

Young boys.

Here's where we get to a part of Krishna culture that was ripe for transgression and outright pedophilia. Krishna consciousness stated as one if its primary principles that followers should not be attached to anything in this material world, which somehow in their minds included children. So children were removed from their families and placed in boarding schools on the community grounds. Or course, none of the adults watching over the children had been properly vetted or trained at all. No one had any idea how many of them were mentally unstable, had histories of violence, or had been victims of sexual abuse themselves. As a result, physical abuse became the norm, including broken bones and lacerations deep enough to require stitches. The common practice of corporal punishment led to mere toddlers being beaten, paddled, punched, and caned with a rubber hose. The physical abuse was equaled only by the emotional anguish that followed in the wake of the same young children being sexually exploited.

And that unconscionable behavior was further enabled by Kirtananda sending so many of New Vrindaban's younger women out on the Pick.

"They also were the mothers of the community," notes Tom, "and while they were sent out to collect money by lying to people, even their youngest children were often living in the school ashram or a nursery. That meant their kids were in harm's way, and many mothers knew it. New Vrindaban became a center for the mistreatment of children, the presence of pedophiles, and the knowledge that Kirtanananda did not particularly see anything wrong with man/boy love."

How did mothers allow this to happen? Well, first off, in Krishna culture they were deemed inferior to men, and second, they had nowhere else to go for the most part. The alternative to living in New Vrindaban was being homeless on the streets.

"I felt so bad for these people," Tom bemoans. "I would drive through there and see all these little kids and people, these people who were just so deluded, they really wanted to believe in something, and the Swami was taking advantage of them. I mean, it just crushed me. I'd think, 'Why can't we just go in here and get these people out of harm's way?' It wasn't that simple, of course."

As for Keith Ham, Kirtanananda, his power had reached a level where he believed himself immune to arrest or prosecution for anything he did and that nothing he did could demean the power he held over his followers. He was seen constantly in the company of young boys, stroking and massaging them in a classic grooming technique. They would be on his lap, and on one occasion when a ranking member walked in on Ham in his cottage, he found one of these boys, seven or eight maybe, sleeping in his bed. The ranking member's presence seemed to startle Ham, but he quickly regained his composure. The fact that the spiritual leader of New Vrindaban was a pedophile was perhaps the worst-kept secret ever. His followers were either in denial or afraid to report what they saw and suspected, maybe a combination of the two.

"There seems to be a special relationship with you and young boys?" Jane Wallace, host of CBS's weekly television news program *West 57th*, asked him in the fall of 1986. "Can you explain that?"

"That is love," came Kirtanananda's curt answer. "Just as I love the boys, God loves us, and the boys love me."

The blinds had yet to be drawn back from the window to reveal the rampant child sexual abuse on the part of Catholic priests, Boy Scout leaders, and even teachers at elite boarding schools. People were still having trouble getting their heads around the fact that any man could descend to such debauchery, which helped explain how the likes of Keith Ham, and other powerful men like him, got away with it for so long.

Which brings us to Steve Bryant. He and his family lived spitting distance from New Vrindaban, and like many locals, Steve knew it only for its communal nature and rural setting. Attracted to Krishna culture from a distance, Bryant decided to move his family close to New Vrindaban and adopt the lifestyle of the smiling folks he saw around town from time to time. They always looked happy, secure, and safe, something Steve decided he wanted for his family. He managed to have it both ways, maintaining his jewelry business on the one hand while providing what he believed was a warm and pleasant environment for his family.

Then Steve returned from a business trip to find that Kirtanananda had arranged for another Krishna devotee, who was about to come into an inheritance that would become the community's (which meant the Swami's) property, to marry his wife to make sure that devotee remained in New Vrindaban until the Swami could get his hands on his money. The weight of regret settled in, and Steve realized he had made a terrible mistake. His wife refused his overtures to flee, so he took off with his kids in tow, only to be chased down before he was able to put much distance between him and the community. The men who accosted him shoved his crying kids into a van and brought them back to New Vrindaban, while Steve himself pressed on, committed now to bringing down the man responsible for the moral cesspool the community had become.

Steve Bryant was no crusader, no hero, but he became the most committed antagonist Kirtanananda had ever come against, determined to expose the truth of a world as superficial as the sheets of gold leaf stretched over that palace on the hill. It wasn't that devotees weren't willing to talk, just not to the police, since they were certain word of their betrayal to the authorities would get back to the Swami, who would excise them from the community or worse.

But they did talk to Bryant, who continued to gather more and more information. No one seemed to doubt that Thomas Drescher had murdered St. Denis, but the one thing Bryant never found was a witness. He did find accusers, who spoke of the rampant abuse of children going on in New Vrindaban, both physical and sexual. Exposing the Swami for what he was and bringing about his downfall became Bryant's sole mission. He was willing to publicly pull back the curtain on the sordid doings that would reveal Kirtanananda as the child molester he was. Only he was so obsessed that he forgot the old axiom that if you shoot at the king, you better not miss.

Bryant missed.

He had written statements people had signed and cassette tapes they had recorded in his presence, attesting to the rot at the core of New Vrindaban. In 1985, he reported his actions and intentions to the West Virginia State Police and went to the sheriff's department and told the sheriff himself he was going to make a dramatic appearance at the Krishna World Conference, which was being held right in Marshall County. He was going to stride in amid an international gathering of Krishna devotees and expose Keith Ham for the fraud, criminal, and pedophile he was, and let the consequences be damned.

The problem was Steve Bryant made for only a single vote on Election Day, while the Krishna community offered up five hundred or more. So the local sheriff, Donald Bordenkircher, who needed those votes, not only forewarned Ham about Bryant's intention, he took Bryant into custody for illegal possession of a firearm and jailed him for the duration of the conference. This after that same sheriff had recommended Bryant get a gun to protect himself, only to then arrest him at the motel where he was staying after he did just that.

Feeling betrayed by the law enforcement body he trusted with the truth was a rude awakening for Bryant. He'd had enough and decided to end his crusade to expose the sordid truths behind the golden veneer of New Vrindaban. His quest had become too dangerous, and with no one in his corner, he headed west for a new start in California, as far away from the Krishnas as he could get.

As soon as Steve Bryant was released from jail, though, Thomas Drescher was waiting. When Bryant drove off, ready to abandon New Vrindaban and his entire life in West Virginia, Drescher was on his tail. Drescher was still there when Bryant reached California, watching when Bryant pulled over beneath a streetlight in West Los Angeles to sleep for the night.

Bryant was smoking a joint when someone tapped on his window. He turned to find Thomas Drescher standing there with a .45-caliber semiautomatic pistol in his grasp. Two shots to the head later, Steve Bryant was dead.

But the threat he posed to Kirtanananda was still very much alive.

"I was very suspicious of the Swami from that first time I met him," Tom Westfall reiterates. "And the more people I got out of there, the more I realized how really bad it was. I learned about the mishandling of children, the sexual abuse, and the scams. But to make a case we needed a conspiracy, we needed definitive proof of those financial crimes I knew were being committed in the Midwest. I tried to get some federal agencies involved, but it just didn't happen. I felt like I was treading water. I had this massive database of information and nowhere to go with it."

In the wake of the murder of Steve Bryant, that all changed. Tom Westfall found a place where that database he'd compiled would be put to good use, at long last...

My office.

CHAPTER 27

Marshall County, West Virginia

Shortly after his murder on May 22, 1986, Los Angeles homicide detectives identified Steve Bryant and contacted the sheriff's department near his last known address in West Virginia.

"The detective out there asked me if I knew Steve Bryant," Tom Westfall recalls, after the call had been routed to his desk. "And I said, yeah, what about him?"

"Well," homicide detective Paul Tippin told Westfall, "he's dead. How much do you know about these Krishnas?"

"And I'm thinking about the file cabinets and the boxes and all the material I had gathered over the years on the comings and goings of New Vrindaban. So I said, 'Kind of a lot.' I told Tippin and his partner Leroy Orozco to look for Thomas Drescher. Look for him at the airport, look for him everywhere. 'Are you sure about this?' he asked me. And I said, 'Yeah, I'm sure.'"[1]

Tippin and Orozco called back a few days later, dumbstruck.

"They couldn't believe," Tom says, "that a deputy sheriff way back there in West Virginia knew who the killer was, what the motive was, and who had ordered the murder. They were on the next plane out here."[2]

By the time the Los Angeles detectives landed, Tom had learned that the West Virginia State Police had an informant inside New Vrindaban named Randall Gorby. At the time, Kirtanananda was in the process of trying to buy up more and more of the land that surrounded the compound, made up of farms that had been in the same families for generations. Some of the farmers were willing to sell, but plenty more didn't trust Ham and had no desire to do business with them. That's where

Gorby came in. He acted as a go-between, a kind of straw man, to provide insulation so the farmers wouldn't have to deal with the Krishnas directly.

Gorby was also friendly with Thomas Drescher, who called him from Detroit days after killing Steve Bryant. Drescher was on the run and getting nowhere with Kirtanananda when it came to being compensated for his work, so he reached out to Gorby to serve as a middleman in that respect as well. Drescher told Gorby that he'd murdered Bryant on orders from the Swami himself, and now he wanted the money he needed to flee the country. As soon as that call ended, Gorby placed another to the West Virginia State Police.

As soon as they landed, Detectives Tippin and Orozco intended to meet up with their WVSP counterparts and then interview Randall Gorby. By the time they landed, though, someone had blown up Gorby's house with him inside. A gas explosion from a line that had been tampered with literally propelled Gorby out of the house and high into the air. Given that what goes up must come down, he didn't enjoy a soft landing. Somehow, he managed to survive but was not expected to live very long with burns over three-quarters of his body. Tippin and Orozco, accompanied by Tom Westfall and a detective from the West Virginia State Police, rushed to the hospital and obtained vital information from Gorby, who not only gave up Thomas Drescher for the murder of Steve Bryant but also that he was hiding out in Kent, Ohio. Gorby actually survived and was placed in the Witness Protection Program. Even though he'd clearly be in no condition to testify, the West Virginia State Police's tap on his phone had provided everything needed to nail Drescher:

GORBY: Do you have a place to go?

DRESCHER: Nothing. Absolutely nothing.

GORBY: Well, I'd really get on 'em. I can't understand them not coming through with it.

DRESCHER: It's just ridiculous because they've got a hundred thousand [dollars] coming in every week.

GORBY: What agreement did you make with...

DRESCHER: Well, it's just that eight figure [$8,000].

GORBY: Yeah.

DRESCHER: I mean it was just like they, a . . . liked it. They actually thought that was a bargain basement price and they were all happy with it.

GORBY: Yeah.

DRESCHER: It was a bargain fuckin' basement. I mean you couldn't go any lower than that . . . . But I don't think he's setting me up. I really don't think [Kirtananada's] trying to set me up.

GORBY: Oh.

DRESCHER: He was with him for ten straight hours.

GORBY: And [Gorrick] gave him? Had the money?

DRESCHER: No. He got it right out of his hand.

GORBY: Oh, from [Kirtanananda]?

DRESCHER: That's right. He counted it out personally.

GORBY: Well, why the hell didn't he give you the full amount, Tom?

DRESCHER: I don't know.

Aware that Hare Krishnas were vegetarians, law enforcement out in Kent, Ohio, were resourceful enough to check out local establishments that specialized in vegetarian fare and, sure enough, they spotted Drescher's vehicle in the parking lot with him still inside, along with plenty of indication he was planning to flee the country and disappear. After being arrested, though, Drescher refused to give up Kirtanananda, which meant all we had was Randall Gorby's deathbed confession, and that wasn't enough for an arrest on its own.

My office quizzed Tom Westfall on what else he had on Keith Ham and the Krishnas, and Tom told us all about how they had traveled across state lines in vans on those fundraising trips to raise money selling fake major college team paraphernalia. Not only had they violated trademark and copyright laws, the crossing of state lines carried a charge of mail fraud as well. That meant we had the Krishnas dead to rights on several violations of the RICO Act. And there was indisputable evidence that Drescher had crossed state lines to commit murder for hire, which made the murder of Steve Bryant a federal crime because interstate commerce laws had been violated.

Kirtanananda was already on our radar, thanks to the case the West Virginia State Police had opened. Now that the Bryant murder had opened up a Pandora's box of violations and crimes, it was time to ramp up those investigative efforts to the next level by putting a task force together that included FBI Special Agent Jeff Banwell and local law enforcement in the person of Tom Westfall, whose database gave us everything we needed to secure a search warrant.

Thanks to intelligence already provided by Randall Gorby, we knew the man in charge of the fundraising activity at New Vrindaban was Dennis Gorrick, whose son, it turned out, was one of the boys Kirtananda had molested. Gorrick was away when we served the warrants on his premises, including his garage, which was stacked with boxes from floor to ceiling. We not only ended up taking a tractor trailer's worth of financial records and paperwork but also boxes and boxes of counterfeit college sports memorabilia like ball caps, bumper stickers, and coffee mugs. Indisputable proof that federal crimes had indeed been committed.

I gave the job of sorting through the massive amount of financial records contained in those boxes to David Bayha, the revenue agent who had worked the Tony Lobise case, my first after being named an Assistant U.S. Attorney for the Northern District. David was a financial forensics expert extraordinaire who now worked for the U.S. Attorney's Office. He was like a maestro when it came to numbers, able to make them sing. Eventually he came up with a number exceeding $10 million the Krishnas had earned on the road through the Pick, a staggering amount considering it had been collected one bill at a time by those young women traversing the country in old vans. We had everything we needed now to secure a federal RICO indictment, which would include the murder-for-hire plot.

By this time, Thomas Drescher was already in a West Virginia prison, serving his sentence for the murder of Steve Bryant. Even though he refused to give up Kirtanananda, we had enough on him to prove conspiracy to commit murder, which became one of the RICO predicate crimes. All we needed was an investigative grand jury that would allow us to issue subpoenas and bring suspects, targets, and witnesses in to testify toward building the grounds for federal indictments.

But not so fast. My old friend Judge Robert Maxwell refused to convene a grand jury on the patently false grounds that the U.S. Attorney's Office had leaked information before a grand jury, indictment, or trial took place. As a result, the lawyer for the Krishnas, Jim Lees, moved to disqualify our office. There were leaks, all right, but I believe they had actually originated with Sheriff Donald Bordenkircher. Those five-hundred-plus votes he was after when he betrayed Steve Bryant were still there for the taking, giving him more than enough motive to work on the Krishnas' behalf. My office, meanwhile, had nothing to gain by leaking.

Nonetheless, a hearing was held on the disqualification motion made by Lees. To give himself cover, Judge Maxwell had a second federal judge, Judge William Kidd, sit with him to rule on Lees's motion. While not granting the Krishna attorney's motion, Judge Maxwell still refused to convene a grand jury. That left me with all this evidence Tom Westfall had provided on the Krishnas, along with all the evidence gleaned from our search of Dennis Gorrick's premises, but no grand jury to present it to in order to fully investigate the case. This was a gross violation of procedure on Maxwell's part, since there is a specific statute in the United States Code that requires a federal judge to convene a special grand jury when requested by the Department of Justice. Unlike grand juries seated on a regular basis, though, Maxwell would have no power over a special grand jury convened on an investigative basis, helping to explain the inexplicable. Three separate times in the spring of 1987, the Justice Department, through Assistant Attorneys General William Weld and John Keeney, certified that a special grand jury was, in fact, needed.

"William A. Kolibash, United States Attorney for the Northern District of West Virginia," Weld wrote on April 8, 1987, in a letter to Judge Maxwell, "has advised me that his office is engaged in several major investigations of criminal activity in the Northern District of West Virginia, involving narcotics trafficking, organized crime, and several other matters, that urgently require the attention of a grand jury. With respect to at least one of these investigations, the statute of limitations will expire in a matter of weeks.... Accordingly, I respectfully request that you authorize a Special Grand Jury to be summoned to investigate criminal activity in the Northern District of West Virginia. It is requested that the Special Grand Jury be empaneled on or before April 17, 1987."

All three times Maxwell ignored what were effectively orders from his superiors, and the special grand jury was not convened. That left my office with no choice but to take the exceedingly rare step of mandamusing Maxwell at the Fourth Circuit. Mandamusing means going to a higher court to get an official to perform their official duty when they refuse to do so, which meant we were asking the Fourth Circuit to order Maxwell to convene a grand jury to investigate the Krishnas because he had no reason not to. Maxwell hired none other than Jim Lees, the lawyer for the Krishnas who had moved to disqualify my office from the case in the first place, to represent him before the Fourth Circuit to oppose our mandamus petition. Such a writ is defined as "an order from a court to an inferior government official ordering the government official to properly fulfill their official duties or correct an abuse of discretion." Maxwell had abused his discretion more times than I could count, but this would be the last time he did so with me, and I beat him one last time.

Instead of actually issuing a writ of mandamus, the higher court issued an opinion that stated something to the effect, "We are sure that Judge Maxwell will do the right thing." The Fourth Circuit didn't want to embarrass him, but the writing was on the wall, so he went ahead and convened the grand jury in July 1987. Had it been up to Maxwell, though, there never would have been an investigation into the sordid activities going on at New Vrindaban.

Keith Ham, Kirtanananda, of course, denied having anything to do with the scheme, which meant we needed witnesses who would testify otherwise. Once those potential witnesses learned they were facing twenty-five years or more on mail-fraud counts, it wasn't hard to make them see the light of day. Kirtanananda was hanging them out to dry, and their only recourse was to implicate him in the massive scheme that had raised millions of dollars in unreported cash for the New Vrindaban community.

While the FBI and my office built the federal case, Tom Westfall set about proving what he'd always believed to be the truth: that Thomas Drescher had murdered Charles St. Denis on the night St. Denis's Chevy Blazer was found parked down the street from a friend's home in Bridgeport, Ohio, after he allegedly fled the compound and disappeared. Charging Drescher with first-degree murder was enough to get him transferred from Ohio to West Virginia, even though the more recent murder of Steve Bryant had taken place in California. (Drescher was actually found guilty of the murder at a second trial in Los Angeles, at which I testified as well, but ended up serving his time in West Virginia.)

Meanwhile, shortly after St. Denis's murder, Dan Reid, the former friend who'd set him up, fled New Vrindaban, and the Los Angeles homicide detectives Tippin and Orozco we were already working with found him in California. He was still living under his own name and doing accounting work for a posh Beverly Hills law firm.

Reid was brought back to West Virginia, where we offered him the opportunity to plead guilty to a lesser charge of involuntary manslaughter, as opposed to first-degree murder, on the condition that he give up Thomas Drescher as the man who had made Charles St. Denis disappear. Reid recounted the gruesome facts of that evening and, in the end, pinpointed the location where he and Drescher had buried the body. Digging up the remains was icing on that particular cake. We had Drescher dead to rights on St. Denis's murder, and when he refused to implicate the Swami in either that killing or Steve Bryant's, he was sentenced to life with no chance of parole.

On top of the murders, we had already heard rumors of sexual molestation and abuse being rampant within the community, but New Vrindaban was so insular, none of the families afflicted ever came forward to report it. As can be the case, though, closing one investigation opens the floodgates on others. All those rumors, it turned out, were true. Since child sexual abuse is not a federal crime, it was sheriff's department detective sergeant Tom Westfall who ran with that.

"I got enough information to get a warrant on one of the teachers. And after I arrested him, and I realized that he was actually part of the victim circle, which is not unusual in sexual assaults of young people, that he had been a student at the school and he too had been molested by teachers or people who were assigned to the school. So I was trying to get a handle on just how many people in the school had been molested. And I had a picture of this group of kids that had turned up in the midst of my investigation. And I said to the teacher I'd charged, 'Could you point out how many of those kids had been molested?' He stopped for a long time. And he looked up to me and said, 'It'd be easier for me to show you the ones that weren't.'"[3]

The picture in question was taken on the steps of the Palace of Gold, the temple the Swami had built to honor Prabhupada, spiritual leader of the Krishna movement. The tragic irony of that was striking, because the lives of these boys had been destroyed in the very shadow of that structure.

Kirtanananda himself was seldom seen outside the company of young boys. One or more of them was always around, often seated in his lap as he conducted the general Krishna business of the day, almost like they were ornaments. Tom Westfall interviewed enough victims to ascertain that the sexual abuse had been taking place for years, well more than a decade, and that Steve Bryant's allegations, if anything, understated the ongoing level of moral depravity.

That said, our focus was trained on building a federal case. We intended to use the sexual abuse to fill out the whole of our narrative because, remember, the motive for Kirtanananda ordering Steve Bryant's death was the very real threat that Bryant was about to reveal the proliferation of such abhorrent behavior taking place at New Vrindaban. Nobody in the community would follow somebody who was involved in that kind of activity. So, under our theory of the prosecution, then, the motive for Bryant's murder was to silence him, to stop this information flow about both the epidemic of sexual molestation and the Swami's active involvement in it.

By that point, Thomas Drescher was serving his sentence at a West Virginia state prison and still refusing to implicate Keith Ham in the murders of Charles St. Denis or Steven Bryant. To strengthen his bonds of loyalty, Ham actually promoted Drescher to the rank of swami to assure he wouldn't talk. That move backfired somewhat, since Krishna followers the world over questioned how a convicted murderer could be worthy of such a sainted position. Kirtanananda's credibility might have been waning. He had been formally excommunicated by Krishna officials in New York as well as prohibited from setting foot in New Vrindaban. Drescher, though, stayed loyal, which didn't stop us from obtaining RICO indictments against Ham in May 1990.

"The founder and leader of a Hare Krishna community was indicted by a federal grand jury Thursday in an alleged scheme to murder, kidnap and beat his followers, authorities said," the *Washington Post* reported on May 30. "Keith Ham, 54, also known as Kirtanananda Swami Bhaktipada, was named on five counts of racketeering and conspiracy to commit murder and six counts of mail fraud. The indictment was handed up by a special grand jury in Elkins. One of the racketeering counts alleges a conspiracy involving the death of Stephen Bryant, a dissident member of the Krishna community who was shot on a Los Angeles street in May 1986."[4]

The grand jury Judge Maxwell hadn't wanted to convene had come through, and we had an ironclad case when we went to trial in Martinsburg's district courthouse before Judge Robert Merhige on March 11, 1991. Even the twenty or so witnesses who appeared for the defense, in contrast to almost seventy for the prosecution, were unable to do anything but enhance the case we were making. And one of our witnesses who testified to being molested by Kirtanananda was the son of Dennis Gorrick, the man in charge of New Vrindaban's illicit fundraising operation who had agreed to cooperate with us in return for a lighter sentence that turned out to be three years. The testimony of those victims helped us establish that the Krishna practice of removing children from the care of their parents at such a young age had created an environment that practically invited pedophilia. And when the defense tried to impeach that theory, it failed miserably, as in the case of Henry Doktorski, a rebuttal witness Jim Lees put on the stand as reported by Doktorski himself in volume 9 of his series on the Swami and New Vrindaban called *Gold, Guns and God*.

> LEES: Having a three-year-old and having been involved in the school system, did you hear allegations of sexual molestation of children in the New Vrindaban community?
> DOKTORSKI: Yes, I first read about it in the newspaper.
> LEES: Based upon your own firsthand information of living there, for those years as a parent, are you satisfied New Vrindaban is a safe place to bring up your child?
> DOKTORSKI: If it wasn't, I would not live there.

On cross-examination, the Assistant U.S. Attorney assisting me on the case, Michael Stein, posed only one question:

> STEIN: How much time has your daughter spent at the ashram, sleeping over at New Vrindaban?
> DOKTORSKI: My daughter lives at home with my wife and I.[5]

At the end of the seven-day trial, the jury found the Swami guilty on eight counts of the indictment, including RICO violations and mail fraud, easily enough to lead to a lengthy sentence in federal prison. The Swami appealed the guilty verdict and was allowed to remain free on bond, pending the results of that appeal. He hired none other than Alan Dershowitz to handle his appeal. Dershowitz, no stranger to taking on unpopular clients like Claus von Bülow and O. J. Simpson, found another in Keith Ham.

In his argument before the Fourth Circuit Court of Appeals, Dershowitz hammered home the fact that the testimony entered into evidence regarding the abuse of women and sexual abuse of children was unduly prejudicial, since those were not crimes the Swami had been charged with, as they are not federal crimes. The appeals court concurred and ordered a new trial, writing in part, "We accept without need of extensive argument that implications of child molestation, homosexuality, and abuse of women unfairly prejudice a defendant. Indeed, no evidence could be more inflammatory or more prejudicial than allegations of child molestation. When evidence of a defendant's involvement in several of these activities is presented to the jury, the risk of unfair prejudice is compounded. In such a case, we fear that jurors will convict a defendant based on the jurors' disdain or their belief that the defendant's prior bad acts make guilt more likely. Furthermore, we are especially sensitive to prejudice in a trial where defendants are members of an unpopular religion."

The justices of the Fourth Circuit had gotten plenty right in my tenure, but I believed then as I believe now that they got this one wrong. Our case had clearly established, beyond all reasonable doubt, that children were being sexually abused at New Vrindaban, that Kirtanananda was guilty of sexually abusing children himself. That, in turn, provided the motive for him to order the death of Steve Bryant out of fear of being exposed for what he was. It wasn't the prosecution that made his behavior "inflammatory" and "prejudicial"; Keith Ham's behavior had done that all on its own. Sometimes the law follows common sense and other times the law defies it.

I had talked with Judge Merhige after the trial was over, and he expressed concern over the testimony about the child abuse he had allowed in. In the federal statutes, the specific law that was cause for consternation was Rule 404B, which covers the rule of evidence, balancing the relevance of that evidence against its prejudicial effects. In the end, the Fourth Circuit had determined that the harm caused by the latter outweighed the clear relevance of Ham's sexual abuse of young boys. Here it was we had a killer in Thomas Drescher who indisputably traveled across the whole country to murder Steve Bryant in Los Angeles and, in the Fourth Circuit's mind anyway, we were *not* supposed to present the evidence as to why? Were we supposed to leave the jury thinking the murder happened in a vacuum, that the Swami had ordered it based on a whim? I knew at that point I'd almost surely not be in office when it came time to retry the Swami, but I remained confident that my successor would prevail. Interestingly enough, the same justification the Fourth Circuit employed in overturning our verdict was later employed by comparable appeals courts in overturning the convictions of both Bill Cosby and Harvey Weinstein, so in that respect I guess we were ahead of the curve.

Ham was allowed to remain free on bail while he awaited a new trial, and in a stroke of ironic counterpoint that would lead to his undoing, he was also allowed to return to New Vrindaban. He was being driven about in a Winnebago motor home outside the commune when a motorist behind the vehicle witnessed the Swami having sex with a boy through an open curtain directly over the bed. He knew immediately who he was looking at, and reports spread in viral fashion that the Swami had sexually assaulted a victim from India or Malaysia he'd taken with him from New Vrindaban for a "ride" in the motor home. That spurred even his most ardent supporters to turn against him. The floodgates opened, and all the accusations of abuse spilled out into the open. The dam, you might say, had finally broken, and the devotees who had bowed to him as God on earth at long last saw Ham as the devil he really was.

Among those devotees was none other than Thomas Drescher, who heard all about the now confirmed allegations from inside his prison cell. When the Swami was retried before Judge Merhige in 1996, a disgusted Drescher took the stand. I had already left the U.S. Attorney's Office by then, and Michael Stein, who'd assisted me on the original trial, took lead when the Swami was retried. I was never informed that it was even happening or consulted in any way. Out of sight, out of mind, I guess.

And since the government now had a smoking-gun witness in Thomas Drescher, the case was pretty much a slam dunk in stark contrast to the one we had built almost entirely on circumstantial evidence, which was always very challenging.

"Did the Swami tell you to kill Charles St. Denis?" Stein asked Drescher, the key question in his two days on the witness stand.

"At first he just waved his hand," Drescher answered in a low, droll monotone, imitating the motion, "and I told him, 'No, no, you can't just wave your hand. You have to tell me. Do you want me to kill Chaka [St. Denis's Krishna name]?' And he said, 'Yes. Kill him.'"

Marshall County Sheriff's Office homicide detective Tom Westfall was the next and final witness for the prosecution. He had just been sworn in and taken the stand when defense counsel rose.

"Your Honor, may we approach the bench?"

The attorneys requested a recess in order to discuss a plea agreement. The jury was dismissed and the courtroom emptied except for Tom, who remained in the witness box, and Judge Merhige himself. The judge looked down at Tom sitting there uncomfortably.

"I think you got him this time, son," he said from the bench.

After the Swami pled guilty to one count of racketeering, mail fraud, and conspiracy to commit murder, Judge Merhige sentenced him to 360 months in prison. The Swami thought he had said *thirty-six* months, which, for a man who never expected to spend a day in jail, caused his mouth to drop.

"Thirty-six months?" he was heard questioning his lawyer, in shock over being sentenced for that long a term.

"No," the lawyer corrected, "*three hundred and sixty months.* Thirty years."[6]

Even though I had no involvement in that trial, the groundwork my office had laid allowed for justice to finally prevail.

"Let me tell you something," Tom Westfall said at the time, "this case never would have happened if it wasn't for Bill Kolibash. I was a man yelling into the wind for years, trying to get someone to listen to me. That only happened when Bill Kolibash decided enough was enough."

Interestingly enough, our investigation wasn't the first time Tom had crossed paths with Thomas Drescher.

"The first time I questioned him after his arrest on the Bryant murder, I remembered how during the Vietnam War he'd been picked up by the military police in Okinawa on a night I was serving as the duty officer.

"'You were in Okinawa, right?' I asked him.

"'Yeah,' Drescher said.

"'You remember the night the MPs brought you into this office?'

"'Yeah. How'd you know that?'

"I told him, 'Because you were five feet away, talking to the MP seated right next to me.' And, let me tell you, there was something that unsettled me about him even back then."

Like Tom Westfall, I kept track of the bigger picture, specifically how our experience with the Krishnas compared to that of other cults that run afoul of the establishment. In Jonestown and Waco, specifically, followers twisted around the finger of a megalomaniac had culminated in terribly tragic endings. But we got the Swami before anything like that could take place at New Vrindaban. And I take great pride in the fact that our efforts, to a large degree, led the Krishna movement to enact sweeping reforms across the globe. Primarily, these included the way children are educated and supervised, along with more checks, balances, and supervision incorporated, so that the debauchery that defined New Vrindaban never happens within the Krishna community again. Basically, by changing the way Krishnas operated at New Vrindaban, throughout the country, and abroad, the movement's leadership conceded the very facts the Fourth Circuit had denied on appeal.

The Swami's health declined rapidly once he was imprisoned, and the sentence was later commuted to twelve years. Ultimately, he was released in June 2004, having served only eight years, and immigrated to India, where he died in 2011.

As for the community that the Swami founded, the Palace of Gold is just a temple now, where services are held and tours are still given. Not that New Vrindaban needs the money; natural gas found beneath the Krishnas' land more than sustains its existence. The reserves were discovered after the Swami had gone to prison, meaning the illegal activity involving the Pick, all those trademark violations, and the mail fraud hadn't really been necessary at all.

The primary teachings of Krishna philosophy remain to this day, including that "one performs all actions as offerings to Krishna and does nothing for one's own sense of gratification."

Keith Ham, aka Kirtanananda Swami Bhaktipada, must have missed that one.

EPILOGUE

Someone took a shot at me my last day on the job. Although I was technically "fired" on President Bill Clinton's January 1992 inauguration, I remained on the job until July 1993 while the administration was in disarray over filling the attorney general position. Actually, I enjoyed bipartisan support to stay in office, but West Virginia was then a Democratic state, so the notion of a leftover from a Republican administration in office staying on just wasn't palpable.

Not that I didn't have my share of supporters, including James Toler, who was a columnist for the *Charleston Gazette*.

"It's been an open secret for many years that the mob was active in Wheeling," he wrote on February 24, 1993. "But nobody ever did much about it until Kolibash came along and started bashing them. He has a proven record of convictions of organized crime figures and his investigations have resulted in dozens of convictions on racketeering, drug distribution and tax charges. He led a lengthy investigation into the Hare Krishna commune that resulted in several convictions for using murder, kidnapping and fraud to protect an illegal multimillion-dollar enterprise."[1]

The *Times West Virginian* agreed, writing on its editorial page that I had "become synonymous with fighting drugs and organized crime. His crusades involving drug dealers and members of the underworld in Northern West Virginia have been well documented."[2]

Well, I'm not sure they were crusades. I was just doing my job, and politics never entered into a single decision I made in how I ran the U.S. Attorney's Office. I had never been overly partisan toward one party or the other, even though plenty of U.S. Attorneys were nothing more than political appointees who hadn't earned their positions based on merit. I wanted to keep the job I'd held for a dozen years and even compiled a forty-seven-page report on my successful prosecutions and pending

Bill Kolibash (center) receiving the 1991 F.E.I.A.A. (Federal Executive Institute Alumni Association) Federal Executive of the Year Award.

cases. Despite an outpouring of support from multiple quarters, though, the Clinton administration opted to appoint a Democratic successor.

My office celebrated my retirement with friends and family on my final day of serving as U.S. Attorney for the Northern District of West Virginia with a dinner at the Hellenic Center in Wheeling. After the dinner, I, along with many of the agents, officers, and staff, continued our celebration at a local "cop bar" called Rose's. I was very humbled by all the accolades and gifts I received that evening, except for one. The next morning I realized that one of the rear tires on my car was flat. The AAA driver who came to slap on the spare showed me a bullet hole in the sidewall. Needless to say, that tire couldn't be salvaged and, to this day, I have no idea who fired the shot. This was a different kind of recognition of my retirement.

Before I stepped down, I tried several other cases, although none of them would approach the magnitude of the Krishnas. My office did take down major gambling operations in the Upper Ohio Valley involving video poker machines owned by brothers John and Benjamin Dobkin that smacked of the old-school brand of strong-arming I had fought against throughout my twenty-year career in the U.S. Attorney's Office. The Dobkins pretty much maintained a monopoly on the vending machine concession for Wheeling and beyond, and they indirectly controlled the local establishments who relied on those machines for a large percentage of their profits. "If you want our cigarette, shuffleboard, bowling, and other machines," they'd say, "then you have to take our poker machines." That's how the brothers forced their machines into all these businesses, in large part as a means to launder money. They were prosecuted for violations of the money laundering and federal gambling statutes in cases that were tried after I left office.

Around that same time, the Christian Science movement did a hit piece on me, I guess because the efforts of my office had basically revealed the true colors of their fellow cultists in the Krishnas. They sent an investigator out here who worked in tandem with none other than Donald Bordenkircher, the Marshall County sheriff who had betrayed Steve Bryant and later might well have been responsible for leaking the information Judge Maxwell blamed me for. They created a sham report they circulated to all the local media, claiming that "U.S. Attorney William Kolibash, head of the U.S. Attorney's Office in the Northern District of West Virginia, and others are involved in various activities that constitute violations of United States laws, codes of ethics and violations and abuses of the civil rights of citizens of the United States of America."

Like I said, a hit job that was long on innuendo and unsubstantiated accusations but short on both evidence and direct testimony.

"Do you have anything you'd like to say in response?" a reporter from a local television affiliate asked me.

"Sure. Run with this story and I'm going to own your TV station."

There was nothing valid or viable to this supposed report, and everyone who mattered knew it. You know you're doing a good job when they come after you that way. The story never aired on that local television station.

As a result of my work on the Krishna case, I was asked to deliver the keynote speech at a convention in Oklahoma City being sponsored by the Cult Awareness Network. That group advocated for victims of cults and drew the ire of groups like the Christian Scientists because the conference sponsors specialized in reprogramming those who'd been brainwashed by cults. They had based their very existence on making people aware of the dangers of cults and preventing harm being done to members they rightfully viewed as victims.

Unlike Tom Westfall's efforts to help spirit away those fleeing New Vrindaban on their own, members of the Cult Awareness Network were known to occasionally kidnap brainwashed cult victims and help them return to their former lives. I could see why that would run afoul of groups like the Christian Scientists, who actually contacted the Justice Department and urged the attorney general to stop me from speaking, which he refused to do. I needed security the whole time I was there because of the very real possibility of violence for good reason: the focus of my presentation was how we were able to dismantle the Krishnas in West Virginia, and I guess the Christian Scientists were afraid somebody would be coming after them next.

Speaking of which, not long after someone put a bullet in my tire, I went to work for the Wheeling law firm of Phillips, Gardill, Kaiser & Altmeyer. I had other offers, some of them considerable, but those would have taken me to Charleston or even Washington, DC. I wanted to stay closer to my family and friends, and the firm needed somebody with my background of litigation experience. They'd had two partners leave, which made the timing perfect, and I was able to handle tax cases and white-collar crime. I had no desire to become a high-profile defense attorney, because I had a prosecutorial mentality that kept me from being sympathetic to criminal defendants, particularly anything involving drugs. By contrast, this was more of a transactional firm whose major clients ranged from banks to the local diocese to the Wheeling Park Commission to Delaware North, which operated the racetrack and casino on Wheeling Island that Big Bill Lias had built up from practically nothing decades before.

When I think back on virtually all the cases I tried as U.S. Attorney, what stands out the most was the teamwork that allowed us to mount so many successful prosecutions. All those RICO cases never could have been made without the likes of the FBI, IRS, West Virginia State Police, DEA, and local law enforcement working in tandem with us, not to mention the investigative grand juries my office helped pioneer. I always told members of our task force that I'd listen to anything they had to say and consider everything they wanted, while jokingly reminding them that I had one more vote than they did. It was never about ego, just results, in stark contrast to the failed prosecutions of the New York gangster John Gotti during the same period my task forces—populated by the likes of Thom Kirk, Tom Burgoyne, Lowell Maxey, Larry Mincks, Jeff Sandy, and Tom Westfall—were taking down Paul Hankish and the Swami.

"The most serious charges in the 1985 Gambino RICO indictment died with [Paul] Castellano and terminally ill Mafia boss Aniello Dellacroce, leaving Gotti to face lesser charges that had little to do with his sudden eminence as a mob boss," an article on Encyclopedia.com noted. "The government's case also was hampered by a bitter jurisdictional dispute between several state and federal law enforcement agencies. Each was building its own case against Gotti. None wanted to share witnesses or information for fear of jeopardizing its own chances for a successful conviction."[3]

Gotti ended up being acquitted in March 1987, and his next prosecution was similarly riddled by the kind of jurisdictional squabbles my office had never faced.

"Secret tapes which purportedly showed Gotti's desire for revenge were imperfect," the same Encyclopedia.com article continues. "The issue was further confused when state and federal prosecutors gave jurors differing transcripts of the same secretly taped conversation."[4]

John Gotti was finally convicted in April 1992 not because the dueling federal and state agencies had a sudden change of heart so much as the testimony of his former associate Sammy "the Bull" Gravano implicating Gotti directly in ten murders.

My daughter, one of this book's coauthors, is a lawyer too, although her career has moved along an entirely different track than mine. And I'm with the same Wheeling law firm today, thirty years later, and enjoy the work and the law as much as I ever have.

In looking back on my career as a U.S. Attorney, perhaps the best encapsulation was provided in an interview I gave to the *Panorama*, the *Dominion Post* newspaper's Sunday magazine, in August 1989.

"My goals are to improve life in this state. I want to create a better lifestyle. I want to create a better climate to come into this state to set up a business. I want this to be a good place to raise children. I think the state needs things for young people to do, for one thing. There are voids here for 18 and 19-year-olds. There's nothing to do. In Wheeling for example, drinking is such a tradition. Drugs are only a step away. I see drugs across the whole spectrum of society. I want to do something about drug dealers. I want to wipe them out."[5]

Nothing I've done since I left the Northern District compared to what I did over those twenty years, especially the final twelve-plus as U.S. Attorney. The only regret I have is that I couldn't save the victims whose lives were destroyed or ended by the likes of the drug dealers, killers, kingpins, and cultists I prosecuted. I could never rest without knowing I had done everything I could to make my city, my state, and my country a better and safer place, which suits me just fine.

Because justice never rests either.

Endnotes

CHAPTER 1

1 "Annual Report 1973," issued by the Internal Revenue Service

CHAPTER 2

1 "Sheriff Donell Beats the Racketeers," (*Reader's Digest*; April, 1980)
2 *Truth... and Consequences: 7 Who Would Not be Silenced,* Greg Mitchell (W. W. Norton; January 1, 1987)
3 "'They Are Not Club Activities': The Hell's Angels and the Early Struggles of the RICO Statute," David Kurlander (CAFE.com; November 11, 2021)
4 "W. Virginia Prosecutor, 24 Indicted in Gambling in W. Va.," Judith Vollmer (*Pittsburgh Press*; February 8, 1979)

CHAPTER 3

1 "Fragging and the United States of Rage," Eugene Linden (The Bulwark; November 22, 2021)

CHAPTER 4

1 "A Judge Who Has Things His Way," James Cramer (*Washington Post*; November 23, 1980)
2 "A Judge Who Has Things His Way," James Cramer (*Washington Post*; November 23, 1980)
3 "A Judge Who Has Things His Way," James Cramer (*Washington Post*; November 23, 1980)
4 "Maxwell Accused of Defying Law," Janet Boyle (*Intelligencer*; November 22, 1980)
5 "No ill will in legal clash, U.S. judge says," Jack McCarthy (*Gazette-Mail*; July 10, 1988)
6 "Reversible judge," (*Charleston Gazette*; October 21, 1988)
7 "Maxwell's Silver Hammer," James Cramer (*American Lawyer*; April, 1981)

CHAPTER 6

1 "Stories in the Shine," Mickie Meinhardt (*The Bitter Southerner*; June 30, 2020)
2 "But Did You Know... Prohibition & Franklin Country, the Moonshine Capital of the World," Patricia Keppel Anderson, Virginia.org
3 "Moonshiner History," uncredited and undated (Moonshiner28)
4 "Moonshine: Big Business in the Backwoods," James J. Nagle (*New York Times*; June 3, 1973)
5 "Lohmann: Varina brothers look back at their moonshining days," Bill Lohmann (*Richmond Times-Dispatch*; January 22, 2017)

6 "Appalachia Moonshiners Are Replacing Their Stills With Marijuana Patches," James Branscome (*Washington Post*; August 8, 1977)
7 "Blood and Whiskey," Peter Carlson (*Washington Post*; May 24, 1998)
8 "Larry R. Mincks, Special Agent with IRS, Recipient of Major Award for Narcotics Probes," Brenda J. Anselene (*Clarksburg Exponent*; November 15, 1985)
9 "Larry R. Mincks, Special Agent with IRS, Recipient of Major Award for Narcotics Probes," Brenda J. Anselene (*Clarksburg Exponent*; November 15, 1985)
10 "Appalachia Moonshiners Are Replacing Their Stills With Marijuana Patches," James Branscome (*Washington Post*; August 8, 1977)

CHAPTER 7

1 "Cocaine: Middle Class High," Michael Demarest (*Time*; July 6, 1981)
2 "What it was really like to be in Miami during the crazy cocaine boom," (*PBS News Hour*; December 21, 2017)

CHAPTER 9

1 "International Financial Terrorism: Organized Crime of the 21st Century," Jeff Sandy (*Counter Terrorist*; June/July, 2016)

CHAPTER 10

1 *Murder Never Dies: Crime and Corruption in the Friendly City*, George Sidiropolis (Headline Books; December 20, 2016)
2 *Murder Never Dies: Crime and Corruption in the Friendly City*, George Sidiropolis (Headline Books; December 20, 2016)
3 "... he maintained a fleet of cars and trucks with the floorboards jerry-rigged to allow for secret compartments to hide the liquor, and even retrofitted a fuel tanker to haul Canadian whiskey all the way to Wheeling." *Murder Never Dies: Crime and Corruption in the Friendly City*, George Sidiropolis (Headline Books; December 20, 2016)
4 *Murder Never Dies: Crime and Corruption in the Friendly City*, George Sidiropolis (Headline Books; December 20, 2016)
5 "The Wheeling Mob: Part 2," Steve Novotney (Weelunk.com; March 28, 2015)
6 *Murder Never Dies: Crime and Corruption in the Friendly City*, George Sidiropolis (Headline Books; December 20, 2016)

CHAPTER 11

1 "Thomas Kirk Takes Down the Top Organized Crime Figure in West Virginia," *Game of Crimes* (Episode 57; July 14, 2022)

CHAPTER 12

1 "Thomas Kirk Takes Down the Top Organized Crime Figure in West Virginia," *Game of Crimes* (Episode 57; July 14, 2022)
2 "Thomas Kirk Takes Down the Top Organized Crime Figure in West Virginia," *Game of Crimes* (Episode 57; July 14, 2022)
3 "U.S.-owned taxi service driven into bankruptcy," (Clarksburg Exponent Telegram, uncredited and undated)

CHAPTER 13

1 "Son, grandson see Robert Kirk's name put on National Law Enforcement Memorial Wall," Bonny Rushbrook (*The Herald-Dispatch*; May 22, 2008)

CHAPTER 15

1 "The Whores, The Help, and The Hooligans," Bill Hogan (Weelunk.com; December 13, 2014)
2 "The Wheeling Mob: Part 3; Harlotry, Husting, and Whoredom," Steve Novotney (Weelunk.com; April 11, 2015)
3 *Murder Never Dies: Crime and Corruption in the Friendly City*, George Sidiropolis (Headline Books; December 20, 2016)
4 "The madam must die: A 1974 death what wasn't what it seemed," Tim Botos and Shane Hoover (*Fayetteville Observer*; October 31, 2019)

CHAPTER 16

1 "Crack Invades the Countryside," Malcolm McConnell (*Reader's Digest*; February, 1989)
2 "Elusive Jamaican Drug Gangs Frustrate Police," Victoria Churchville (*Washington Post*; February 23, 1988)
3 "U.S. Captures 120 in Gang Roundup," *New York Times* archive (*New York Times*; October 14, 1988)
4 "Jamaican Gangs Wage War Over Drugs, Area Police Say," Linda Wheeler and Keith Harriston (*Washington Post*; November 19, 1987)
5 "Crack Invades the Countryside," Malcolm McConnell (*Reader's Digest*; February, 1989)
6 "Born Fi' Dead: A Journey Through the Jamaican Posse Underground," Laurie Gunst (Cannongate Books 3rd edition; January 1, 2003)
7 "The Federal Bureau of Alcohol, Tobacco and Firearms (ATF) estimated that there were at least 40 Jamaican posses with more than 13,000 members operating in the United States," from "Afro-Lineal Organized Crime" (New Jersey State Commission of Investigation; March, 1991)
8 "A Jamaican Invasion in West Virginia," Mark Miller (*Newsweek*; March 28, 1988)
9 "Crack Invades the Countryside," Malcolm McConnell (*Reader's Digest*; February, 1989)
10 "Crack Invades the Countryside," Malcolm McConnell (*Reader's Digest*; February, 1989)
11 "U.S. Captures 120 in Gang Roundup," *New York Times* archive (*New York Times*; October 14, 1988)

CHAPTER 17

1 "More indictments expected in bust of five-state drug ring," UPI Archives (UPI; July 7, 1987)

CHAPTER 18

1 "Lancaster native, retired FBI agent, honored as Good Samaritan," The Item (*Telegram & Gazette*; July 23, 2021)
2 "Respected, beloved Sheriff Tom Burgoyne dies at age 82," D.K. Wright (WTRF.com; January 26, 2003)

CHAPTER 19

1 "The Mob Bombing Heard Around the Valley," Steve Novotney (Lede; January 18, 2022)
2 "The Wheeling Mob Part 5: Dynamite, Trained Monkeys, and Dead Broke," Steve Novotney (Weelunk.com; May 9, 2015)
3 *Murder Never Dies: Crime and Corruption in the Friendly City,* George Sidiropolis (Headline Books; December 20, 2016)
4 *Murder Never Dies: Crime and Corruption in the Friendly City,* George Sidiropolis (Headline Books; December 20, 2016)
5 "The Wheeling Mob Part 5: Dynamite, Trained Monkeys, and Dead Broke," Steve Novotney (Weelunk.com; May 9, 2015)
6 "The Wheeling Mob Part 5: Dynamite, Trained Monkeys, and Dead Broke," Steve Novotney (Weelunk.com; May 9, 2015)
7 "The Wheeling Mob Part 5: Dynamite, Trained Monkeys, and Dead Broke," Steve Novotney (Weelunk.com; May 9, 2015)
8 *Murder Never Dies: Crime and Corruption in the Friendly City,* George Sidiropolis (Headline Books; December 20, 2016)
9 "The Wheeling Mob Part 1: The Bosses, Bookies, and Burgoyne," Steve Novotney (Weelunk.com; October 1, 2016)

CHAPTER 20

1 *Murder Never Dies: Crime and Corruption in the Friendly City,* George Sidiropolis (Headline Books; December 20, 2016)
2 *Steel City Mafia: Blood, Betrayal and Pittsburgh's Last Don,* Paul N. Hodos (The History Press; April 17, 2023)
3 *Steel City Mafia: Blood, Betrayal and Pittsburgh's Last Don,* Paul N. Hodos (The History Press; April 17, 2023)

CHAPTER 22

1 "Hankish accomplices sentenced," uncredited (*Pittsburg Post-Gazette*; September 1, 1990)

CHAPTER 23

1 *Krishnas: Gurus. Karma. Murder,* from executive producers Joseph Freed, Allison Berkley, Tara Long, David Holthouse and Tim Clancy; produced by Entertainment One Reality Productions, LLC. and Marwar Junction Productions (Released by Peacock; October 23, 2023)
2 "Not What Krishna Had in Mind," Anne Fadiman (*New York Times*; November 20, 1988)
3 *Krishnas: Gurus. Karma. Murder,* from executive producers Joseph Freed, Allison Berkley, Tara Long, David Holthouse and Tim Clancy; produced by Entertainment One Reality Productions, LLC. and Marwar Junction Productions (Released by Peacock; October 23, 2023)
4 *Krishnas: Gurus. Karma. Murder,* from executive producers Joseph Freed, Allison Berkley, Tara Long, David Holthouse and Tim Clancy; produced by Entertainment One Reality Productions, LLC. and Marwar Junction Productions (Released by Peacock; October 23, 2023)

CHAPTER 26

1 *Krishnas: Gurus. Karma. Murder,* from executive producers Joseph Freed, Allison Berkley, Tara Long, David Holthouse and Tim Clancy; produced by Entertainment One Reality Productions, LLC. and Marwar Junction Productions (Released by Peacock; October 23, 2023)
2 *Krishnas: Gurus. Karma. Murder,* from executive producers Joseph Freed, Allison Berkley, Tara Long, David Holthouse and Tim Clancy; produced by Entertainment One Reality Productions, LLC. and Marwar Junction Productions (Released by Peacock; October 23, 2023)

CHAPTER 27

1 *Krishnas: Gurus. Karma. Murder,* from executive producers Joseph Freed, Allison Berkley, Tara Long, David Holthouse and Tim Clancy; produced by Entertainment One Reality Productions, LLC. and Marwar Junction Productions (Released by Peacock; October 23, 2023)
2 *Krishnas: Gurus. Karma. Murder,* from executive producers Joseph Freed, Allison Berkley, Tara Long, David Holthouse and Tim Clancy; produced by Entertainment One Reality Productions, LLC. and Marwar Junction Productions (Released by Peacock; October 23, 2023)
3 *Krishnas: Gurus. Karma. Murder,* from executive producers Joseph Freed, Allison Berkley, Tara Long, David Holthouse and Tim Clancy; produced by Entertainment One Reality Productions, LLC. and Marwar Junction Productions (Released by Peacock; October 23, 2023)
4 "Hare Krishna Leader Tied to Murder Plot," uncredited (*Washington Post*; May 30, 1990)
5 "Gold, Guns, and God: Swami Bhaktipada and the West Virginia Hare Krishnas—Volume 9: Pushed Out Completely," Henry Doktorski (Independently published; February 27, 2023)
6 *Krishnas: Gurus. Karma. Murder,* from executive producers Joseph Freed, Allison Berkley, Tara Long, David Holthouse and Tim Clancy; produced by Entertainment One Reality Productions, LLC. and Marwar Junction Productions (Released by Peacock; October 23, 2023)

EPILOGUE

1 "Prosecutors Deserve to Keep Their Jobs," James Toler (*Charleston Gazette*; Friday, 24, 1993)
2 "Kolibash and Carey should retain posts," uncredited (*Times West Virginian*; February 18, 1993)
3 "John Gotti Trial: 1992," uncredited and undated (Encyclopedia.com)
4 "John Gotti Trial: 1992," uncredited and undated (Encyclopedia.com)
5 "Kolibash: 'I try to do what's right,'" Torsten Ove (*Dominion Post Sunday Magazine*; August 6, 1989)

Acknowledgments

For their friendship and support in the making of a book, a career, and a life, I'm eternally grateful to Stanley Prieser, James Companion, Dean Paul Selby, Steve Jory, Debbie Koshenka, John McCabe, David Faber, Bill Meckel, Basil Lockhart, Coach Etz Rine, Coach Mike Young, the family of Tom Burgoyne, Larry Mincks, Jeff Sandy, Thom Kirk, Lowell Maxey, and Tom Mucklow. Finally, a special thanks to my wife and kids, the most important jury of them all.

About the Author

William A. Kolibash was born on February 12, 1944, in Wheeling, West Virginia. He spent his high school years at Wheeling's own The Linsly School and was awarded a scholarship to Brown University from which he received a Bachelor of Arts degree in 1966.

Following his graduation from Brown, Bill attended West Virginia University College of Law and received his Juris Doctorate degree in 1969. Following his graduation from law school, he was commissioned as a captain in the United States Army Judge Advocate General's Corp. Upon being honorably discharged, he began his civilian legal career as an Assistant United States Attorney in the Northern District of West Virginia, during which he prosecuted several high-profile corruption cases and as a result received the Department of Justice's Special Commendation Award for outstanding services in 1980. After serving several months as the court-appointed U.S. Attorney, he was nominated by President Ronald Reagan and approved by the United States Senate as the presidentially appointed United States Attorney for the Northern District of West Virginia in 1982.

The many awards he received during his service as U.S. Attorney include Federal Executive of the Year in 1991, the same year he was awarded the Distinguished West Virginian by Governor Gaston Caperton. Bill's tenure as a United States Attorney ended in July of 1993, after which he entered private practice until his retirement in 2024. He is married to the former Rita Scanlon with whom he has three children, including the coauthor of this book, and six grandchildren.